Publisher

Published by

THE BIBLE FOR TODAY PRESS
900 Park Avenue
Collingswood, New Jersey 08108
U.S.A.

Church Phone: 856-854-4747
BFT Phone: 856-854-4452
Orders: 1-800-John 10:9
e-mail: BFT@BibleForToday.org
website: www.BibleForToday.org
fax: 856-854-2464

**We Use and Defend
the King James Bible**

**July, 2005
BFT3230BK**

Copyright, 2005
All Rights Reserved

ISBN #1-56848-048-2

Publisher's Foreword
July, 2005

It is with a great deal of personal delight that our Bible For Today Press has been enabled to publish *Early Manuscripts, Church Fathers, and the Authorized Version*. This hardback volume was formerly two separate volumes produced in copy machine format.

The present production has been long in coming. Each page of the former two volumes had to be scanned carefully into electronic format and then checked for spelling and many other details. This laborious work was undertaken by Mr. James Grumblatt, Dr. and Mrs. H. D. Williams, and the BFT Director.

The funds for this massive undertaking have been supplied by a close friend of our Bible For Today ministry. We thank him very much for his willingness to make these vital truths available to the public in an even more attractive and convincing form.

The author of this work, Dr. Jack Moorman, is one of the missionaries supported by our *Bible For Today Baptist Church*. He has been laboring faithfully for many years in the United Kingdom both as a Baptist Pastor and as a distributor of many thousands of gospel tracts in England and in some areas of Europe.

In my opinion, Dr. Moorman is the world's greatest living scholar who is defending the King James Bible and its underlying Hebrew, Aramaic, and Greek Words. He has the evidence to back up that defense, and knows how to put it in writing.

Sincerely yours for God's Words,

D. A. Waite

Pastor D. A. Waite, Th.D., Ph.D.
Director, Bible For Today, Incorporated

Early Manuscripts, Church Fathers, and the Authorized Version

WITH MANUSCRIPT DIGESTS
AND SUMMARIES

J. A. Moorman

TABLE OF CONTENTS

PUBLISHER'S DATA	i

PUBLISHER'S FOREWORD	ii

	PAGE
EARLY MANUSCRIPTS and THE AUTHORIZED VERSION	9 - 312

	PAGE
PREFACE, ACKNOWLEDGMENT, DEDICATION	9 - 10

SECTION ONE	11 - 36

THE BATTLE FOR THE DOCTRINAL HEART OF SCRIPTURE	11

CHAPTER	TITLE	PAGE
I.	ADOPTIONISM: THE DARK SECRET Removal of the Name "Jesus" Removal of "Lord" and "Christ" What Lays Behind This Disassociation	13 - 22 14 - 16 17 - 20 20 - 22
II.	THE "FIRST RULE" IN TEXTUAL CRITICISM	23 - 24
III.	THE "STANDARD TEXT" AND CATHOLIC COOPERATION	25 - 28

IV.	THE CRITICAL TEXT: "ECLECTIC" OR BOUND TO ALEPH-B An Actual Count	29 - 32 31
V.	THE REMARKABLE ALTERATIONS OF CODEX SINAITICUS	33 - 36

SECTION TWO	PAGE
	37 - 118

A SUMMARY OF MANUSCRIPT EVIDENCE TWELVE SUMMARIES STANDARDS OF COMPARISON	37 40 -118 38

SUMMARY	TITLE	PAGE
I	THE PAPYRI FRAGMENTS	40 - 44
II	THE OLD UNCIALS (1)	45 - 49
III	THE OLD UNCIALS (2)	50 - 51
IV	THE "ALPHABET" AND "O" UNCIALS	52 - 62
V	THE CURSIVE MANUSCRIPTS	63 - 64
VI	FAMILIES ONE AND THIRTEEN	65 - 66
VII	THE OLD LATIN	67 - 72
VIII	JEROME'S VULGATE Editions Rather than Individual Manuscripts The Vulgate Summary	73 - 77 73 74 - 75 76

4 Early Manuscripts, Church Fathers, & the Authorized Version

IX	THE SYRIAC VERSIONS	78 - 87	
	Peshitta	78 - 79	
	Sinaitic and Curetonian	80 - 81	
	Philoxenian and Harclean	81 - 83	
	Palestinian	83 - 84	
	Summary	85 - 87	
X	THE COPTIC VERSIONS	88 - 95	
	Sahidic	88 - 90	
	Bohairic	90	
	Minor Coptic Versions	91	
	Summary	92 - 94	
	Overall Margin for Three Primary Versions	95	
XI	THE GOTHIC, ARMENIAN AND ETHIOPIC VERSIONS	96-103	
	Gothic	96-98	
	Armenian	98-99	
	Ethiopic	99-100	
	Summary	101-103	
XII	THE FATHERS TO CHRYSOSTOM	104-118	
	Selective Citation	105-106	
	The Burgon and Miller Material	106	
	A Disadvantage for the Traditional Text	107	
	Tatian's Diatessaron	107-110	
	Summary	111-118	

	PAGE
SECTION THREE	119-312

A MANUSCRIPT DIGEST OF 356 DOCTRINAL PASSAGES	119-312
Format, Symbols and Abbreviations	119-121
The Digest	122-312

Table of Contents 5

| EARLY CHURCH FATHERS and THE AUTHORIZED VERSION | PAGE 313 - 432 |

| INTRODUCTION | 314 - 315 |

CHAPTER	TITLE	PAGE
I.	TEXTUAL CRITICISM AND THE CHURCH FATHERS	317 - 328
	The Search for a "Good Critical edition"	318
	Frederic Kenyon	318 - 320
	Bruce Metzger	320 - 322
	Kurt Aland	322 - 324
	IGNTP	324 - 326
	Gordon Fee	326 - 327
	Conclusion	327
II.	SOME INFLUENTIAL PATRISTIC WORKS	329 - 334
	Eusebius	329
	Jerome	329 - 330
	Gennadius	330
	"A Catholic Enterprise"	330
	Angelo Mai	331
	Jacques Paul Migne	331
	The Berlin and Vienna Editions	332
	Dean Burgon's Index	332 - 333
	The Roberts, Schaff Editions	333 - 334
III.	GUIDELINES FOR THE DEMONSTRATION	335 - 338

CHAPTER	TITLE	PAGE
IV.	THE SUMMARY, WITH BIOGRAPHICAL SKETCHES: Alexander Ambrose Aphrahat Athanasius Athenagoras Basil Clement Cyprian Cyril Dionysius Ephraem Eusebius Gregory, Nazianzen Gregory, Nyssa Gregory-Thaumaturgus Hilary Hippolytus Ignatius Irenaeus Justin Martyr Malchion Methodius Novatian Origin Polycarp Pontius Tatian Tertullian Victorinus Anonymous Works Apocryphal Works Chronological Summary Geographic Summary	339 - 364 359 - 361 362 - 364

Table of Contents

CHAPTER	TITLE	PAGE
V.	THE DIGEST All passages Cited are "Distinctly Byzantine" An Invitation 149 Doctrinal Passages	365 - 432 365 365 366 - 432
	SELECTED BIBLIOGRAPHY	433 - 438
	INDEX	439 - 448
	ORDER BLANK PAGES	449-454
	ABOUT THE AUTHOR	454

PREFACE, ACKNOWLEDGMENT, DEDICATION

The Authorized Version of the Scriptures is the <u>receptus</u> of doctrinal truth. It is fuller and more distinct doctrinally than any other version. The first *profitable* outcome of inspiration is <u>doctrine</u> (II Tim. 3:16). The first purpose of Scripture is to establish doctrine. It is not surprising that the doctrinal heart of Scripture should have borne the fury of Satan's attack through the centuries, and especially during the Second and Third. A number of early witnesses show the scars of this warfare in the disfiguring, defacing and deletion of doctrinal truth. God, however, has been faithful to His promise and there has always been a <u>Traditional Text</u> in which truth remained pure and full. And, even here, when the attack reached its full fury, if there was any scattering or diminishing, the Holy Spirit who had promised to *guide into all truth* (John. 16:13) would show where to find the missing part.

When we come to the King James Bible, we feel that we have come home! We know that it is the final chapter of the Traditional Text. We know that whatever may have been scattered or diminished along the way has been brought home and clarified in its pages. The fact that the AV has been the *sole* Standard these past 400 years, and conscious of the many Scriptural promises concerning preservation, we have certainty and confirmation as to this assurance.

The present volume places before the reader an entire range of evidence, and demonstrates how the early manuscripts, versions, and fathers bear witness to the doctrinal heart of the Authorized Version. With some revision this work combines the author's *Early Manuscripts and the Authorized Version*, and *Early Church Fathers and the Authorized Version*. These were published by The Bible for Today in 1990 and 1992.

A battle has raged over the doctrinal heart of Scripture. As early as the days of the Apostle Paul, there were *many* who were seeking to *corrupt the word of God*, (II Cor. 2:17). This corruption and defacement is especially obvious in several of the very early manuscripts. Their surprisingly good current condition, and scarcity of similar types of manuscripts, is clear proof that they were wisely avoided in the transmission and recopying process. Yet more recent times, have seen them brought out of their dusty hiding places to form the basis of modern bibles.

The following presentation represents something of a breakthrough. Here the reader is able to accurately access how the different strata of an entire range of manuscript evidence votes with respect to 356 doctrinal passages that are present in the AV but missing from modern bibles.

In preparing this material, I acknowledge my debt and gratitude to those choice servants who labor in the defense of the Received Text and Authorized Version; to all missionaries who go the extra mile in making certain that their foreign language translation is based on the Received Text; and to all who stand, like the pastor, whose letter I received, placed I John 5:7 after his signature.

I am very thankful for the *huge* effort of my wife in typing the original drafts; and to Dr. H. D. and Patricia Williams, and James Grumblatt for their massive labor of much retyping and placing the material into an electronic format.

Most notably we mark the fact that for many years Dr. D. A. Waite has stood at the forefront in the defense of the Standard Bible and Traditional Text. His efforts have been tireless. His voice often the first to be heard. His work has had a beneficial effect around the world, with many being alerted to this crucial issue. His founding of the Dean Burgon Society has provided a forum for others to enter into the defense. With gratitude, this volume is dedicated to a true and consistent champion of the faith, Dr. D. A. Waite.

Jack Moorman
London, 2005

SECTION ONE
THE BATTLE FOR THE DOCTRINAL HEART OF SCRIPTURE

The repeated argument that "not one doctrine" is affected by the current controversy between the Authorized Version and Modern Versions, is of course, completely wide of the mark. There has not been a "wholesale" removal of doctrine from these new Bibles. You can still teach the Deity of Christ, or the Second Coming, or the Trinity from the New International or New American Standard Versions. But, you will do so with greater difficulty! You will have to look harder! You will find some key component parts missing! And, you may find yourself having to explain some things "you never knew before"! See, *only begotten God* in *NASV* at John 1:18.

In this first section, we look at some areas which are not so well-known among God's people. In fact, I think we have here some *depths of Satan* (Rev. 2:24) which go far deeper than most have imagined.

CHAPTER I
ADOPTIONISM: THE DARK SECRET BEHIND
THE TEXT OF THE MODERN VERSIONS

It has long been known that names and titles of Christ occur less frequently in the NIV/NASV than in the Authorized Version. In the AV, the complete signature is given to our Saviour's Person. When the Bible writes this in full, it is "the Lord Jesus Christ."

Notice how substantial the amount of omission is in two of the prominent versions.

	NASV	NIV
Lord	35	35
Jesus	73	36
Christ	43	44
Total Omissions	156	115

This can hardly be brushed aside in the way the following attempts do:

> One common objection...is that in a relative few cases the names "Christ" and "Lord" are omitted when referring to Jesus. (A tract by Homer Kent, President of Grace Theological Seminary, *The King James Only*).

The removal of "Christ" and "Lord" are a strike against our Saviour's deity in every place it occurs. But what are we to say about the removal of "Jesus", the "name which is above every name", but the name which, nevertheless, speaks of our Lord's humanity.

As we now show, "Jesus" is often removed from an *association* with other titles or works of Deity. In other words, "Jesus" is frequently made to stand alone, or not at all!

REMOVAL OF THE NAME "JESUS" FROM ASSOCIATION WITH TITLES AND WORKS OF DEITY

Jesus is removed from:

MATTHEW	
4:12	the prophecy of the great light (12-16)
4:18	the call to discipleship (18-22)
4:23	the miracle working ministry in Galilee (23-25)
8:29	association with the title "thou Son of God"
12:25	healing of the blind and dumb demoniac (22-30)
13:36	the interpretation of "wheat and tares" (36-43)
13:51	association with the title "Lord" (which is also removed)
14:14	the immediate account of a miracle
14:22, 25, 27	much of the account of walking on the sea
15:16	the discourse about defilement (10-20)
15:30	the immediate account of a miracle
16:20	association with the title "the Christ"

MARK	
1:41	the immediate account of a miracle
5:13	the immediate account of a miracle
5:19	association with the title "Lord"
6:34	the "feeding of the 5,000" (32-44)

Chapter I--Adoptionism: the Dark Secret Behind Modern Versions

7:27	healing of the Syrophonician woman's daughter (24-30)
8:1	the "feeding of the 4,000" (1-9)
8:17	the discourse concerning leaven (14-21)
11:14	the "cursing of the fig tree" (12-14)
11:15	the "cleansing of the Temple" (15-19)
12:41	the account of the widow's mite (41-44)
14:22	the account of the Last Supper (22-25)

LUKE	
7:22	the answer of miracles to John the Baptist (19-23)
9:43	an account of miracles and coming crucifixion (43-45)
10:21	a prayer of union with the Father (21-22)
13:2	an exhortation to repent (1-5)
24:36	the upper room appearance to the disciples (36-53)

JOHN	
3:2	a confession of His miracles
5:17, 19	a declaration of union with the Father (17-47)
5:14	immediate association with "that prophet"
13:3	a statement of union with the Father

ACTS	
3:26	association with the title "His Son"
9:29	association with the title "Lord"
19:10	association with the title "Lord"

16 Early Manuscripts, Church Fathers, & the Authorized Version

ROMANS	
15:8	association with the title "Christ"
16:18	association with the titles "Lord" and "Christ"

1 CORINTHIANS	
5:5	association with the title "Christ"
16:22	"Jesus Christ" association with the title "Lord"

II CORINTHIANS	
4:10	association with the title "Christ"
5:18	association with the title "Christ"

COLOSSIANS	
1:28	association with the title "Christ"

II TIMOTHY	
4:22	"Jesus Christ"... association with the title "Lord"

I PETER	
5:10	association with the title "Christ"
5:14	association with the title "Christ."

REMOVAL OF "LORD", "CHRIST" AND OTHER TITLES OF DEITY FROM IMMEDIATE ASSOCIATION WITH THE NAME JESUS

The underlined words are removed from Modern Bibles

MATTHEW	
13:51	Jesus saith unto them, Have ye...Yea, <u>Lord</u>
23:8	Then spake Jesus (verse 1)...for one is your Master, <u>even Christ</u>
28:6	for I know that ye seek Jesus...Come see the place where the <u>Lord</u> lay

MARK	
1:1	The beginning of the gospel of Jesus Christ, <u>the Son of God</u>
9:24	Jesus said unto him, if thou canst believe .. <u>Lord</u> I believe
11:10	Blessed be the kingdom of our father David, that cometh <u>in the name of the Lord:</u> ... And Jesus entered

LUKE	
9:57	<u>Lord</u> I will follow thee ... And Jesus said
9:59	<u>Lord</u>, suffer me first ... Jesus said
23:42	And he said unto Jesus, <u>Lord</u>, remember me

JOHN	
6:69	We believe and are sure that thou art <u>that Christ</u>, the Son of the living God. Jesus answered...

ACTS

15:11	through the grace of the Lord Jesus <u>Christ</u>
16:31	Believe on the Lord Jesus <u>Christ</u>
19:4	that they should believe on ... <u>Christ</u> Jesus
20:21	faith toward our Lord Jesus <u>Christ</u>

ROMANS	
6:11	but alive unto God through Jesus Christ <u>our Lord</u>
16:20	The grace of our Lord Jesus <u>Christ</u> be with you

I CORINTHIANS	
5:4	In the name of our Lord Jesus <u>Christ</u>
5:4	with the power of our Lord Jesus <u>Christ</u>
9:1	have I not seen Jesus <u>Christ</u> our Lord
16:23	The grace of' our Lord Jesus <u>Christ</u> be with you

II CORINTHIANS	
4:10	Always bearing about in the body the dying of the <u>Lord</u> Jesus
11:31	The God and Father of our Lord Jesus <u>Christ</u>

GALATIANS	
6:17	for I bear in my body the marks of the <u>Lord</u> Jesus

I THESSALONIANS	
2:19	in the presence of our Lord Jesus <u>Christ</u> at his coming
3:11	and our Lord Jesus <u>Christ</u> direct our way unto you
3:13	at the coming of our Lord Jesus <u>Christ</u>

II THESSALONIANS	
1:8	that obey not the gospel of our Lord Jesus <u>Christ</u>
1:12	That the name of our Lord Jesus <u>Christ</u> may be glorified

I TIMOTHY	
1:1	and <u>Lord</u> Jesus Christ which is our hope
5:21	I charge thee before God, and the <u>Lord</u> Jesus Christ

II TIMOTHY	
4:1	I charge thee therefore before God, and the <u>Lord</u> Jesus Christ

TITUS	
1:4	from God the Father and the <u>Lord</u> Jesus Christ

HEBREWS	
3:1	consider the Apostle and High Priest of our profession, <u>Christ</u> Jesus

1 JOHN	
1:7	the blood of Jesus <u>Christ</u> his Son cleanseth
4:3	And every spirit that confesseth not that Jesus <u>Christ is come in the flesh</u> is not of God

II JOHN	
3	and from <u>the Lord</u> Jesus Christ

REVELATION	

| 12:17 | and have the testimony of Jesus <u>Christ</u> |
| 22:21 | The grace of our Lord Jesus <u>Christ</u> be with you all. |

Here we have 86 examples where the Modern Versions disassociate the name "Jesus" from other titles and acts of Deity. These are examined further in the Manuscript Digest.

WHAT LIES BEHIND THIS DISASSOCIATION?

The separation of "Jesus" from "Christ" occurs far too often to look for any cause other than deliberate editing in certain N.T. manuscripts. That there was a strong movement in the early centuries which could result in such a systematic editing, there can be no doubt! The foremost error regarding the Person of Christ, is of course, to deny His true Deity and true Humanity. The chief means by which this was done, and which finds expression down to our own day, is technically known as "ADOPTIONISM" or "Spirit Christology." Here: Jesus of Nazareth, an ordinary man of unusual virtue, was "adopted" by God into divine Sonship by the advent of the "Christ-Spirit" at His baptism. Therefore, Jesus became Christ at His baptism, rather than, the fact that He was always the Christ from eternity. Though united for a time, Jesus and Christ were thus said to be separate personages.

This heresy is expressed in a number of ways. *Hastings Encyclopedia of Religion and Ethics* (Under "ADOPTIONISM") cites the following early example:

> The Holy Spirit...is regarded as the preexistent Son ... The Redeemer is the virtuous man chosen by God, with whom that Spirit of God was united. As He did not defile the Spirit, but kept Him constantly as His companion, and carried out the work to which the Deity had called Him...He was in virtue of a Divine decree, adopted as a son ... (*The Shepherd of Hermas*).

Many names and groups are associated with this wicked teaching, foremost of whom were the Gnostics.

The liberal J.N.D. Kelly writes:

> There was a great variety of Gnostic systems, but a common pattern ran through them all. From the pleroma, or spiritual world of aeons the divine Christ descended and united Himself for a time (according to Ptolemy, between the baptism and the passion) to the

Chapter I--Adoptionism: the Dark Secret Behind Modern Versions

historical personage...These were tendencies on the fringe, yet Gnosticism at any rate came within an ace of swamping the central tradition. (*Early Christian Doctrines*, London: Adam & Charles Black, 1958, pp. 141,42).

Ponder carefully Kelly's statement about how near this came to *swamping the central tradition*! In the Summaries we will be looking more closely at Egypt; but notice for now that Kelly's mention of Ptolemy and Gnosticism takes us to that city which gave such force and rise to the Gnostic error - Alexandria.

The Digest in Section Three shows clearly that it is the small group of Alexandrian manuscripts which consistently disassociate "Jesus" from "Christ". Along with Aleph and B, Papyri 46 follows the same trend. This favorite papyri among editors of the Critical Text covers parts of Romans to Hebrews, and dates from 200 AD, making it just about the oldest manuscript we have. But, in I Cor. 15:47, *it reveals its dark secret!*

the second man is <u>the Lord</u> from heaven	AV
the second man is from heaven	Aleph* B
the second man is <u>the spirit</u> from heaven	P46

Very much in line with what *The Shepherd of Hermas* said!

As we near the end of the New Testament, and the Spirit of the Living God is setting out His final admonitions and warnings, we now begin to understand better one passage in particular --

> And every spirit that confesseth not that <u>Jesus Christ is come in the flesh</u> is not of God: and this is that spirit of Antichrist...(I John 4:3).

In fact there is a fivefold warning at the end of the Bible concerning this heresy! See I John 2:22; 4:3; 5:1; 5:5; II John 7,9.

This then, is the dark secret of the Modern Bibles: they are based on manuscripts tainted by the heresy of "ADOPTIONISM.", and this completely undermines the doctrinal heart of Scripture.

CHAPTER II
THE "FIRST RULE" IN TEXTUAL CRITICISM

The Westcott and Hort theory produced a table of about eight or ten "canons" by which Textual Criticism operates, and which greatly affects the Bible's doctrinal heart. You will not have to look at these "rules" for long before realizing that they are "weighted" in the direction of their own predetermined preference for the Alexandrian Text. For example: if the Alexandrian Text is shorter than the Traditional, then one firm rule is "The shorter reading is to be preferred." And, if above ninety percent of the manuscripts support the Traditional Text and the remaining ten percent must be divided between the Alexandrian (which struggles to get even 3%), Western and Caesarean texts, then of course "numerical preponderance counts for nothing, the Traditional Text is merely one of four competing 'text types'". And, should it be pointed out that the Alexandrian Text is less distinct doctrinally: then it is an established fact that "there are no signs of deliberate falsification of the text for doctrinal purposes during the early centuries." And, on it goes! A number of authors have exposed this partiality, and in our *Missing in Modern Bibles,* (See also *Modern Bibles the Dark Secret*), I give a simplified overview of these "canons". But, let it be noted, that it is their "FIRST RULE" that allows them to get away with the other rules!

Textual Criticism has long played a perverse game with what they are only too aware is substantial pre-350AD evidence for the Traditional Text. To them, the Traditional Majority is always that of a *derived* text (and that, simply because they say so!). With respect to the early centuries, it is not allowed to stand on its own. The pre-350AD evidence which is plainly there, is in the majority, and witnesses strongly to the Traditional Text, is not a witness at all, but is made to be merely *secondary sources* which were later developed into the Traditional Text.

When they say, "there are no distinctive Byzantine readings before 350", it is in fact circular reasoning, for by their logic, if it is before 350, then it cannot be Byzantine! It is much like the evolutionist dating the strata by the fossils, and the fossils by the strata. The pre-350 era is solely the domain of Aleph and B, and the few manuscripts which support them. The mass of manuscripts as represented by the Authorized Version must not be allowed to intrude into that era. Their evidence is ruled out of court.

What, however, are they to do with the clear and substantial evidence to the contrary? Here they have been forced to a second line of defense: "Well, there may be Byzantine readings before 350, but there is no Byzantine Text"! To this we naturally reply that given the large number of passages involved, how can you have one without the other?

I think you will see from the evidence in the following, how wickedly dishonest this line of argument is. There, in many hundreds of places, we have called upon the early witnesses to vote between the Traditional Text and that of Aleph-B. The results are convincing; but it must also be said, that in the early centuries there was indeed a warfare over the doctrinal heart of Scripture, and that in more recent times our opponents have been very adept at "moving the goal posts"!

CHAPTER III
THE "STANDARD TEXT" AND ROMAN CATHOLIC COOPERATION

In recent years Kurt Aland has encouraged the use of the term "Standard Text" for the critical edition (Nestle) of which he has been the chief editor. Whether others will be quite so ready to call it that, is not clear. However, it is clear that the "Standard Text" has become the *first* Greek edition since the Reformation over which Catholics and Protestants could cooperate fully. It has been an "ecumenical break through" which has made the doctrines of the Bible "more acceptable to all." In fact, the earlier editions of the Nestle text were technically "off limits" to the Catholic Church, with backing instead being given to the editions of three of their own scholars - Vogels, Merk and Bover.

> ... they were intended to meet the overwhelming "competition" of the popular Nestle edition which was circulating widely even in Roman Catholic circles. The fact that the Nestle text was produced by the Bible Societies, which were still under official Catholic proscription, only aggravated the situation. (Kurt Aland and Barbara Aland, *The Text of the New Testament*, Grand Rapids: Eerdmans, 1987, p. 26).

Except for some differences in paragraphing, punctuation and spelling, the texts of the two most popular critical editions — Nestle Aland and United Bible Societies — are now identical. This is primarily through the efforts of Kurt Aland, director of the Institute for New Testament Textual Research in Munster, West Germany; and Eugene Nida, Translations Secretary of the American Bible Society. For many years Aland has been editor of the Nestle Text, which by 1963 had reached its 25th edition. This has always been the most popular critical edition and is based firmly on the Aleph B text of Westcott and Hort.

The United Bible Societies' edition is of more recent origin. In 1955 through the initiative of Nida, a committee was established to prepare an edition especially for missionary translators. Those invited to participate were Matthew Black of St Andrews, Scotland, Bruce Metzger of Princeton, Allen Wikgren of Chicago University, as well as Kurt Aland who would now be working on both editions.

It should be noted that this is the <u>United</u> Bible Societies text. Initially three societies sponsored the project — the American, National of Scotland and Wurtemberg of W. Germany. These were joined by the Netherlands Bible Society and the British and Foreign Bible Society. But, in fact, it became the Greek text of the worldwide United Bible Societies, a union of national societies which dates back to the thirties. It was envisaged that it become the standard base for all future translation work carried out by these national societies. It has furthermore become an <u>interconfessional</u> text, as it is officially recognized by the Roman Catholic Church. At about the time the first edition was published (1966), Carlo Martini — rector of the Pontifical Biblical Institute of Rome, and later Archbishop of Milan, <u>and Cardinal</u> — was invited to serve on the editorial committee.

Kurt Aland writes:

> What of the present scene where the reader of the Greek New Testament now meets the new "Standard text"? By this we mean the text officially published and distributed by the United Bible Societies and also officially by the Catholic Church - a significant new factor in the present scene. (*Ibid*, p. 30).
> In any event, the new "Standard text" is a reality, and as the sole text distributed by the United Bible Societies and by the corresponding offices of the Roman Catholic Church - an inconceivable situation until quite recently. (*Ibid*, p. 35).

The first edition was published in 1966, and as stated in the preface, the work was carried out "on the basis of Westcott and Hort's edition". A second edition appeared two years later. "Only a few changes were introduced" (Aland p. 33), but these set the stage for the common text. Further changes were agreed, and with the publication of *UBS 3* in 1975 and *Nestle Aland 26* in 1979 the quest for textual identity between the two editions was realized.

This has all resulted in a marked increase of Roman Catholic involvement in Bible Society work:

> It was disclosed in the 1987 Annual Report of the United Bible Societies (p. 193) that "of the 573 current UBS projects of Scripture translation, there is active Roman Catholic participation in 161, and there have been over 160 interconfessional Bibles and New Testaments published since 1968." This represents a massive increase in Roman Catholic influence over the work of Bible translation in the past twenty years. (*Trinitarian Bible Society Quarterly Record*, April—June 1989, p. 12).

Chapter III--The "Standard Text" & Roman Catholic Cooperation

Yet, many missionaries, pastors and Bible colleges who claim to be conservative and fundamental use the "Standard Text" as their standard too!

CHAPTER IV
THE CRITICAL TEXT: "ECLECTIC," OR BOUND TO ALEPH AND B

Driving through Birmingham, England, I passed an "establishment" called "The Artful Dodger". And, frankly, there is not a better way to describe Textual Criticism. It shifts, it turns, it establishes, it overturns, it rewrites, it restates, it examines, it ignores, etc. Textual Criticism would have us believe that it is the arbiter of the kind of Bible we should read; but all it can offer is a provisional, preliminary and eclectic kind of "Bible". It is in their use of "eclectic" that new meaning has been brought to the word, "artful".

The well-known statement in the *NIV* introduction claims:

> The Greek text used in translating the New Testament was an eclectic one (viii).

According to the dictionary definition eclectic means:
 1. Selecting what is considered best from different systems and sources. 2. Composed of elements selected from diverse sources.

Most involved in Textual Criticism would accept this as a reasonable description of their approach to the N.T. Text. In reading their material, you will find that some claim to be "more eclectic than others". Yet, despite all that we hear about this approach, when it comes to the current Critical Text — has it really been a case of "selecting what is considered best from different sources"? Hardly at all! The primary source of the *NA 26, UBS 3* has altered very little since F.J.A. Hort wrote:

> Accordingly, with the exceptions mentioned above, it is our belief (1) that readings of Aleph B should be accepted as the true readings until strong internal evidence is found to the contrary, and (2) that no readings of Aleph B can be safely rejected absolutely, though it is sometimes right to place them only on an alternative footing, especially where they receive no support from the Versions or the Fathers. (*The New Testament in the Original Greek Introduction and Appendix*, New York: Harper Bros., 1882, p. 225).

But, does not the introduction to *NA 26* tell us that the narrow base used by Westcott and Hort is now finished?

> The view is becoming increasingly accepted today that...neither Codex Vaticanus nor Codex Sinaiticus (nor even P75 of two hundred years earlier) can provide a guideline we can normally depend on for determining the text. The age of Westcott—Hort and of Tischendorf is definitely over. (*Nestle Aland -26th Edition*, 1981, p 43*).

This is simply not the case! Despite their statements about "eclecticism", and a "broadening of the manuscript base" very little of substance has changed in the latest Critical Edition. It is still the Aleph-B text of Westcott and Hort.

Notice how J. K. Elliott, a frequent reviewer of the *UBS* and *NA*, comes around to this conclusion:

Commenting first on the earlier UBS editions he writes:
> As for the UBS text itself, it claims to be eclectic. In a sense this is demonstrably so, in so far as it does not regularly follow only a few MSS in the way Tischendorf (8) or Westcott and Hort do. Sometimes readings appear which do not reflect the text of the traditional "best" MSS ("A Second Look at the United Bible Societies' Greek N.T.", *The Bible Translator*, 26 (1975), p 327).

However, after giving ten examples of departures from the "best MSS" (Aleph and B), he continues:
> The cult of MSS ... is a questionable principle, especially in a text which purports to be eclectic. Metzger's <u>Commentary</u> p. 271 states that the text of Acts is intended to be eclectic, but in practice it is the shorter Alexandrian text which has usually been printed (*Ibid*).
> Preference for Aleph B has caused the editors to print the Attic form <u>ephee</u> found in these MSS at Mark 9:12, 38; 10:20, 29; 12:24; 14:29. (*Ibid*, p. 332).

Regarding the third edition of UBS, Elliott says:
> ...the general verdict of UBS 3rd edn. is that its text is closer to Westcott and Hort's text. It is in many ways a "safer" text than the first and second UBS editions insofar as many more of the readings of Codex Vaticanus and Codex Sinaiticus appear in UBS 3rd edn. ("The United Bible Societies Greek New Testament: A Short Examination of the Third Edition", *The Bible Translator*, 30 .1979 p. 138).

It should be pointed out, though, that in order to bring the text of NA-26 into line with UBS-3, it had to depart from a number of the Aleph B readings in NA-25.

Chapter IV--The Critical Text: "Eclectic," or Bound to Aleph & B

...as if to underline their reluctance at abandoning the readings of NA 25, the editors frequently bracket the newly added text...The resultant text...is, however, still close to Hort. (Elliott, "An Examination of the Twenty - Sixth Edition of Nestle Aland Novurn Testamentum Graece," *Journal of Theological Studies*, 32 '1981, p. 22).

AN ACTUAL COUNT

The key determinate in the Westcott and Hort theory is that a reading supported by both Aleph and B should virtually always be incorporated in the text. When they divide preference will generally be given to B. Taking into account that the Vaticanus MS omits I Timothy - Philemon, Hebrews 9:15 - end and Revelation; I counted <u>216</u> instances in the NA-26 apparatus where it's text departed from an Aleph-B reading. In most cases this would also represent a departure from the Hort text. The count was of the original readings of Aleph and B, not subsequent scribal alterations.

> 216 departures over 559 pages of text, or
> one departure for every 2.6 pages, or
> about one departure in every 32 verses

How can this be called "eclecticism"? Well, if you are very "artful" it can be! Aleph and B do not always provide a comfortable bed for the modern "standard" text to rest upon. They frequently disagree, and in other places the evidence against them is such that it cannot be ignored by the critical editors. It is because, and *only* because of these two factors, that Textual Criticism has had to exercise its "eclectic facilities". If Aleph and B were more in agreement, the word "eclectic" would not be mentioned! In short, the "Standard Text" is nearly as bound to Aleph and B, as the one drafted by Westcott and Hort over one hundred years ago. And, it is these two manuscripts which most corrupt the doctrinal heart of the Bible.

CHAPTER V
THE REMARKABLE ALTERATIONS IN CODEX SINAITICUS

That a battle raged in the early centuries over the doctrinal heart of Scripture is nowhere more manifest than in the scriptorium where Codex Aleph was copied! Among the early manuscripts it seems to have far more than the usual number of corrections and alterations. Indeed, Scrivener speaks of this manuscript being "disfigured with corrections" (*Plain Introduction*, p 90). Two of our summaries show that these alterations generally move away from Aleph's characteristic Alexandrian base to the kind of text underlying our Authorized Version.

In the doctrinal passages of the Manuscript Digest the Aleph-correctors support the AV by a margin of:

$$70 - 19$$

In Nestle Aland-26 they side with the Traditional text against Codex Vaticanus by:

$$473 - 181$$

The question naturally arises, and given the early date of Aleph © 350), it is one of the most important that can be asked in textual criticism: When in relation to the actual penning of the manuscript were the alterations made? Prior to 1934, when Aleph was acquired by the British Museum, the two scholars most able to give a first hand opinion of its paleography were Constantine Tischendorf and Kirsopp Lake. They believed that Aleph in its Old and New Testaments and Apocrypha was the work of four scribes designated A, B, C, D. They postulated that many different hands were involved in the corrections: some at the time of production, some during the 5th/7th century, and others later.

With the benefit of new techniques including ultraviolet lamps, H.J.M Milne and T.C. Skeat of the British Museum were able to undertake a far more thorough investigation. Their findings were published in *Scribes and Correctors of Codex Sinaiticus* (London, 1938). They. concluded that in fact Aleph was the work of three scribes rather than four — A, B and D; and that the New Testament was penned mainly by Scribe A with a few portions going to Scribe D.

Scribe A	Nearly all of the New Testament
Scribe D:	Matthew 16:9 - 18:12; 24:36 - 26:6 Mark 14:54 - 16:7 Luke 1:1 - 18 I Thessalonians 2:14 - 5:28 Hebrews 4:16 - 8:1 Revelation 1:1 - 5

Coming to the correctors, Milne and Skeet were persuaded that the numerous corrections in Aleph were carried out by fewer hands than previously thought, and reinforced the conclusion of Tischendorf and Lake that <u>many were carried out shortly after the manuscript's completion</u> (see *Scribes and Correctors*, pp. 40 - 50). Before the manuscript left the scriptorium it was corrected by the scribes themselves, and in fact, by the scribes designated above as A and D (Ibid, p. 41). The importance of this conclusion is not difficult to see:

> These early corrections...can all be recognized with ease and certainty as the product of the scriptorium, and as all are in consequence contemporary with the main script, <u>they stand in this respect on more or less the same footing for the purpose of textual criticism</u>. (*Ibid*, p 40; emphasis mine).

Regarding the nature of these alterations, Milme and Skeat indicate that in the Old Testament it was merely a case of the scribes correcting their work with reference to the single (probably) exemplar they were using.

> In the New Testament, however, there are signs of a further revision, of actual collations <u>with another textual tradition</u>. (*Ibid*, p 45, emphasis mine).

Thus, all was not lost in that long ago scriptorium, the penmen of this corrupted Alexandrian manuscript were able to correct it in numerous places with the God-given text that underlies our King James Bible. Of course, the correcting didn't go nearly far enough, but that which did take place was noteworthy.

It remains to be pointed out that Tischendorf, followed by Lake divided the correctors of Sinaiticus into five chronological groups and, not to be confused with the original scribes, they were designated A, B, C, D, E. Of these, the British Museum researchers concluded:

Chapter V--The Remarkable Alterations in Codex Sinaiticus 35

The A and B corrections we have shown to be contemporary with the manuscript, since they are attributable to the scribes of the text themselves. The C correctors have been assigned by some to the fifth, by others to the seventh century, and lack of comparative material enforces caution upon whoever would decide between the two dates. The medieval D and E correctors are of slight importance. (*Ibid*).

In the Manuscript Digest, drawing upon the citations of *NA 26*, A and B have been designated Aleph 1,2; while C is Aleph 3, (D and E are not cited). We will not here be able to study the correctors of the other early uncials, but what has been seen in Aleph sets the stage, and opens up a very strong and early line of evidence in behalf of the Traditional Text and it's doctrinal heart.

SECTION TWO
A SUMMARY OF MANUSCRIPT EVIDENCE

There has been a vast amount of valuable and painstaking research into the manuscript evidence of the New Testament. Over the years in the midst of a busy church planting/tract distribution/Bible Institute schedule, I have tried to gather what is most valuable from the past and keep up with the more important current research. It is easy to be buried beneath it all! In my view there needs to be a brief, definitive summary of the manuscript evidence: something that would allow us to see exactly where the Old Latin stands, or the uncials (all of them), or the church fathers, etc. For example, if you want to look into the characteristics of the Old Latin manuscripts, Herman Hoskier's *Genesis of the Versions* (London 1911) is one of the most important works to consult. But even if you read it through - and I wonder that anyone ever has - it would be difficult to get a good overview of the subject because of his failure to adequately summarize.

Nevertheless, the lack of summary in Hoskier's enormous research is far to be preferred to the partial, selective, and biased conclusions made in behalf of the Alexandrian Text: e.g. "Manuscript A has a good text in Acts." "A study of Mark 11 shows a Casearean tendency." "The Vulgate text is inferior in the Gospels," etc. This enables Textual Criticism to dismissively reject and withhold evidence that rightly belongs to the Traditional Text. In the same vein they have said, "Witnesses should be weighed not counted." Of course they should be both weighed and counted; and I think the following will show why *they have had a problem with counting*.

It is believed that these summaries will help the student come to firm conclusions as to the entire range of manuscript evidence.

TWELVE SUMMARIES

1.	Papyri
2., 3.	Early Uncials - judged by two criteria
4.	The "Alphabet" and "0" Uncials

38 Early Manuscripts, Church Fathers, & the Authorized Version

5.	Cursives
6.	Families 1 and 13
7.	Old Latin
8.	Vulgate
9.	Syriac
10.	Coptic
11.	Gothic, Armenian, and Ethiopic
12.	Church Fathers to Chrysostom, UBS Evidence

These provide a full picture and any others to be added would be of a more secondary nature.

STANDARDS OF COMPARISON

In the first instance we want to know whether these witnesses support the Doctrinal Text of the Authorized Version or the diminished text of the Modern Versions. The material gathered into the Manuscript Digest is brought to bear on this question. Where available evidence was not consistently or fully cited for the doctrinal passages, as in the case of the Old Latin and Church Fathers, I have instead shown how they vote in a large number of passages where the Traditional Text (Byzantine Majority) stands against readings supported by Aleph and B. In this latter, many of the doctrinal passages would be included. In the case of the Old Uncials both criteria of comparison were used. The basis of comparison is always stated at the beginning of each summary.

The basic sources for the information compiled in the Digest and Summaries were the Greek New Testaments of: Tischendorf-8th, Nestle Aland-26th, United Bible Societies-3rd, and the manuscript charts given in *The Text of the New Testament* by Kurt and Barbara Aland. Legg on Matthew and Mark, and the *IGNTP* on Luke 1-12 were cited. The author's other digest in *KJVMT* was also used at times, here citations were gathered from von Soden, Hodges and Farstad, Aland's *Synopsis* on the Gospels, and Hoskier on Revelation.

Most of the summaries are based on the citations gathered into the Manuscript Digest from these sources. Turning to the Digest you will see that the witnesses are divided under the headings AV and NIV. Whereas material on the AV side is always that which supports the Authorized Version; "NIV," though usually referring to the reading adopted in the *New International*

Section Two--A Summary of Manuscript Evidence

Version, may on occasion refer to a reading in the footnote or that of the *New American Standard Version*. This is always stated. Therefore while it is usually AV against NIV, in a number of places it is AV versus readings that have found some acceptance in the Modern Versions. It should also be noted that while the Byzantine Majority usually supports the AV side, and Aleph-B the NIV side, there are times when these witnesses switch and divide.

SUMMARY I : THE PAPYRI FRAGMENTS
Basis of Comparison : Doctrinal Passages from the Manuscript Digest

Our oldest extant manuscripts are the papyri. They are the remains of a kind of text which did not live very long, and rather than spread widely among God's people suffered an early death and burial, in the sands of Egypt. In his valuable *The Byzantine Text-Type and New Testament Textual Criticism*, Harry Sturz has shown how frequently the earliest papyri support the kind of distinctive Byzantine readings found in the Authorized Version. By "distinctive Byzantine", he means readings found in the mass of later manuscripts, but not supported by Aleph, B and one or two other early witnesses. These papyri/majority readings have caused a real problem for those holding to the Alexandrian Text. However, in the specifically doctrinal passages the papyri will more generally side with the Aleph and B against the majority.

As with Aleph and B - their doctrinal definition stripped away - the papyri were soon discarded by early believers, with few copies made. After examining a number of heretical readings in early Egyptian manuscripts,

Edward Hills concludes:
> Thus we see that it is unwise in present day translators to base the texts of their modern versions on recent papyrus discoveries or on B and Aleph. For all these documents come from Egypt, and Egypt during the early Christian centuries was a land in which heresies were rampant. So much was this so that, as Bauer (1934) and van Unnik (1958) have pointed out, later Egyptian Christians seem to have been ashamed of the heretical past of their country and to have drawn a veil of silence across it. This seems to be why so little is known of the history of early Egyptian Christianity. In view, therefore, of the heretical character of the early Egyptian Church, it is not surprising that the papyri, B, Aleph, and other manuscripts which hail from Egypt are liberally sprinkled

with heretical readings. (*The King James Version Defended*, Des Moines; The Christian Research Press, 1984, p. 134).

THE SUMMARY

Only those papyri cited in the Manuscript Digest are listed. The approximate date, mainly by century is given in the second column. (A small "c" stands for circa.) The general section of the N.T. - in which what is usually only a fragment - is given in the third column.

E = Gospels (Evangelists)
A = Acts
P = Epistles of Paul including Hebrews
G = General Epistles
R = Revelation

The specific portions of the N.T. covered by the papyri are recorded in *Nestle Aland 26*. The fourth column (containing numbers in parentheses) shows the times a papyri fragment *appears* to be extant for a passage in the Manuscript Digest, but for some reason Aland has not cited it. The first number (where two are given) represents a fair amount of likelihood; the second, doubt. Otherwise, a single number is given, with or without a question mark.

Papyri	Date (Century)	Section	Times extant but not cited	AV	"NIV"
P3	VI/VII	E			1
P5	III	E	(1?)		2
P8	IV	A			1
P11	VII	P	(3?)		2
P13	III/IV	P	(1)		3
P15	III	P			1
P20	III	E	(1?)		
P21	IV/V	E			1
P25	IV	E		1	

Section Two--A Summary of Manuscript Evidence

P26	c 600	P			1
P34	VII	P	(1)		
P35	IV?	E			1
P36	VI	E			1
P37	III/IV	E			2
P38	c 300	A			1
P41	VIII	A	(2)	1	
P44	VI/VII	E	(2)		
P45	III	EA	(5?)	9	13
P46	c 200	P	(4, 7?)		37
P47	III	R			7
P49	III	P			1
P50	IV/V	A		1	
P59	VII	E	(1?)		
P60	VII	E	(2)		1
P61	c 700	P	(1?)		
P63	c 500	E		1	
P64	c 200	E	(1?)		
P66	c 200	E	(1)	9	27
(P67)	part of P64	E			1
P69	III	E			1
P71	IV	E	(1?)		
P72	III/IV	G	(1?)	3	12
P74	VII	AG	(7, 3?)	2	14

P75	III	E	(4, 4?)	11	50
P77	II/III	E		1	
P79	VII	P	(1)		
P81	IV	G	(1?)		
P83	VI	E	(1?)		
P84	VI	E	(1)		
P86	IV	E	(1?)		
P88	IV	E			1
TOTALS			(26, 32?)	39	182

    A manuscript like P75 is fairly similar to Codex B, and when it supports the AV side you can usually expect to find B in support also. Only seven of the 88 papyri are more than small fragments.

    This is the only summary chart among the twelve showing a paucity of support for the AV doctrinal text. In the Christian Book Stores of 2nd/3rd Century Egypt you had to do a little shopping around before finding a Traditional Text Bible ... but they were there!

SUMMARY II: THE OLD UNCIALS
(1)
Basis of Comparison: Every Reading in NA - 26 Where the Traditional Text Opposes Vaticanus

In this summary we draw upon the apparatus of Nestle Aland 26 and show the results when the other old uncials are asked to cast a vote in the many places where the Byzantine Majority opposes Codex B. Since this cursive majority is a chief supporter of the Authorized Version, and since Codex B easily ranks foremost among the supporters of the Modern Version text: should we not pit them together and allow Codices Aleph, A, C, D along with their correctors to join the conflict? The "Five Old Uncials" have formed the basis of textual criticism during these past two hundred years, but to my knowledge this particular comparison has not been made. Keep in mind, also, what was said about the Aleph correctors in Section I.

I have attempted to note every place in the NA apparatus where the two rivals oppose each other. (B does not have I Timothy - Philemon, Hebrews 9:15 to end, and Revelation). Here are the results: first for each manuscript, and then the combined totals:

	With the Majority	With Vaticanus
CODEX - ALEPH (IV)		
THE GOSPELS		
Original	757	1504
Corrected	183	124
ACTS		
Original	155	333

Corrected	43	12
EPISTLES OF PAUL		
Original	381	513
Corrected	223	30
GENERAL EPISTLES		
Original	130	161
Corrected	24	15
TOTALS		
Original	1423	2511
Corrected	473	181
Combined	1896	2696

With the Majority	With Vaticanus

CODEX A (V)		
GOSPELS		
Original	1704	211
Corrected	13	0
ACTS		
Original	203	283
Corrected	9	2
EPISTLES OF PAUL		
Original	134	166
Corrected	4	2

TOTALS		
Original	2443	1049
Corrected	29	2
Combined	2472	1051

CODEX C (V)		
THE GOSPELS		
Original	882	566
Corrected	229	14
ACTS		
Original	148	156
Corrected	25	4
EPISTLES OF PAUL		
Original	304	265
Corrected	40	4
GENERAL EPISTLES		
Original	102	114
Corrected	15	5

TOTALS		
Original	1436	1101
Corrected	309	27
Combined	1745	1128

CODEX D 05 (V)

THE GOSPELS

Original	1120	783
Corrected	20	3

ACTS

Original	178	101
Corrected	10	8

TOTALS

Original	1298	884
Corrected	30	11
Combined	1328	895

CODEX D 06 (VI)

EPISTLES OF PAUL

Original	449	369
Corrected	287	10
Combined	736	379

TOTALS FOR ALEPH, A, C, D-05, D-06

THE GOSPELS

Original	4463	3064
Corrected	445	141

ACTS

Original	684	873
Corrected	87	26

Section Two--A Summary of Manuscript Evidence

EPISTLES OF PAUL		
Original	1268	1313
Corrected	553	44
GENERAL EPISTLES		
Original	366	441
Corrected	43	22
TOTALS		
Original	6781	5691
Corrected	1128	233
Combined	7909	5924

The impression is often given that these five (actually six) oldest and most famous uncials give conclusive support to the text of the modern versions. Nothing could be further from the truth! B strongly supports it. But the support of Aleph is hardly overwhelming: from 2-1 in the Gospels and Acts to about 10-7 in Romans to Jude, with its correctors supporting the Traditional Text by 5-2. And then A, C, and the two D manuscripts give overall majority support to the AV side.

What was said earlier about "partial, selective, and biased conclusions" is given a revealing example in Kurt Aland's assessment of Codex A:

> The text is of uneven value...inferior in the Gospels, good in the rest of the New Testament. (*The Text of the New Testament*, Grand Rapids: Eerdmans, 1987, p. 107).

To Aland, this manuscript from the early 400's is "inferior in the Gospels" because it gives overwhelming support to the Traditional Text! But how can he call it "good in the rest of the N.T." when it moves only marginally to the side of Codex B?

Therefore, if the Modern Version Text cannot get conclusive support from the "Five Old Uncials"-the so-called *best manuscripts*- where is it going to get it? We will have to leave this to others to look for the answer.

SUMMARY III: THE OLD UNCIALS (2)
Basis of Comparison : Doctrinal Passages in the Manuscript Digest

When we leave the overall textual picture given in the previous summary of the "Five (Six) Old Uncials" and concentrate more on their doctrinal passages, we see them weakening somewhat (especially in Revelation). This helps to explain why Codex C became a palimpsest, and others were virtually ignored during a thousand years of transmissional history.

	AV	"NIV"
CODEX ALEPH		
Original	58	290
Corrected	70	19
TOTAL	128	309
CODEX A		
Original	140	153
Corrected	3	0
TOTAL	143	153
CODEX B (Missing I Tim., - Phile; Heb. 9:14 - end; Rev.)		
Original	21	294

Section Two--A Summary of Manuscript Evidence

Corrected	5	2
TOTAL	26	296

CODEX C		
Original	90	129
Corrected	41	3
TOTALS	131	132

CODEX D-05 (Gospels and Acts)		
Original	77	110
Corrected	6	2
TOTAL	83	112

CODEX D-06		
Original	30	56
Corrected	38	2
TOTAL	68	58

Therefore, while B, and to a lesser extent Aleph are on the side of the diminished text, the combined figures for the four other uncials reveal a stand-off (425-455). Hardly the overwhelming support Modern Version proponents claim from these sources! Therefore we ask, if they cannot get decisive support from the "Five Old Uncials", where are they going to find it? Just about everywhere else we look in these summaries shows that they are on the minority side of the evidence.

SUMMARY IV:
THE "ALPHABET" AND "0" UNCIALS
Basis of Comparison: Doctrinal Passages in the Manuscript Digest

Beginning with Aleph (01), A (02), B (03) on down to 0274, we have at least 274 uncial manuscripts, many of which contain only a small part of the New Testament. The "0" system of numbering was adopted in the early part of the 20th Century, with the first 45 uncials in the list retaining their previous Roman or Greek letters of designation. Sinaiticus - Aleph is the only instance where a Hebrew letter is used.

The list did not extend beyond the "Alphabet" uncials in Tischendorf's day, but it is to his credit that he consistently cited the 40+ uncials available to him. Later editors have been much more selective in their presentation of the "0" uncials. Usually it has been a case of concentrating on those which show divergence from the Traditional Text and ignoring the rest. Thus, it is not possible to give as full a picture as we would like. However, Aland's material compensates for this, and allows us to at least show whether, and how many times, a manuscript is extant for the passages in the Digest. Given the readiness of the critical editors to list everything possible for their text, it can be reasonably assumed that most of what appears in the fourth column of these next two lists will support the Doctrinal Text of the AV.

The first number (where two are given) in the fourth column represents the times a passage is extant though not cited for the manuscript. Here, Aland has specifically shown that the manuscript contains the <u>verse</u> in question. In the second there is far more uncertainty as he indicates the <u>chapter</u> in which the verse is being sought is incomplete. Where only a single number is given, the "?" indicates this latter, and without "?" the former.

The Alphabet and O uncials give important insights into the kind of manuscript that was being copied between the fifth and ninth centuries. *They leave no question about the matter!*

THE "ALPHABET" UNCIALS

UNCIAL	DATE	Section	Times Extant But Not Cited	AV	"NIV"
Dabs	IX	P		50	30
E-07	VIII	E		169	9
E-08	VI	A		16	8
F-09	IX	E		148	4
F-010	IX	P		29	48
G-011	IX	E		168	6
G-012	IX	P		29	48
H-013	IX	E		145	6
H-014	IX	A		15	3
H-015	VI	P		3	5
I-016	V	P	(19)	5	6
K-017	IX	E		164	18
K-018	IX	APG		90	18
L-019	VII	E		73	93
L-020	IX	APG		122	16
M-021	IX	E		168	13
M-022	VI	E	(13,1?)	31	8
O-023	VI	E	(1,18?)	6	1

P-024	VI	E		17	4
P-025	IX	APGR	(1)	101	60
Q-026	V	E	(2)	10	1
R-027	VI	E	(4)	10	4
S-028	949	E		171	10
T-029	V	E	(5)	3	11
U-030	IX	E		170	8
V-031	IX	E		162	14
W-032	V	E	(5)	92	76
X-033	X (IX/X)	EG		107	20
Y-034	IX	E	(84,1?)	80	6
Z-035	VI	E		4	9
Gamma 036	X (IX)	E		139	14
Delta 037	IX	E		138	39
Theta 038	IX (VIII/IX)	E	(6)	111	48
Lambda 039	IX (VII/IX)	E		79	5
XI-040	VI*na* VIII*ubs*	E	(5)	2	11
Pi-041	IX	E		143	24
Sigma 042	VI	E		76	12
Phi-043	VI	E	(5,5?)	54	12
Psi-044	VIII/IX	EAPG	(30)	131	85

Section Two—A Summary of Manuscript Evidence

Omega 045	IX (VIII)	E	(85,1?)	77	5
Totals			(265,26?)	3308	818

These important witnesses move strongly to the side of the AV Doctrinal Text: by at least 4 - 1. Coming now to the "0" uncials I have only listed those which are known to be extant among the passages in the Manuscript Digest.

THE "O" UNCIALS

UNCIAL	DATE	Section	Times Extant But Not Cited	AV	"NIV"
046	X	R		6	
047	VIII	E	(163, 11?)	1	2
048	V	APG	(12)	3	11
049	IX	APG	(70, 6?)	30	4
050	IX	E	(1)	2	
051	X	R	(4)	5	
053	IX	E	(1)	4	1
054	VIII	E	(1)	6	
055	XI	EG	(181)		
056	X	APG	(122)	27	2
060	VI	E	(2)		
061	V	P	(1)	1	1
063	IX	E	(5)	18	1
064	VI	E	(6)		
065	VI	E	(1)		
067	VI	E	(2, 3?)	3	2
068	V	E		1	
070	VI	E	(11)	3	2

Section Two--A Summary of Manuscript Evidence 57

071	V/VI	E			1	
073	VI	E	(2)			
074	VI	E	(1)	4	2	
075	X	P	(52, 1?)	2		
078	VI	E	(2)	2		
079	VI	E	(1)	1		
083	VI/VII	E	(6)		5	
084	VI	E			2	
085	VI	E			2	
086	VI	E			2	
088	V/VI	P			2	
090	VI	E		2		
091	VI	E			1	
093	VI	AG	(1)			
095	VIII	A			1	
096	VII	A				
097	VII	A				
099	VII	E		1		
0102	VII	E	(3)	2		
0103	VII	E	(3)			
0104	VI	E	(2)	2		
0105	X	E		1		
0106	VII	E	(3)	3	2	
0107	VII	E	(2)	1	2	

0111	VII	E	(1)		1	
0112	VI/VII	E		2		
0113	V	E			4	
0114	VIII	E	(1)			
0115	IX/X	E	(1)	2		
0116	VIII	E	(6)	5	1	
0117	IX	E	(1)	3		
0119	VII	E		1		
0120	IX	A		1		
0121a	X	P		1	1	
0121b	X	P	(1)	3	1	
0122	IX	P		1		
0124	VI	E		6	4	
0125	V	E			1	
0130	IX	E	(3)	2		
0131	IX	E	(1)		1	
0132	IX	E	(1)			
0133	IX	E	(3, 30?)	4		
0134	VIII	E	(2)			
0135	IX	E	(5)	8		
0136	IX	E			1	
0137 (Part of 0136)	IX	E		1		
0138	IX	E		5		

Section Two--A Summary of Manuscript Evidence

0141	X	E	(39)		2
0142	X	APG	(123)	26	4
0143	VI	E	(1?)		
0144	VII	E	(1?)		
0146	VIII	E	(1)		
0148	VIII	E		1	
0149 (Apparently the same as 0187)	VI	E			1
0150	IX	P	(84, 1?)		
0151	IX	P	(89, 3?)		
0154	IX	E	(1, 4?)		
0155	IX	E			
0156	VIII	G			2
0157	VII/VIII	G	(1, 1?)		
0160	IV/V	E	(1)		
0161	VIII	E		1	
0163	V	R			1
0165	V	A	(1)		
0167	VII	E	(1)		
0170	V/VI	E			1
0171	IV	E	(1)	1	
0175	V	A			1
0176	IV/V	P		1	
0179	VI	E			1

0180	VI	E			1	
0181	IV/V	E	(1, 1?)		1	
0186	V/VI	P	(1)			
0187	VI	E	(1)			
0188	IV	E			1	1
0197	IX	E			2	1
0199	VI/VII	P	(1)			1
0201	V	P				
0202 (Part of 070)	VI	E	(1?)			
0204	VII	E	(1)			
0206	IV	G	(2)			
0208	VI	P	(1)			1
0209	VII	APG	(2)		2	
0211	VII	E	(179, 1?)			1
0212	III	E	(2)			
0220	III	P			1	
0230	IV	P	(2)			
0232	V/VI	G	(1)			2
0233	VIII	E	(7, 113?)		6	1
0240	V	P				1
0241	VI	P	(1)		1	
0242	IV	E	(3)		1	
0243	X	P	(4)		2	4

Section Two--A Summary of Manuscript Evidence

0245	VI	G	(1)		
0246	VI	G			
0247	V/VI	G	(1)		
0248	IX	E	(18?)		
0250	VIII	E	(3, 1?)	13	2
0251	VI	G	(1)		
0257	IX	E	(13, 40?)		
0262	VII	P	(1)		
0266	VI	E	(1)		1
0272	IX	E	(3)		
0273	IX	E	(1)		
0274	V	E	(2)		2
TOTALS			(1265, 218?)	238	111

Selective citation gives a disproportionate picture here. If, as the fourth column shows, the manuscripts were <u>fully</u> cited, the 2 - 1 margin could easily become 10 - 1 in favor of the Doctrinal Text. You may rest assured that if the 1265+ non-cited readings gave even 10% support to their side, the critical editors would have been quick to show it.

Only a few of these uncials are from the fifth and sixth centuries, but here also the evidence moves convincingly to the Doctrinal Text. Limiting this comparison to manuscripts which are adequately cited (at least 20 times) and fully cited (a minimum of non-citations in comparison to citations), we find:

				AV	"NIV"
E-08	VI			16	8
N-022	VI		(13, 1?)	31	8
P-024	VI			17	4
W-032	V		(5)	92	76
Sigma-042	VI			76	12
Phi-043	VI		(5, 5?)	54	12
TOTALS				286	120

Excluding the one uncial which mounts a challenge (W), the other five vote for the Doctrinal Text by well over 4-1. Thus in the entire list of 274 uncials, very few of those which are adequately cited give clear support to the diminished text of the Modern Versions. The text that was buried in the sands of Egypt found little reception during this period of manuscript transmission.

SUMMARY V:
THE CURSIVE MANUSCRIPTS
Basis of Comparison:
Doctrinal Passages in the Manuscript Digest

During the 9th century, scribes abandoned the uncial script for the small-lettered cursive (minuscule) in their production of New Testament manuscripts. About 2,800 cursives are now known to exist and these overwhelmingly side with the Doctrinal Text of the Authorized Version.

The textual implications of this transition of scribal practice has often been overlooked.

Jakob van Bruggen explains:
> It is assumed that after this transliteration process the majuscule was taken out of circulation...The import of this datum has not been taken into account enough in the present New Testament textual criticism. For it implies, that just the oldest, best and most customary manuscripts come to us in the new uniform. (*The Ancient Text of the New Testament*, pp 26,27;. cited in *The Identity of the New Testament Text*, Wilbur Pickering, Thomas Nelson Publ. 1980, p. 131).

Does it not seem likely that scribes of the Ninth Century would be in a better position to decide on the "oldest and best manuscripts" than textual critics of the Twentieth? Why during this changeover did they so decisively reject the text of Vaticanus and instead make copies of that text which now underlies the AV? It makes you think does it not!

In giving a relative picture of what proportion of cursive support a reading has, the *Nestle Aland 26* gives four indicators:

>   Majority
>   pm = a great many (permulti)
>   al = others (alii)
>   pc = a few (pauci)

According to Aland, " *al* is somewhere between *pc* and *pm*, but much closer to *pc*; *pm* refers to a large group of the majority text when it is divided, and accordingly can be found in support of more than one variant." (*NA 26*, p. 63*).

Aland, at his Institute for New Testament Textual Research, has most of the cursives on microfilm and is better placed than anyone to give a firsthand picture of their relative support. However, the methods he has used in arriving at these conclusions have not to my knowledge been published. In fact it seems to be something of a secret.

> The Munster Institute has compiled a list of 1000 test readings by which to determine MSS of the Majority type, so as to "weed out" such MSS from necessity for further study, (in accord with their anti-Majtxt theory); however, when Dr. Jakob van Bruggen... tried to secure even a copy of that list, permission was denied! (*How Many manuscripts are Necessary to Establish the Majority Text*, unpublished paper by Maurice A Robinson, 1978, p. 2).

Nevertheless, Aland's - *Majority, pm, al, pc* - are the best we have to go by for the present, and they certainly leave us in no doubt where the cursives stand in the AV - "NIV" debate over 356 doctrinal passages.

	AV	**"NIV"**
Majority	304	25
pm	25	23
al	10	61
pc	27	247

The Doctrinal Text of the Authorized Version receives Majority or *pm* support for 90% of its 356 doctrinally distinct passages, whereas 86% of the cursive support for the diminished text is only *pc* or *al*. On this subject, I would also like to recommend to you the author's *When The KJV Departs From The "Majority" Text*, available from the Dean Burgon Society.

SUMMARY VI:
FAMILIES ONE AND THIRTEEN
Basis of Comparison:
Doctrinal Passages in the Manuscript Digest

Textual Criticism has long sought to find cursives among the 2,800 which diverge substantially from the Traditional Text. It has been a difficult search! Not many have been found, and those few that do divert have had the most made of them. For example, MS 33 is close to Vaticanus in the Gospels, this led Hort and others to call it "the best of the minuscules", "the queen of the cursives." But alas, the "Queen" loses her crown in the rest of the N.T. for it reverts back (or nearly so) to the Traditional Text. Rarely, if ever, is there consistent or anything approaching complete divergence.

The *UBS 3* (pp XIX, XX) lists 62 cursives which are claimed to "exhibit a significant degree of independence from the so-called Byzantine manuscript tradition." At a later time it would be interesting to examine *just how significant* the departure is. Suffice it for now, to give an example of two groups of cursives which because of their "significant degree of independence" have long been held in favor among textual critics.

Family 1. Early in the twentieth century Kirsopp Lake identified a family of witnesses that includes manuscripts 1, 118, 131 and 209, all of which date from the 12th to 14^{h} centuries. Textual analysis of the Gospel according to Mark indicates that the type of text preserved in these minuscules often agrees with that of Codex Theta and appears to go back to the type of text current in Caesarea in the 3rd or 4^{h} centuries.

Family 13. In 1868...William Hugh Ferrar, discovered that four medieval manuscripts, namely 13, 69, 124 and 346 were closely related textually...It is known today that this group (the Ferrar group) comprises about a dozen members (including manuscripts 230, 543, 788, 826, 828, 983, 1689 and 1709) ... this family also has affinities with the Caesarean type of text. (Bruce H. Metzger, *The Text of the New Testament*, 2nd edition, Oxford: Clarendon Press, 1968, p. 63).

The textual affinities of these two families apply only to the Gospels. The *NA 26* from which the figures below are derived indicates that at least 18 manuscripts are included. Caesarea, you will recall, was a kind of halfway house textually to Alexandria.

Their consensus vote on the doctrinal passages in the Gospels is as follows:

	AV	"NIV"
Family 1 (5+NSS)	100	61
Family 13 (13+MSS	151	21
TOTALS	251	82

Thus, these "favored" cursives move to the side of the AV Doctrinal Text by 3 - 1. By themselves, the 13 manuscripts of Family 13 support the AV by 7-1.

SUMMARY VII: THE OLD LATIN
Basis of Comparison:
All places in UBS 3 where Byzantine readings oppose those of Aleph - B

We now look at the various language versions into which the New Testament was early translated. In some instances it was a direct translation (more or less) from the Greek. While in others, the work was done in more of a secondary fashion; i.e. from the Syriac or Latin, but still no doubt with the Greek at hand.

We will not be able to go into many of the intricate questions of the origin and early history of these versions, but rather to touch on the main points and to show on which side they line up. I would though like to encourage our readers to seek out some of the main facts of early versional history. Let it be said that with several, it is a *study in corruption*, supported by the "official" church, and very early bearing marks of heresy. Other versions, we can gladly report, came from a burning desire to spread the pure word of God. As the roots of the Authorized Version go back to a Tyndale or Wycliffe, so it is to God's humble people with a heart for the Bible that we look, rather than the lofty church "fathers". Versional History is by far the most important and stirring chapter in church history. It is an account that often winds along the trail of blood, and should be told more fully.

It seems likely that the Old Latin was translated in the Syrian Antioch by missionaries going to the West. Existing manuscripts certainly show a strong Syrian and Aramaic tendency. This being the case, the Old Latin is associated with that city which is the missionary center of the Book of Acts, and had immediate concourse with those centers in Asia Minor which received the Epistles of Paul. History is so unanimous to Antioch being the fountainhead of the Traditional Text that it has been called the *Antiochan Text*.

The 55 - 60 OL manuscripts which remain for us today show varying amounts of corruption, and frequently disagree among themselves. As such they are but an imperfect reflection of the original Old Latin Text. The OL of North Africa show some of the strange cases of addition and subtraction associated with the so-called Western Text, while those of Europe are generally favorable to the Received Text.

It is the branch of the Old Latin used in northern Italy that attracts our interest most, and establishes one of the crucial chapters in Bible transmissional history. This version, known as the Itala, is associated with the Christians of the Vaudois - the valleys of northern Italy and southern France. These noble believers withstood every attempt to bring them into the Catholic Church. From the days of Pope Sylvester (early 300's) unto the massacres of 1655, they were slaughtered, their name blackened, and their records destroyed; yet in those days they generally remained true to the Scriptures. They are known by a number of names, but best as the Waldensians. Research into the text and history of the Waldensian Bible has shown that it is a lineal descendant of the Old Latin Itala. In other words, the Itala has come down to us in the Waldensian form, and firmly supports the Traditional Text.

The following list shows the textual affinities of virtually all of the OL manuscripts. The parentheses in column 3 indicates that though the MS contained at least part of that section, citations were not available or taken from it.

SUMMARY

Number	Date	Section	Traditional	A'ph-B	Pre A.D. 600 Traditional	Aleph-B
a-3	IV	E	137	60	137	60
a2-16	V	E	1	1	1	1
ar-61	IX	(E)AP G(R)	94	79		
aur-15	VII	E	143	70		
b-4	V	E	129	58	129	58
beta-26	VII	E	3	4		
c-6	XII/XIII	EAPG (R)	170	87		
d-5	V	EAG	131	84	131	84
d-75	V/VI	P	47	31	47	31
dem-59	XIII	(A)PG (R)	71	43		
div--	XIII	P (G)R	25	22		
e-2	V	E	68	50	68	50
e-50	VI	A	46	20	46	20
e-76	IX	P	48	29		
f-10	VI	E	160	38	160	38
f-78	IX	P	46	35		
ff-66	X/XI	G	1	2		

Early Manuscripts, Church Fathers, & the Authorized Version

ff1-9	X	EAG	39	32		
ff2-8	V	E	128	51	128	51
g-77	IX	P	36	35		
g1-7	IX	E(A)P G(R)	47	21		
gig-51	XIII	(E)AP G(R)	48	26		
gue-79	VI	P	2	0	2	0
h-12	V	E	45	12	45	12
h-55	V	AG(R)	8	3	8	3
haf--	X	(R)	-	-		
i-17	V	E	35	16	35	16
j-22	VI	E	2	2	2	2
k-1	IV/V	E	11	30	11	30
l-11	VII/VIII	E	141	59		
l-67	VII	(E)AP G(R)	7	8		
m--	IV-IX	(E)AP G(R)	8	9	8	9
mon-86	X	P	6	10		
n-16	V	E	13	6	13	6
o-16	VII	E	1	0		
p-20	VII	E	1	1		
p-54	XIII	(E)AP GR	22	17		
ph-63	XII	A	10	6		

pi-18	VII	E	1	0		
q-13	VII	E	156	31		
q-64	VII	G	2	3		
r-57	VII/VIII	A	3	4		
r1-14	VII	E	97	39		
r2-28	VIII/IX	E	0	0		
r1,2,3-64	VII	P	8	14		
rho-24	VII/VIII	E	0	0		
s-21	V	E	3	0	3	0
s-53	VI	AG	4	10	4	10
t-56	XI	(E)AP G(R)	23	19		
t-19	VI	E	3	1	3	1
v-25	VII	E	0	0		
v-81	800	P	2	1		
w-83	XI	P	0	0		
x--	IX	P	51	34		
z-65	VIII	P(G)R	57	39		
TOTALS			2340	1252	981	482

The Old Latin supports the Traditional. Text against Aleph-B by about 2 - 1. If the cut-off date is moved back to 600 AD, we still have 2-1, and if back to 500AD, the numbers are 712 - 371. The one pre 400AD manuscript *a-3* gives 137 - 60 support to the text underlying our King James Bible.

Most of the above represents the European text of the OL, while according to Hort *e* and *k* (in the Gospels), and *f* and *q* (in the Gospels) are that of the African and Itala respectively. Certainly among the manuscripts which are adequately cited, k shows the weakest support for the Traditional Text while f and q give the strongest. (See Metzger, *Early Versions*, pp 326, 27).

e	7 - 5
k	1 - 3
f	4 - 1
q	5 - 1

Augustine of Hippo (N. Africa, died 430) is clear as to which he thought was the best:

> Now among the translations themselves the Italian (Italia) is to be preferred to the others, for it keeps closer to the words without prejudice to clarity of expression. (quoted in Metzger, pp 291).

SUMMARY VIII: JEROME'S VULGATE
Basis of Comparison: Indications of full or partial support as recorded in the Manuscript Digest

EDITIONS RATHER THAN INDIVIDUAL MANUSCRIPTS

Until now the summaries have been based on evidence of the manuscripts themselves. Generally it has been the <u>individual</u> manuscripts which have provided our conclusions. And even where we have had to use the estimated or consensus citations for the cursives, the points of reference have been reasonably certain. In the remaining summaries, though, it will unfortunately have to be a more secondary and subjective line of evidence - the editions! Here, an editor decides on a text which he believes is best supported by the manuscripts available to him. He may have done his work objectively, with actual reliance upon the Lord. He may have taken into account the necessary criteria: the age of the witnesses, a long line of traditional acceptance, number, geographic spread, variety of types of sources, etc. But, if a Westcott and Hort philosophy colors his judgment and he attempts to make the versional text fit into the Aleph-B mold - then we have serious problems. I am afraid that most of the editions that we are now going to consult are of this latter kind. The classic example is of course the modern critical Greek edition: it is based far more on a particular theory of the text than overall manuscript evidence. We will also increasingly see the hand of Rome and that version we are now to look at, the Latin Vulgate, as becoming a major influence.

It would be far better to show a breakdown of the older versional MSS (as with the Old Latin) then to have to rely upon an edited text. But as this information is not so readily available, we will have to use this source - but with caution and discernment!

THE VULGATE

We would have to be more than a little naive than to believe the account that the main reason Pope Damasus commissioned Jerome (in 383) to produce a new Latin Bible, was his concern over the differing Old Latin texts. It is likely that the Pope's chief concern was that there be a new translation which in format (inclusion of the Apocrypha), and text was more suitable to the rising power of the Roman Church. Nor should too much weight be given the idea that Jerome was "an independent scholar unfettered by the strictures of the Church." In fact, during the year immediately before the translation work began, he was the Pope's secretary at Rome! And, Jerome certainly leaves no doubt in his preface as to what his first motivation for the work was: "The command laid upon him by Damasus, the Supreme Pontiff". (Metzger, pp 334,35).

Questions about the kind of Old Latin and Greek texts Jerome used have long engaged scholars. This is made difficult by the wide variance in existing Vulgate MSS, and frequent mingling with the Old Latin which continued to be used through the centuries. Many of the conclusions are contradictory, while the research of H. J.Vogels (1928) - which seems to have held the field better than most - concludes that the sources were closer to our Traditional Text than originally thought (*Ibid*, pp 355,56). Nevertheless this is the Bible of Rome! It was kept from the common people. And, its 10,000 extant manuscripts scattered throughout the libraries and theological institutions of Europe and beyond have done their leavening work.

The Vulgates primary interest for us is the light it may throw on the Old Latin Text. As for it's earliest manuscripts, Metzger lists one from the 5th Century, two from the 6th, and several others from the 7th or early 8th Centuries.

EDITIONS

The editions of the Vulgate to which citation is occasionally made in *Nestle Aland 26* are:

1. **The Sixtine Edition**: This first authoritative edition was completed in May 1590 by a team under the direction of Pope Sixtus V, and seems to move surprisingly in the direction of the Traditional Text. Sixtus died on 27 August, and by 5 September all sales were stopped and the copies bought up and destroyed.

2. **The Clementine Edition**: The hurried replacement issued by Pope Clement VIII in 1592 differed from the Sixtine in about 3000 places. It remains to this day the edition of the Roman Catholic Church.

3. **The Wordsworth and White Edition**: Begun in 1877 by an Anglican scholar, John Wordsworth and carried on by his assistant, Henry White, it was completed (by others) in 1954. It contains an apparatus with the variant readings

Section Two--A Summary of Manuscript Evidence

of Vulgate and Old Latin MSS, and is an important source for anyone wanting to pursue the Latin evidence.

4. The "Stuttgart" Edition: A joint Protestant-Catholic production that was issued in Germany in 1969. To my knowledge it is the only Vulgate Edition which does not have I John 5:7,8 in its text.

THE SUMMARY

Drawing upon the evidence gathered in the Digest, Vulgate support is either "Full" or "Partial." "Full" means that most or all of the manuscripts and editions support the reading. Whereas "Partial" indicates that a significant minority of evidence supports the reading.

This then is how the Vulgate reacts to the doctrinal passages of the Authorized Version:

AV		"NIV"	
FULL	PARTIAL	FULL	PARTIAL
THE GOSPELS			
113	14	64	11
ACTS			
7	3	14	4

ROMANS TO HEBREWS			
28	19	51	12
JAMES TO JUDE			
6	10	20	6
REVELATION			
3	7	12	7
TOTALS			
157	53	161	40

Thus, the Vulgate supports the AV by a little less than 2 - 1 in the Gospels, with the same margin being reversed in Acts to Revelation. The total picture is one of a standoff. The Vulgate is therefore a kind of *halfway house* between the Received and Aleph-B text. This explains why the Vatican was so reluctant to let scholars have access to Codex B, for while it could be used against the Received Text of the Protestants, it also undermined their own Vulgate.

SUMMARY IX: THE SYRIAC VERSIONS
Basis of Comparison: Doctrinal Passages from the Manuscript Digest

As noted above, the importance of Antioch in the early transmissional history of Scripture cannot be overstated. It was the fountainhead of missionary activity. It had direct contact with the Apostles, and concourse with those centers who received the autographs of Scripture. It was famous for its literal exegesis. It was the home base of the Traditional Text. As the early centuries of the Christian era can be summed up as a "tale of two cities", in every respect Antioch stands in opposition to Alexandria!

THE PESHITTA

By all accounts the origin of the standard Syrian Version, the Peshitta, is to be found in the mid or even early 2nd Century (see for example Scrivener, *Plain Introduction*, p. 311ff). As the version witnesses strongly to the Traditional Text, attempts have been made to move it from the 2nd to 5th Century, putting in its place two really pitiful manuscripts known as the Curetonian and Sinaitic Syriac. The Peshitta was then declared (without a trace of evidence) to be a revision carried out by Rabbula, Bishop of Edessa, in about 425. The answer to this re-writing of textual history is well known. In Rabbula's day the Syrian church was split into two opposing sides known as the Monophysites (led by Rabbula) and the Nestorians. Both sides, though bitterly opposed to each other, used the Peshitta as their standard and only Bible. It is impossible to believe that the side opposed to Rabbula would at the same time wholeheartedly embrace the version he "revised." Nor can we believe that a version so widely accepted in that era had been only recently produced.

The number of Peshitta MSS is frequently put at 300. However, this refers to C. R. Gregory's list of 1902. Their number is now known to be much higher. It is also pointed out that the Book of Revelation as well as the smaller of the General Epistles are missing from the Peshitta MSS. This, however, should not be taken for granted. Early Syrian fathers quote Revelation! What were they quoting from

Section Two--A Summary of Manuscript Evidence 79

if not the Peshitta? Or which version of Revelation did the revisors of the Peshitta have before them? Certainly a source as the following should be consulted with regard to this inquiry.

"An Index of Syriac Manuscripts containing the Epistles and the Apocalypse", *Studies and Documents*, xxxiii, Salt Lake City, 1968.

Metzger (*Ibid*, pp 49-51) lists eleven of the more noteworthy Peshitta MSS: two are from the 5th Century, five from the 5th or 6th and four from the 6th. He then points out that nearly fifty others have been assigned to the 6th century.

Tischendorf, whom I have used in the Manuscript Digest, cites the edition of Leudsen and Schaff (1708) for his Peshitta evidence. The two editions cited today by critical editors, and therefore also reflected in our Manuscript Digest, are:

1. Tetraevangelium Sanctum Juxta Simplicem Syrorum Versionem. This edition of the four Gospels, by Philip Pusey and G. H. Gwilliam, was published in 1901. It is based upon 42 MSS, and also has a Latin translation on the facing pages. We get to feeling a little uneasy when Metzger tells us that its "resultant text agrees, to a very remarkable extent" with the first Peshitta edition of 1555 (*Ibid*, p.55). In this, Johann Widmanstadt collaborated with one Moses Mardinesis, "who had been sent as a legate to Pope Julius III. Moses brought with him a manuscript of the Syriac New Testament, which served as the basis of the printed volume ... In the Latin preface Widmanstadt expresses the hope that the edition might help promote the union of Christendom", (*Ibid*, pp. 52,53). Thus this first editor of the Peshitta was certainly no friend of the Reformation. It would be important to know whether any Catholic bias entered his text, and to what extent it affected the editions that followed.

2. The New Testament in Syriac. The British and Foreign Bible Society published an edition in 1920 which utilized a text prepared by C. H. Gwilliam in Acts to Hebrews, James, I Peter and I John. The remaining general epistles were taken from an edition of John Gwynn (1909), with his edition of Revelation (1897) also included. These latter two are not of the Peshitta at all, but rather the "Philoenian" Syriac (see below).

When *Nestle Aland 26* cites the Peshitta, it is always the text of Gwilliam; for it cites the *Tetraevangelium...* in the Gospels, and the Bible Society edition for the remainder of the N,T. (excluding II Peter, II, III John, Jude, Revelation). Thus, the only convenient view given today of the Peshitta (besides Tischendorf) is through the glasses of George Henry Gwilliam. And there are reasons for concern as to whether they have been colored by other factors.

THE SINAITIC AND CURETONIAN SYRIAC

Textual Criticism would have us believe that two manuscripts discovered in the latter half of the 19th century represent the "Old Syriac," the "primal" version of the Syrian Church from whence the Peshitta is only a revision.

It is hard to think of a less promising locality for a Peshitta "replacement" to be found than the monastery dedicated to St. Mary Deipara in the Nitrian Desert of Egypt! Yet, this was the source of the bundle of manuscripts William Cureton of the British Museum examined back in 1842. Among them was a MS of the Gospels in a hitherto unknown Syriac text.

Metzger describes the *stampede*:
> As soon as the text of the leaves was made available to scholars, it became obvious that the newly found version was a rival claimant to the priority of the Peshitta version. In fact, Cureton went so far as to suppose that in this version he had discovered the original of St. Matthews Gospel. (*Ibid*, p. 37)!!!

A second "Old Syriac" MS of the Gospels was found near the close of the century in St. Catharines Monastery at Mount Sinai (also the home of Codex Aleph). It was a palimpsest, with the Gospel text having been erased in the 8th Century, and twelve "Lives of Female Saints" written in its place. What does that say about 8th Century opinion concerning "a rival claimant to the Peshitta"?

The Cureton is thought to have been written about the middle of the 5th Century, with the Sinaitic about a half century earlier. Metzger concedes that though they "are far from containing identical texts, they agree often enough to make it convenient to cite their readings over against the text" of what he calls "the later Syriac versions", (meaning primarily the Peshitta!), (*Ibid*, p 39). In fact both are but another example of that small group of early MSS which through the influence of Alexandria have been stripped of substantial doctrinal content. Our summary shows that this is more apparent in the Sinaitic than Curetonian. For example, the Sinaitic in Matthew 1:16 denies the Virgin birth:

> Joseph, to whom was betrothed Mary the virgin, begot Jesus who is called the Christ.

These are the only two "clear" examples of the so-called Old Syriac to be found, and Metzger's attempt to explain this scarcity in comparison to the hundreds of Peshitta manuscripts betrays how weak the position is. (*Ibid*, pp 45-47*)*. In fact, Aland now admits "that the Old Syriac ... derives not from the II century but from the IV century". (NA - 26, p 54*).

Keep in mind how necessary this "Old Syriac exercise" has been for Textual Criticism: a 2nd Century Peshitta completely undermines their theory of early priority going to the Aleph - B Text.

THE PHILOXENIAN AND HARCLEAN SYRIAC

Separated by just over a century, the city of Mabbug in southwestern Asia Minor had two bishops whose names are associated with versions of the Syriac New Testament. The latter of these was Thomas of Harkel, who after fleeing an Arab invasion found refuge at a monastery near Alexandria. There, in 616, he completed a translation known to us as the "Harclean." And, with this we introduce one of the more complex accounts in the history of the Bible's transmission!

At the end of the Gospels, Thomas wrote a subscription (colophon) in which he refers back to the earlier translation of his predecessor, Philoxenus.

> This book of the four holy Gospels was translated out of the Greek into Syriac with great diligence and labor in the city of Mabbug, in the year of Alexander of Macedonia 819 (A.D. 508) in the days of the pious Mar Philoxenus, confessor Bishop of that city. Afterwards it was collated by me, the poor Thomas, by the help of two (or three) approved and accurate Greek Manuscripts ... (Scrivener, *Plain Introduction*, p. 326).

I think we will see that the "poor Thomas" did a far better work in his version, then the "pious Philoxenus." In fact, Philoxenus though commissioning the new translation does not seem to be the actual translator. Around the year 550, a certain Moses of Aghel translated into Syriac the writings of Cyril of Alexandria.

In his preface he refers to the translation of Philoxenus and has some revealing things to say:

> ... if the reader finds quotations from the holy scriptures in this translation of Cyril let him not be worried if they do not agree with MSS in Syriac, seeing there is great variation between the editions and traditions of the scriptures. If the reader wants to verify this, should he come across the edition of the New Testament and of the Psalter which the late chorepiskopos Polycarp made in Syriac for the faithful teacher Aksenaga (=Philoxenus) of Mabbug worthy of blessed memory, he will be amazed at the difference between the Syriac (ie Peshitta) and the Greek. (Sebastian Brock, "The Resolution of the Philoxenian/Harclean. Problem," *New Testament Textual Criticism* ...

Essays in Honor of Bruce Metzger, Ed. Eldon J. Epp and Gordon D. Fee, Oxford: Clarendon Press, 1981, p. 325n).

This Moses seems to be saying that the reader will be amazed at the difference between the Peshitta and the Greek underlying the new version associated with Philoxenus. Indeed there is quite a difference!

As to the motivation behind the revision, Brock is quite certain:
From these four passages it is evident that theological considerations were uppermost in Philoxenus' mind when he sponsored the new (or rather revised) translation. (*Ibid*, p 329).

And Metzger comes to the same conclusion, but needs to be read here with more than a little salt:
It appears that Polycarp sought to make a more theologically accurate rendering of the Greek than the current Peshitta rendering. (*Early Versions*, p. 65).

A dry wind seems to have blown upon the Philoxenian. Moses' statement above "should he come across the edition," indicates that forty years after its publication, it was not common *to come across it*! Certainly little remains in the manuscript record. And Thomas' knowledge of it is due more to the shared associations with Mabbug than anything else. The summary below shows that if Thomas' version is to be understood as a revision of the Philoxenian, then it is a revision which strongly moves back to the text of the Peshitta.

This latter view seems far preferable to that of Joseph White (the version's editor) and others, that Thomas made only a slight revision and added notes to the margin. According to this view, the manuscripts we have today are really those of the Philoxenian with minor adjustments by Thomas. But their alignment with the Peshitta; and as Brock has shown, their essential disagreement with the other writings of Philoxenus - namely his Scripture quotations in *Commentary on the Prologue of John* - militate convincingly against the idea.

The Harclean version covers the entire N.T. (Metzger, p. 69), including the four smaller General Epistles and Revelation. There is but one edition, that which Joseph White completed in 1803. It was based chiefly on an 11th century manuscript (*Ibid*, p. 72) and we hope it was a good representative, for some sixty Harclean manuscripts are now known to exist. The standard critical editions (Tischendorf, NA, UBS) cite White for Matthew to Jude, but as he omitted Revelation, the so-called *de Dieu* manuscript is used for the Harclean evidence of that book. This manuscript, named after the man who published it in 1627, is one of sixteen of the Apocalypse known to exist (*Ibid*, p. 68n). But, whether it is a good manuscript is another matter, for as our summary shows it uncharacteristically votes against the AV Text. The fact that the *de Dieu* found a home in the Polyglot Bibles which began to appear after the publication of the Authorized Version, further puts us on guard. Most of these "multi-versions" were funded by Rome as an attempt to undermine Protestant faith in the AV through the display of variants. (See Theodore P. Letis, *Edward Freer Hill's Contribution to the Revival of the Ecclesiastical Text*, masters thesis pending publication, p. 41ff).

Does this help to explain why White did not include Revelation in his edition?

If anything remains of the actual Philoxenian, it is in a late manuscript of II Peter, II, III John, and Jude published by Edward Pococke in 1630; and in a 12th/13th Century manuscript of Revelation purchased by a certain Earl of Crawford in 1860. The "Pococke Epistles" and "Crawford Apocalypse" are cited in *NA 26* and *UBS 3* as the "Philoxenian". This seems to be the current consensus, but the issue of their identity is still debated.

THE PALESTINIAN SYRIAC

Our last Syrian version to be mentioned comes to us in an Aramaic dialect used in Palestine during the earlier centuries of the Christian era. Many have tried to reconstruct historical events in Palestine in such a way as to push it back to a 5th Century origin.

But, as Arthur Voobus with his usual candor concludes:
...that means that the version must have existed already before 700 A.D...This means the version did not exist in the fourth century...This leaves the following two centuries open for the date of the origin ... Unfortunately there is nothing which would give us a hint that the version existed in the fifth century... (*Early Versions of the New Testament, Stockholm*: Estonian Theological Society in Exile, 1954, p. 126).

Unlike the Peshitta or Harclean, the Palestinian takes its place with the Sinaitic, Curetonian and Philoxenian in coming down to us with only the barest manuscript witness. And, as to where it was found, I think you'll find the story has a familiar ring! Apart from a few fragments, the version is extant in three dated Gospel lectionaries, designated A,B,C. "A" dated A.D. 1030 was in the Vatican Library; while "B" and "C", dated 1104 and 1118, were discovered in the Monastery of St Catherine on Mount Sinai. The homes of B and Aleph!

Regarding the other fragments, Metzger sums up:
Beside the three primary witnesses to the Palestinian Syriac version, fragments of the text of the Gospels have survived in non-

lectionary manuscripts, as well as portions of Acts, of all the Pauline Epistles (including Hebrews) except 2 Thessalonians and Philemon and of James and 2 Peter, some passages in more than one witness. The most recent acquisitions have come to light at Khirbet Mird; these include fragments from Luke (3:1,3-4), Acts (10:28-9, 32-41), and Colossians (1:16-18, 20ff). (*Early Versions*, pp. 79, 80).

As explained above with the 17th century polyglots, it must always be noted *who* is willing to raise the finances to publish a given manuscript. The fact that Rome in 1861 funded a "sumptuous edition with Latin translation" of the Vatican Palestinian (*Ibid*, p. 78) leads us to put a question mark over it.

Indeed as our summary also indicates:
The Palestinian Syriac version shows a textual type which when compared with the Greek families, is closest to the standard Byzantine text. But it does not go all the way with this text. (Voobus, p. 128).

In our view the Palestinian Syriac was a halfway-house which either purposely or through carelessness tended to undermine the God-honored Text.

THE SUMMARY

	AV	"NIV"
THE GOSPELS		
Peshitta	152	32
Sinaitic	55	81
Curetonian	43	41
Philoxenian	--	--
Harclean	161	21
Palestinian	62	38
ACTS		
Peshitta	16	9
Sinaitic	--	--
Curetonian	--	--
Philoxenian	--	--
Harclean	15	11
Palestinian	0	1
ROMANS TO HEBREWS		
Peshitta	60	24
Sinaitic	--	--
Curetonian	--	--
Philoxenian	--	--

Harclean	66	22
Palestinian	3	8

JAMES TO JUDE		
Peshitta*	9	9
Sinaitic	--	--
Curetonian	--	--
Philoxenian**	3	8
Harclean	15	16
Palestinian	0	1

REVELATION		
Peshitta	--	--
Sinaitic	--	--
Curetonian	--	--
Philoxenian	4	17
Harclean***	5	16
Palestinian	--	--

TOTALS		
Peshitta	237	74
Sinaitic	55	81
Curetonian	43	41
Philoxenian	7	25
Harclean	262	86
Palestinian	65	48

*   James, I Peter, I John only
**   II Peter, II, III John, Jude only
***   de Dieu manuscript

In company with the other early versions, warfare raged over the doctrinal heart of the Syriac Bible. Keep in mind that four of the above have only traces of MS support, whereas the Peshitta (350+ MSS) and Harclean (60 MSS), demonstrate a widespread usage in the early Eastern church. And, viewed against our concern that the <u>editions</u> of the Peshitta and Harclean may not adequately represent their manuscript testimony, the margin to each is quite convincing.

SUMMARY X: THE COPTIC VERSIONS
Basis of Comparison: Doctrinal Passages from the Manuscript Digest

Given its proximity to Alexandria, we would expect the Egyptian Coptic versions to be almost completely hand-in-glove with the text of that city. This, however, is not entirely the case. Here, in this summary is listed the evidence for versions belonging to seven Coptic dialects. The two most important are the Sahidic, originally associated with Southern Egypt, and the Bohairic of northern Egypt. As we must now come again to $2^{nd}/3^{rd}$ Century Egypt, it cannot be stated too strongly that we have come to the worst possible place to look for a Bible!

Even Bruce Metzger, a supporter of the Alexandrian Text, is compelled to catalogue the vast amount of religious corruption which came from Egypt:

> Among Christian documents which during the second century either originated in Egypt or circulated there among both the orthodox and the Gnostics are numerous apocryphal gospels, acts, epistles and apocalypses. Some of the more noteworthy are the Gospel according to the Egyptians, the Gospel of Truth, the Gospel of Thomas, the Gospel of Philip, the Kerygma of Peter, the Acts of John, the Epistle of Barnabas, the Epistle of the Apostles, and the Apocalypse of Peter. There are also fragments of exegetical and dogmatic works composed by Alexandrian Christians, chiefly Gnostics during the second century. We know, for example, of such teachers as Basilides and his son Isidore, and of Valentinus, Ptolemaeus, Heracleon, and Pantaenus. All but the last-mentioned were unorthodox in one respect or another. In fact, to judge by the comments made by Clement of Alexandria, almost every deviant Christian sect was represented in Egypt during the second century. Clement mentions the Valentinians, the Basilidians, the Marcionites, the Peratae, the Encratites, the Docetists, the Haimetites, the Cainites, the Ophites, the Simonians, and the Eutychites. What proportion of Christians in Egypt during the second century were orthodox is not known. (*Early Versions*, p.101).

Yet, this is the home of our Modern Bibles! The Jews of Egypt who heard the Gospel on the Day of Pentecost (Acts 2:5,10) would have returned with that same Gospel to their homeland. No doubt sound local churches were established, pure copies of Scripture made available, and a witness maintained amid the philosophic and theological corruption for which Egypt was notorious. Sadly *our* records are of the corruption; but God knew His own in that land, they were not lost from His records. There was always a silver cord of redemption, even in Egypt.

THE SAHIDIC COPTIC

"The earliest Christians used Greek, but soon the new faith found adherents outside the Hellenized section of the population - which it must be remembered, was only a fraction in comparison with the number of native inhabitants who used only the Egyptian language." (*Ibid*, p. 103,4). Though the Sahidic dialect is generally associated with southern (or upper) Egypt: in the centuries before the birth of Christ, it became the standard literary language of the educated classes throughout the entire country. Thus, Sahidic would have been more acceptable in Alexandrian circles than the other more "rustic" dialects. Sahidic began to wane in the 8th/9th Centuries, and gave way to the increasingly popular Bohairic, first in the Delta and then the rest of Egypt.

Unlike the Old Latin or Peshitta, the Coptic comes down to us in only a relatively few and scattered fragments. This fact is especially significant when we consider how much better the climatic conditions were in Egypt for the preservation of manuscripts. Yet even with this advantage, it didn't last! This is clearly the mark of a text that was discarded. It was not until the beginning of the 20th Century that enough material was available for Musei Balestri to publish an edition of the Sahidic N.T. which even approached being complete. This, you should notice was published in Rome in 1904! Prior to this, Tischendorf had to use the partial editions of Munter (1789), Woide (1799), and Schwartze (about 1850).

The edition used by *NA 26* is that of George W. Homer —
> The Coptic version of the New Testament in the Southern Dialect, otherwise called Sahidic and Thebaic, Oxford, 1911-29.

But here too, it was only by "piecing together widely scattered scraps of text" that Homer was able to produce an edition containing "almost every verse of the N.T."; and "one must beware against attributing to the edition any measure of homogeneity" (*Ibid*, p. 109n).

Metzger (pp. 110-114) lists fourteen Sahidic manuscripts containing usually no more than small portions of individual N.T. books. Three are from perhaps the 3rd/4th Centuries; five from the 4th, three from the 4th/5th, one from the 5th, and two from about 600. These last two are much fuller: one contains the fourteen Epistles of Paul (incl. Hebrews), and the other is of Acts and John. A number of $9^{th}/10^{th}$ Century MSS contain much of the Gospels and other N.T. portions.

Given the likelihood of more general interaction with the Alexandrian "scholarship", it is not surprising to find in our summary that the Sahidic differs more sharply from the Traditional Text than the other Coptic versions. Bohairic, though more indigenous to Alexandria, does not differ as much.

THE BOHAIRIC COPTIC

As with Sahidic, the roots of the Bohairic dialect reach far back into the pre-Christian era. It was the language of Northern or Lower Egypt. It was "spoken in the environs of Alexandria, in the Delta, and from the coastal regions to Memphis ... It has been called Memphitic". (Voobus, p. 229). Unlike Sahidic, it remained a provincial dialect until the $8^{th}/9^{th}$ centuries, when it began to be used throughout the entire country. "Of the several Coptic dialects, Bohairic is the only one that continues to be used today as the liturgical language of the Coptic Orthodox Church." (Metzger, p. 121).

Bohairic was not the "collegiate" language that Sahidic was. This may help to explain why it's scriptures were not so strongly "Alexandrian."

Compared with the Sahidic, where we have mainly fragments and very few manuscripts, the Bohairic is represented by a number of reasonably full manuscripts. But, very little is available before the 9th Century. The relative dampness of lower Egypt in contrast to the drier Sahidic - South may explain this. Metzger mentions a small portion of Romans which goes back to the beginning of the 4th Century, and a half-chapter of Philippians of the $4/5$. The most extensive early manuscript is a nearly complete Gospel of John from the 4th Century. This was found in the drier climate of Upper Egypt. But see below on "Proto-Bohairic."

Tischendorf for his Bohairic evidence used the editions of David Wilkins (1716), and N.G. Schwartze (about 1850) for the Gospels. Critical editions today use George Homers –

The Coptic version of the New Testament in the Northern Dialect, otherwise called Memphitic and Bohairic, Oxford, 1898—1905.

Again, the objectivity of an editor in his presentation of the manuscript evidence and traditionally accepted readings, must never be taken for granted. Whenever possible, it is far better to know what the individual MSS say than to rely upon the composite text in an edition.

The Sahadic and Bohairic are generally dated from the 3rd or 4th Centuries, with the Sahadic thought to be the somewhat earlier. There were, no doubt, pure copies of God's Word circulating in Egypt during the century before the two "official" versions took root.

Section Two--A Summary of Manuscript Evidence   91

THE MINOR COPTIC VERSIONS

Citations from five other Coptic translations have been gathered in The Manuscript Digest, with their evidence reflected in the Summary. Manuscript remains are very fragmentary and are mentioned only occasionally in *NA 26*, but they seem to be quite early, not far removed in time from the two primary versions. What little we do have often moves more in the direction of the Traditional Text.

1. PROTO BOHAIRIC : This seems to refer only to the 4th Century MS of John's Gospel which was mentioned above among the Bohairic MSS. It is known as Papyrus Bodmer III, and has certain features which indicate the copyist may have been a Gnostic (Metzger, p. 125).

2. MIDDLE EGYPTIAN : Two manuscripts (4th/5th Centuries) containing a large portion of Matthew and Acts have been found. A third (5th Century), containing portions of Paul's Epistles, is now thought to be closer to the Sahidic. The Matthew and Acts MSS witness quite strongly for the Traditional Text.

3. FAYYUMIC : Though *NA 26* seems to cite the version belonging to this dialect only occasionally, quite a lot of scattered portions are available. Metzger (p. 120) lists the following:

        22 from the Gospels, 6th-9th Centuries
        2 from Acts, one early 4th/5th, and the other late
        14 from Epistles of Paul, 5th-9th
        3 from the General Epistles, 5th-7th

4. ACHMIMIC : Very little remains. Metzger lists three fragments with small portions of Matt. 11, James 5, and Gal. 5. These are dated from the $4^{th}/5^{th}$ Centuries; a fourth, more sizeable portion, contains parts of Luke and is from the 4th Century. Only one citation from this Version has been noted in the Manuscript Digest.

5. SUB-ACHMIMIC : Our main source for this dialect is a nearly complete Gospel of John dating from the 5th Century. "The handwriting bears a rather strong resemblance to that of Codex Vaticanus, allowance being made for the circumstance that one is on papyrus and the other on vellum." (Metzger, p. 116). Our summary shows that it is not nearly so diverse from the AV as Codex B.

THE SUMMARY

Here is how the two major, and five minor Coptic Versions (where extant) vote as regards the Doctrinal Text of the Authorized Version. Indications of "partial" support are shown for the Sahidic and Bohairic.

	AV	'NIV'
GOSPELS		
Sahidic	42	105
partial	8	8
Bohairic	50	72
partial	63	52
Proto-Bohairic	5	8
Mid-Egyptian	16	11
Fayyumic	7	11
Achmimic		1
Sub-Achmimic	8	10
ACTS		
Sahidic	4	19
partial		1
Bohairic	4	19
partial	2	2
Proto-Bohairic		
Mid-Egyptian	6	
Fayyumic		

Section Two--A Summary of Manuscript Evidence

Achmimic		
Sub-Achmimic		
ROMANS TO HEBREWS		
Sahidic	16	52
partial	3	2
Bohairic	27	59
partial	4	3
Proto-Bohairic		
Mid-Egyptian		
Fayyumic	3	6
Achmimic		
Sub-Achmimic		
JAMES TO JUDE		
Sahidic	3	22
partial	2	
Bohairic	12	17
partial		2
Proto-Bohairic		
Mid-Egyptian		
Mid-Fayyumic		
Achmimic		
Sub-Achmimic		
REVELATION		
Sahidic	3	5
partial		

Bohairic	6	14
partial		1
Proto-Bohairic		
Mid-Egyptian		
Fayyumic		
Achmimic		
Sub-Achmimic		
TOTALS		
Sahidic	68	203
partial	13	11
Bohairic	99	181
partial	69	60
Proto-Bohairic	5	8
Mid-Egyptian	22	11
Fayyumic	10	17
Achmimic		1
Sub-Achmimic	8	10
TOTALS	294	502

Unlike the Syriac, where we are comparing the massively attested Peshitta (350+ MSS) against 2 MSS of the "Old" Syriac, we have for each of the above Coptic versions only small amounts of available evidence. Current information shows the Egyptian Coptic moving against the AV by about 5 - 3.

THE OVERALL MARGIN FOR THE THREE PRIMARY VERSIONS

	AV	"NIV"
Old Latin	2	1
Syriac	3	1
Coptic	3	5

The one dissenting voice comes from the version with the least manuscript evidence!

SUMMARY XI:
THE GOTHIC, ARMENIAN, AND ETHIOPIC
Basis of Comparison: Doctrinal Passages from the Manuscript Digest

Our final three versions, though not being in the first rank of antiquity, nevertheless played a vital role in the early transmission history. The Gothic Version was translated from the Greek in the mid 4th Century by Ulfilas the missionary to the Goths. The few remaining MSS bear strong witness to the Traditional Text despite their influence from the Latin. The same is true of the 5th Century Armenian version. Over 1200 MSS survive, though here too, we see considerable influence from the Latin Vulgate. And the 6th Century Ethiopic demonstrates something of a victory for the Traditional Text in an area close to Egypt.

THE GOTHIC VERSION

During the 2nd and 3rd Centuries the Goths came from the wilds of Scandinavia into the plains of southeastern Europe to the north of the Lower Danube and west of the Black Sea. From here they made frequent raids into the crumbling remains of the Roman Empire, and eventually invaded Rome itself in A.D. 410. Given their warlike nature, Augustine reflected the general feeling of thankfulness that the Goths had been Christianized before the sack of Rome. Earlier, in one of their forays into Cappadocia, Asia Minor, Christian captives were brought back and settled in Dacia (Romania). From among these were the grandparents of Ulfilas (little wolf), the "Apostle of the Goths".

Ulfilas' great accomplishment was to translate the Old and New Testaments into the language of the very people who deported his forebears. The work (about A.D. 350) necessitated the adaptation of Greek and Latin characters into the first Gothic alphabet. Thus, he was the forerunner of the many missionaries who had first to create an alphabet before translation work on the Bible itself could begin.

Section Two--A Summary of Manuscript Evidence 97

His translation was taken directly from the kind of Greek manuscripts found in the vast majority today. This witnesses powerfully to the fact that in 350 there were many Traditional Text MSS, and that these had held a place of esteem among God's people. Ulfilas' roots in Asia Minor, should also be noted here. The path from Antioch, to Asia Minor, to the world beyond was the route of the God-honored Text.

The one shadow over this happy account, is the oft-repeated inference that "in theology Ulfilas was hospitable to Arianism, or semi-Arianism". (Metzger, pp. 376,77). Except of course in the more obvious cases, this kind of charge should not be accepted unless given with clear evidence, (which Metzger and others I have before me have not given). We cannot go into the case of Ulfilas here, but only to point out that Rome has long used this epithet against men who had absolutely nothing to do with Arianism.

Metzger describes the impressive early history of the Gothic Version and the sudden demise of it's language:

> About a century after the death of Ulfilas, the Ostrogothic chief Theodoric invaded northern Italy and founded a mighty empire, the Visigoths being already in possession of Spain. Since the use of Ulfilas' version can be traced among the Goths of both countries, it must have been the vernacular Bible of a large portion of Europe. Many manuscripts of the version were certainly produced during the fifth and sixth centuries in the writing schools of northern Italy and elsewhere, but only eight copies, most of them quite fragmentary, have survived... The Ostroigothic kingdom in Italy was of relatively brief duration (A.D. 488-554), and by the middle of the sixth century it was overthrown, succumbing to the power of the eastern Roman Empire. The survivors left Italy, and the Gothic language disappeared leaving scarcely a trace...Interest in Gothic manuscripts was completely lost. Many of them were taken apart, the writing scraped off, and the expensive parchment used again (*Ibid*, pp 377,78; emphasis mine).

Regarding the remaining manuscripts, Voobus says:
> ...the existing manuscripts testify to some corruption from Latin sources, very naturally arising during the occupation of Italy by the Goths (p. 405).

This Latinization is certainly seen in the little that does remain. The best known MS is Codex Argenteus (5th/6th Century), it contains the four Gospels, but in the Latin order - Matthew, John, Luke, Mark. Several verses from the end of Luke are extant in the leaf of a 6th Century Gothic-Latin MS. The few remaining Gothic manuscripts are all palimpsests thought to have been rewritten at a monastery in Bobbio, Italy. Their underlying text reveals scattered portions of the Epistles of Paul and Matthew. No portion of Acts, Hebrews or Revelation remains.

The 1908 editions of W. Streitberg is used in *NA 26*. Our chief concern is to what extent the remaining MSS have departed from the original Gothic through influence of the Vulgate. They support the AV by nearly 3-1, but there is reason to believe that the margin in the original would have been much greater.

THE ARMENIAN VERSION

Few people have known the turmoil of the Armenians. In other places there has been a "water barrier" between the Moslem East and European West, but here it is but a land frontier — traditionally sandwiched between the Roman and Persian Empires. And, like the Jews, the Armenians have long known the meaning of the word "Pogrom".

When we look at the areas mentioned in Acts 2:9, we are getting close to Armenia; and it is likely the Gospel was taken there after the Day of Pentecost. There are records of Syriac speaking missionaries going to this land of Noah's Ark in the 3rd Century. According to Scrivener, Armenian believers used the Peshitta before they had a version of their own. (*Plain Introduction*, p 407).

> H.S. Miller gives a good summary account of the Version's beginnings:
> About 406 Mesrob, a great missionary and writer, succeeded in inventing an Armenian alphabet of 36 letters, thus laying the foundation for Armenian literature as did Ulfilas for the Gothic. He had a helper, Sahak (Isaac),with assistants, made translations from the manuscripts, Syriac and Greek, which they had (411). Returning from the Council of Ephesus (431), two of his students brought from the Imperial Library at Constantinople copies of the Greek Bible. A fresh translating and recasting from these manuscripts produced a version (about 436). (*General Biblical Introduction*, Houghton: The Word-Bearer Press, 1960, p *254).*

Thus, whether from Syria or Constantinople, we see the convergence of the Traditional Text upon the new version. But, as Scrivener explains, with many of the surviving manuscripts there is something of a problem:

> ...that like the Memphitic its existing codices are comparatively modern and differ widely in the text they represent; and that their very close resemblance to the Vulgate Latin has lent countenance to a tradition, in itself sufficiently probable, that on the submission of the Armenian Church to that of Rome, King Haitho (1224-70) revised the Armenian version by the Latin: it seems to be ascertained that he did

translate into Armenian and insert in his national Bible the Prefaces in the Vulgate (*Plain Introduction*, p 408).

Vulgate influence may well explain why this version and some others agree much more closely with the Traditional Text in the Gospels than they do in the remainder of the N.T. For example, my summary shows the Armenian supporting the AV by 2-1 in the Gospels, but it swings slightly against it in the remainder of the N.T. Compare this with the 2-1 support the Vulgate gives to the AV in the Gospels, only to reverse the margin in the remainder!

In 1959 Erroll F. Rhodes compiled a list of 1244 Armenian MSS. Further information about collections in the Soviet Union show that the total figure is much higher. The oldest (of the Gospels) is dated 887. Metzger lists a further six MSS from the 9th or early 10th Centuries.

The first printed edition was published in 1666 by an Armenian cleric, A.D. Uscan. It is said to be based on an Armenian manuscript connected with King Haitho, which as indicated above had been revised in the direction of the Latin Vulgate. Metzger speaks of seven places, including the addition of John 8:1-11 and I John 5:7, "where Uscan's text agrees with the Latin Vulgate against all known Armenian manuscripts". (*Early Versions*, p. 170n).

Our information here has some gaps, and is a little contradictory. For example we are not certain if King Haitho damaged the Armenian, or if it was done before him. But, given the probability that 2000 Armenian MSS currently exist: what percentage with regard to John 8:1-11 and I John 5:7 was Metzger referring when he said "all known Armenian manuscripts"?

The edition used by critical editors today is that of John Zohrab (1789), and is based on a 1319 MS that was in the Mechitarist Monastery at Venice. It has an apparatus in which as many as 30 MSS are cited in the Gospels with a lesser number elsewhere.

When the two editions disagree, Uscan invariably goes with the AV, and Zohrab against! All of which is an example of the warfare that rages over God's Word, but the Lord has promised to "guide into all truth," John 16:13.

THE ETHIOPIC VERSION

H.S. Miller gives the "official" account of how "Christianity" came to Ethiopia:
> We are told that it was introduced there in the time of Constantine (about 330) by two Tyrian missionaries from Alexandria, Frumentius and Aedesius. The latter afterwards returned to Tyre, but Frumentius continued the work, went to Alexandria and there was consecrated bishop and head of the Ethiopian Church (*General Biblical Introduction*, p 252).

This comes from the *Ecclesiastical History* of Rufinus in the 4th Century. However, I would much rather follow the trail of those chariot wheels in Acts Chapter Eight! It was the view of Iranaeus (died 202), and even Eusebius (339) that the Ethiopian eunuch introduced the Gospel to that land (Metzger, p. 217n). Ethiopian tradition claims that the first Ethiopic Bible was already available when Frumentius preached there. (Voobus, p. 248). Editions such as *UBS 3* give a 6th Century date. There is no clear indication from history, but there is a clear testimony from Scripture: *Have they not heard? Yes verily, their sound went into all the earth, and their words unto and their words unto the ends of the world.* Rom. 10:18. And, this happened sooner rather than later! *He sendeth forth his commandment upon earth: his word runneth very swiftly.* Psa. 147:15.

Several thousand Ethiopic MSS are known to exist, but most are very late. Metzger lists the earliest (the four Gospels) as from the 10th Century, two are from the 11th, and the rest from the 14th and later. Two editions are cited today: the Rome edition, edited by three Abyssinian monks in 1549, and that of the British and Foreign Bible Society (1830), prepared by Thomas Pell Platt. This later was revised by Franz Praetorius at the request of the Swedish Evangelical Society in 1899. It will not be a surprise to discover that when the editions differ, the *Rome* will invariably support the Modern Version Text while Platt and Praetorius stands with the Authorized Version.

THE SUMMARY

	AV	"NIV"
THE GOSPELS		
Gothic	66	22
Armenian	113	55
Uscan	13	0
Zohrab	0	11
Ethiopic	111	58
Rome	1	10
Platt-Praet.	10	2
ACTS		
Gothic	--	--
Armenian	12	12
Uscan	0	0
Zohrab	0	0
Ethiopic	7	11
Rome	0	4
Platt-Praet.	4	1
ROMANS TO HEBREWS		
Gothic	44	18
Armenian	43	38
Uscan	7	0

Zohrab	0	6
Ethiopic	27	44
Rome	0	17
Platt-Praet.	16	1
JAMES TO JUDE		
Gothic	--	--
Armenian	8	19
Uscan	1	1
Zohrab	1	1
Ethiopic	10	14
Rome	0	3
Platt-Praet.	3	0
REVELATION		
Gothic	--	--
Armenian	9	8
Uscan	4	0
Zohrab	0	3
Ethiopic	5	13
Rome	0	0
Platt-Praet.	0	0

TOTALS		
Gothic	110	40
Armenian	185	132
Uscan	25	1

Section Two--A Summary of Manuscript Evidence

Zohrab	1	21
Ethiopic	160	140
Rome	1	34
Platt-Praet.	33	4
TOTALS	**515**	**372**

The Authorized Version is the clear victor in the Gothic, Armenian and Ethiopic Versions. Yet, with our present evidence, the actual margin of victory cannot be clearly seen. The further one goes in these matters, the more the hidden hand of Rome is seen in the editions. Ten thousand Vulgate manuscripts scattered throughout Europe and the Mediterranean regions have done their leavening work!

SUMMARY XII:
THE EARLY CHURCH FATHERS TO CHRYSOSTOM
Basis of Comparison : All places in the UBS-3 where Byzantine readings oppose those of Aleph-B; and the evidence of Burgon and Miller

Scripture quotations contained in the commentaries and theological works of early preachers, writers and church leaders give an important testimony to the kind of text that prevailed in the early centuries. Do they witness to the full Doctrinal Text underlying the Authorized Version, or is it the diminished text of Alexandria? F.J.A. Hort seemed very confident in declaring that little of the Byzantine majority could be found in patristic quotation before Chrysostom (died 407). But, this well-known assertion may have stemmed more from a sense of necessity than confidence. For without it, the entire critical theory collapses.

Frederic Kenyon recognized this:
> Hort's contention, which was the cornerstone of his theory, was that readings characteristic of the Received Text are never found in the quotations of Christian writers prior to about A.D. 350. (*Recent Developments in Textual Criticism of the Greek Bible*, pp. 7,8, quoted from W. H. Pickering, p 36).

One hundred years after Hort, this is still asserted. D. A. Carson is an example:
> The ante-Nicene fathers unambiguously cited every text type except the Byzantine (*The King James Version Debate*, Grand Rapids: Baker Book House, 1979, p. 47).

Now, that certainly is a confident statement! However, if you want an example of a textual "escape artist" you need to read this same author on page 110. Here Carson gives his response to the substantial evidence gathered by

Section Two--A Summary of Manuscript Evidence   105

Burgon and Miller that ante-Nicene fathers not only quote the Traditional Text, but they quote it predominantly.

> Textual critical scholars have responded to this in various ways. First of all, detailed critical editions of the fathers had not been prepared in Miller's day. Many Byzantine readings in the late manuscripts of the fathers may well be due to assimilation to the Byzantine text-type in the post-Nicene period. Of course there is a danger of arguing in a circle here; so let us be conservative and suppose that there were but few assimilations. It then follows that many Byzantine readings are found in the ante-Nicene fathers. However, that fact by itself still proves nothing...

I will have to let you buy the book to get the rest of his "reply". But notice, Carson is tacitly conceding that considerable Byzantine quotation may well take place in the early fathers, and that "assimilation" cannot be used to explain away the fact.

It is now one hundred years since Burgon gathered his quotations, and it has yet to be shown that any of the "critical" editions present an appreciably different overall picture than the sources he used.

Edward Hills was in no doubt about this:
> In regard to my references to the Church Fathers, I am sure that if you examine the notes to my KING JAMES DEFENDED and my BELIEVING BIBLE STUDY, you will see that I have taken care to look up all of Burgon's references in the most modern editions available. During the years 1950-55 I spent many weeks at this task...Whether Pickering looked up all Burgon's references or not, I do not know. At any rate, Fee's rebuttal is a very ancient one, rather out of date, namely, the attempt to invalidate Burgon's patristic references by alleging that the editions of the Church Fathers which he used were old and out of date. Fair-minded naturalistic scholars, however, like Rendel Harris (1909), have recognized that Burgon's arguments cannot be so easily disposed of. In fact, the newer German editions of the Church Fathers differ little from those of the 17th and 18th centuries. Certainly not enough to affect Burgon's arguments. (Theodore Létis, *Edward Freer Hill's Contribution* ... pp. 174,75).

SELECTIVE CITATION

The big problem in using the evidence of the fathers as presented in the current critical editions of the Greek New Testament is not assimilation but *selective citation*. Have the critical editors searched as diligently through the voluminous works of the fathers for evidence on the Traditional side as on the

Alexandrian? Of course not! Their search and selection is guided by their own dictum, "no Byzantine evidence before A.D. 350". They have silenced and stifled the patristic voice in the Traditional Text! It was for this reason that patristic evidence in this first part of this book was not included in the Manuscript Digest.

For the purpose of this twelfth summary, it has been helpful to draw upon the substantial patristic citation presented in *UBS 3*, though, as we say, with the likelihood that the TR has not been given a fair hearing. A much fuller and fairer presentation is given in the second half of this volume. Nevertheless, here, as an "accepted" critical edition has been called to give evidence on the early fathers, the results are certainly interesting!

THE BURGON-MILLER MATERIAL

I would strongly recommend that you purchase *The Traditional Text of the Holy Gospels* by Burgon and Miller (available from the Dean Burgon Society), and read carefully Chapter 5. Here, one cannot help but be impressed and feel gratitude to the authors for their extreme care and diligence in bringing to bear a vast amount of pre-400 A.D. patristic quotation upon this question.

Two tests were carried out. In the first, the fathers are asked to give their voice on a wide range of passages in the four Gospels. These were taken from Scriveners *Cambridge Greek Testament* (1887). This is an edition of the Received Text, where readings disputed by Westcott and Hort are printed in darker type. The results clearly favored the Traditional Text.

Overall, before A.D. 400   3-2 (2,630 - 1,753)

Early, before A.D. 225   2-1 (151 - 84)

In the second test, the same fathers were asked to testify on 30 well-known passages, such as Mt. 1:25, Mark 1:2, Mark 16, John 1:18, etc.

Overall, before A.D. 400   3-1 (530 - 170)

These figures include citations from one or more works a father may have written. On page 97, they describe the care they took to avoid assimilation. If anything, in this and other respects, they were guilty of the kind of selectivity that favored the other side. For example, they declined to cite the *Diatessaron*, which *UBS* does cite!

In the following, I have not included a number of names from their list to whom only one or two citations are given. This accounts for the slight difference in our totals.

A DISADVANTAGE FOR THE TRADITIONAL TEXT

Most early writers who wrote prolifically, and whose writings are available for us today, were associated with the areas where the shorter text was prevalent (Alexandria), and where most of the divergences have been noted in the manuscripts (North Africa and the West). Not as much literature came from those areas of Asia Minor, Macedonia, Achaia and Syria, which were most closely associated with the original autographs, and where the Traditional Text flourished. In fact, it seems like the further the early writers were from the autographs the greater was their literary output! Yet, even with this disadvantage, the Traditional Text is shown to prevail among the early fathers.

Before presenting the list, there is one work that requires special notice.

TATIAN'S DIATESSARON

Here we have what is without question the chief enigma of early transmissional history: a harmony of the Gospels dating back to 170 AD, widely used throughout the East and West, strongly supportive (at least in the present MSS) of the Traditional Text, yet compiled by a man who is reported to have been a heretic!

Tatian was from the east of Syria or Mesopotamia, and brought up in heathenism. He was converted under Justin Martyr and became his disciple at Rome © 155). Tatian remained in fellowship with the Christians there until sometime after Justin's martyrdom (between 163 and 167). Leaving Rome, he may have paused for a time in Greece, and then at Alexandria where he is said to have taught Clement. Afterwards, he returned to Mesopotamia © 172) and founded an ascetic, vegetarian sect called the "Encratites" (continent ones). They also taught that marriage was sinful. In mentioning the Encratites, Eusebius (*Hist. Eccl.* IV, 29) refers to Tatian as its first leader, and also gives the earliest mention we have (early 4th Century) of his harmony. (F.F. Bruce *The Books and the Parchments*, London: Pickering and Ingles, 1962, pp. 195, 96*)*.

Sometime after 176 Tatian wrote his famous *Oration to the Greeks*. Metzger says there is much in this that runs counter to the contention that he was a gnostic (*Early Versions*, p. 33). However, the following quotations would put strong doubt on that conclusion:

...better aeons above the heaven. They enjoy unapproachable light. (20:1-2)

...the Logos descended to Jesus and was mingled with his soul; the Logos dwelt in him as in a temple. (15:2).

Compare this last statement with the account on ADOPTIONISM in Section One. Between the years 180 and 185, Irenaeus of Lyons condemned three errors in Tatian's teaching:

> (1) He invented certain invisible 'aeons' like those of the Valentinians; (2) he denounced marriage as 'corruption and fornication'...(3) he denied the salvation of Adam (*Adv. Haer.* 1:28.1) (Robert M Grant, "The Heresy of Tatian", *Journal of Theological Studies*, 5-1954, p. 62 ff).

There has long been a question as to whether Tatian compiled his harmony before leaving Rome, or after arriving in Mesopotamia. Though, he came into sharp conflict with the Roman Bishop, Soter (166-175), there seems to be no other way to account for its rapid spread in the West than to decide on Rome.

With some reservation Voobus says:
> The spread of his Harmony in Rome is conceivable only by supposing that Tatian composed it in Rome, before his quarrels disqualified him as a member of the church. (*Early Versions*, p. 4).

It is also debated whether it was first written in Greek or Syriac. This question turns to a certain extent on where it was written: if in Rome, then Greek would seem the more likely. Its title *Dia-tessaron* (through the four) is Greek. Its oldest known fragment © 240 A.D.) which was found in the Roman fortress-town of Dura-Europos on the Euphrates, is Greek. Voobus, however, is persuaded that further research into the Dura fragment shows the underlying base to be Syriac. The question remains unsettled. But, it does seem more natural, especially when we consider the form of it's composition, to suppose that Tatian drafted it in Greek from four Greek Gospels.

One thing is clear: when we see the Diatessaron in the West, its Old Latin base is unmistakable; and in the East, it is part-in-parcel with the Syriac Peshitta. This latter point is a real problem for the critical view, which has tried to move the Peshitta from the 2nd into the 5th Century. Textual research over the past century has wasted a great deal of paper and ink trying to resolve this "problem"!

The Diatessaron is one of the earliest witnesses we have to the text of the Gospels, and it witnesses strongly for the Traditional Text! Tatian's theological decline (probably mainly after he compiled it) does not seem to affect as much in the harmony as is sometimes suggested. Metzger for example lists eight examples, mainly to do with two of Tatian's hobbyhorses - eating and marriage. Certainly, the error that does exist, would not affect the overall textual complexion.

The late date of many manuscripts should not cause concern that the Traditional Text had been "assimilated" into the Diatessaron. The nature of the work militates strongly against this idea. It was not a four-columned harmony which could later be exchanged by block to a different kind of text; but rather a single account tightly woven with the strands of the four Gospels.

It is evident that Tatian went about composing his Diatessaron with great diligence. Probably, he worked from four separate manuscripts, one for each of the Gospels, and as he wove together phrases, now from this Gospel and now from that, he would no doubt cross out those phrases in the manuscripts from which he was copying. Otherwise it is difficult to understand how he was able to combine so successfully phrases from four documents into a remarkable cento which reminds one of delicate filigree work. (Metzger, pp 11,12).

To exchange the shorter Alexandrian Text for the fuller Traditional in such a work would have taken quite an editor! In fact, the Diatessaron may in those early centuries have been a corrective against textual corruption of the Gospels manuscripts; and give a partial explanation as to why some MSS show the Gospels with less corruption than Acts to Revelation.

SOURCES USED FOR THE DIATESSARON

The *UBS 3* cites eleven different sources (which I have shown in the following list) in its presentation of the Diatessaron evidence. Though many of these witnesses are late, their geographic distribution is impressive. The following information is derived from Metzger (pp. 10-25).

1. Other Greek Editions, Mainly Arabic Sources: Frequently the *UBS* apparatus cites "Diatessaron" without a superscript indicating its source, (see p. xl). This material has probably been taken from other Greek editions (e.g. von Soden, etc.) where, in turn, no indication of the particular version of the harmony is given. Here, the *UBS* indicates, "it usually refers to the Arabic version".

2. Arabic: There are two editions of the Arabic Diatessaron. The first was published by A. Ciasca (later Cardinal) toward the close of the 19th century, and was based on two manuscripts of the 13th and 14th centuries. A more recent edition (1935) is by A.S. Marmardji, and is based an a late MS dated 1795, with variant readings from the two MSS of Ciasca's edition. The *UBS 3* does not tell us which of these it used.

3. Quotations by Ephraem: Indicates that the source of the quote is from the Syriac or Armenian edition of Ephraem's commentary on the Diatessaron (see below), or another of his writings, but which is not specified.

4. Quotations preserved in the Syriac text of Ephraem's Commentary on the Diatessaron: Ephraem of Syria (died 373) wrote a commentary on Tatian's harmony in the Syriac language. About three-fifths of it is preserved in a 5th/6th Century MS. It was apparently not his intent to cite and comment on every part

of the harmony.

5. Quotations preserved in a later Armenian translation of Ephraem's Commentary on the Diatessaron: In addition to Ephraem's comments, the actual Scripture portion was taken from two Armenian MSS of the Diatessaron dated 1195. A comparison of the Syriac and Armenian texts indicates that the latter represents, on the whole, a reliable rendering of the original.

It will be noted that as far as our Summary is concerned, the *UBS* evidence from Ephraem was too sparse to be of much use.

6. Codex Fuldensis: This is one of the oldest (546) manuscripts of the Vulgate, and contains the entire N.T.; but in the place of the four Gospels, it has a harmony based on the Diatessaron. While the actual text is that of the Vulgate, it was clearly based on an Old Latin edition of the Diatessaron. H.J. Vogels estimated 600 instances of O.L. readings (Voobus p 11). Here too, the *UBS 3* cites it only a few times.

7. Tuscan - Old Italian: Twenty-four MSS in the Tuscan dialect contain the harmony. The oldest is from the 13th century.

8. Venetian - Old Italian: One MS (14th century) preserves the Diatessaron in the Venetian dialect.

9. Liege - Old Dutch: The Leige Diatessaron dates from about 1280.

10. Stuggart - Old Dutch: Of the Flemish dialect and written in 1332.

11. A Persian Harmony: In 1547, near the Tigris River, a Jacobite priest copied a harmony of the Gospels from a parent manuscript dating back to the 13th Century. This in turn has been taken from an earlier (some would say very early) Syrian base. Like Tatian's this harmony has the four Gospels combined into one account. However, the order of the paragraphs is substantially different.

Section Two--A Summary of Manuscript Evidence

THE SUMMARY

Here then is how the church fathers vote in all places where *UBS 3* shows Byzantine readings opposing those of Aleph-B, (i.e. where Aleph and B agree). Here also, as explained above, is the more comprehensive material gathered by Burgon and Miller. The figures on the left in those two columns are those of the Traditional Text, with the Aleph-B support listed on the right. The date of a father is usually of his death. *Latin* = a Latin quotation from a father who generally used Greek. *Manuscript(s)* = containing a fathers Scripture quotation which differs from that given in the printed editions of his work.

			UBS		Burgon-Miller	
SECOND CENTURY						
NAME	**DATE**	**LOCATION**	**T T**	**Aleph B**	**T T**	**Aleph B**
Didache and *Patres Apostolici*	100?				11	4
Heraclean	125	Alexandria		1	1	7
Marcion	130	Rome	16	6		
Justin Martyr	165	Palistine A. Minor, Rome	4	1	17	20
Athenagoras	177	Athens		1	3	1
Theophilus	180	Antioch	1	3	2	4
TOTALS			21	22	34	36

112 Early Manuscripts, Church Fathers, & the Authorized Version

NAME	DATE	LOCATION	T T	Aleph B	T T	Aleph B
Diatessaron	170	Rome, Syria				
		1. Other Greek Editions? Mainly Arabic Sources	66	12		
		2. Arabic	50	19		
		3. Quotations by Ephraem	1			
		4. Quotations preserved in the Syriac text of Ephraem's Commentary	2	3		
		5. Quotation preserved in the Armenian translation of Ephraem's Commentary	1	1		
		6. Codex Fuldensis	1	4		
		7. Tuscan - Old Latin	4	5		
		8. Venetian - Old Italian	3	1		
		Old Italian (agreement of two above)	12	10		
		9. Liege - Old Dutch	1	4		
		10. Stuttgart - Old Dutch	2			
		Old Dutch (agreement of the two above)	17	9		
		11. A Persian Harmony	23	2		
		TOTALS	183	70		

Section Two--A Summary of Manuscript Evidence

			UBS		Burgon-Miller	
THIRD CENTURY						
Name	Date	Location	T T	Aleph B	T T	Aleph B
Irenaeus Latin	202	Lyons	10 24	11 22	63	41
Clement	215	Alexandria	25	39	82	72
Tertullian	220	Carthage	20	28	74	65
Hippolytus	225	Rome	7	2	26	11
Novation	251	North Africa			6	4
Origen Latin Manuscript	254	Alexandria, Caesarea	75 39 1	112 51	460	491
Cyprian *de Rebaptismate* from among Cyprians works	258	Carthage	22 2	19 1	100	96
Dionysius the Great	265	Alexandria	3	3	12	5
Synodical Epistle of Antioch Council	269				3	1
Archelaus	278	Mesopotamia		1	11	2
Gregory-Thaumaturgus	270	Pontus in Asia Minor	1	1	11	3
Methodius	111	A. Minor, Tyre	3	6	14	8

Name	Date	Location	T T	Aleph B	T T	Aleph B
Clement of Rome	III-IV	Rome	2	8	7	
TOTALS			232	298	880	806

			UBS		Burgon-Miller	

FOURTH CENTURY

Name	Date	Location	T T	Aleph B	T T	Aleph B
Adamantius Manuscript	300	Asia Minor, Syria?	21	9		
Victorinus	304	Pettau, near Lyon		1	4	3
Pamphilus	310	Caesarea		1	5	1
Peter Manuscripts	311	Alexandria	1	43	7	8
Alexander	328	Alexandria			4	
Juvencus	330	Spain	2	2	1	2
Arius	336	Syria, Alexandria		1	3	1
Eustathius	337	Antioch		1	7	2
Jacob	338	Nisibis in Mesopotamia	3			
Eusebius Manuscripts	339	Caesarea	35	301	315	214
Firmicus Maternus	348	Sicily		1	3	1
Serapion	362	Egypt		1	5	1
Victorinus, Marius	362	Rome	11	8	14	14
Aphraates	367	Persia, Syria	7	2		

Section Two--A Summary of Manuscript Evidence

Hilary	367	Poitiers in France	24	31	73	39
Caesarius - Nazianius	369	Cappadocia	3	1		
Pacianus	370	Barcelona			2	2
Lucifer	370	Cagliari	15	14	17	20
Zeno	372	Verona			3	5
Ephraem	373	Syria			37	10
Athanasius Latin *Orations Against Arius*	373	Alexandria	17	20	122	63
				2	57	56
Titus	378	Bostra	1	4	44	24
Basil the Great Manuscript	379	Cappadocia	45	17	272	105
				1		
Apos. Const. Canons	380	Syria	16	6	61	28
Evagrius Ponticus	380	Constantinople, etc.			4	
Faustinus	380	?			4	
Philastrius	380	Italy, other			7	6
Ambrosiaster	384	Rome?	48	41		
Optatus	385	Numidia in Algeria		1	10	3
Priscillian	385	Spain	4	1		
Cyril	386	Jerusalem	10	13	54	32
Gregory-Naz.	390	Cappadocia	4	2	18	4
Macarius	391	Egypt			36	17

116 Early Manuscripts, Church Fathers, & the Authorized Version

Amphilochius	394	Iconium			27	10
Gregory - Nyssa	394	Cappadocia	3	5	91	28
Ambrose Manuscript	397	Milan	221	19	169	77
Didymus Latin	398	Alexandria	271	181	81	36
Quaestions	IV				13	6
TOTALS			303	261	1570	818

Section Two--A Summary of Manuscript Evidence

			UBS		Burgon - Miller	
Name	**Date**	**Location**	**T T**	**Aleph B**	**T T**	**Aleph B**
EARLY FIFTH CENTURY TO CHRYSOSTOM						
Macarius, Magnes	400	Magnesia in Asia Minor			11	5
Philo	401	Carposia			9	2
Epiphanius	403	Cyprus	23	21	123	78
Gaudentius	406	Brescia in N. Italy	1	3		
Chromatius	407	Aquilea in N. Italy	1	2		
Chrysostom	407	Constantinople	204	56		
TOTALS			229	82	143	85
GRAND TOTAL			968	733	2627	1745

Excluding those fathers (as Tatian) who are located in a number of areas, the ratio of fathers from Alexandria and the West to those of the East is about 3-2. These same are also shown to have a greater literary output. Despite these disadvantages and ignoring for the moment questions of selective citation and so-called "assimilation", the early fathers give their overall vote to the Traditional Text which rose in the East.

There was warfare over the Text of Scripture, but the outcome was not left in doubt - there is a Victor!

SECTION THREE
A MANUSCRIPT DIGEST OF 356 DOCTRINAL PASSAGES

The Digest records the bare facts of a warfare that has raged through the centuries over the doctrinal heart of the New Testament. From the beginning, the pressure has been upon God's people to surrender the doctrinal edge of their Sword. Many have wavered, and a brief survey of the Digest shows this has always been the case - first to one side, then the other. Many casualties can be counted. Certainly, when we contend at the Bible's doctrinal heart we have entered the quick of the battle.

The 356 doctrinal passages listed here are what makes the Authorized Version unique among today's "Bibles". Despite the enemy's rage against these precious lines of truth - in one manuscript, out of another - they have all come home to their rightful place in the pages of the King James Bible. The Digest is, therefore, not only a record of the substantial support the AV commands, but is also a chronicle of the warfare and journey of this precious deposit of doctrinal truth down to us today.

As with Israel:
> And Moses wrote their goings out according to their journeys by the commandment of the Lord; and these are their journeys according to their goings out. (Num. 31:2).
> And he brought us out from thence that he might bring us in. (Deut 6:23).

God did the same with His Word! Relative to this Digest, it is important to keep in mind the basic principles of Bible preservation. Some of these I have attempted to set out in *Modern Bibles - The Dark Secret* and also page 27 of *When the KJV Departs from the 'Majority' Text*. Both are available from the Dean Burgon Society.

FORMAT, SYMBOLS AND ABBREVIATIONS

Our recent publication *8000+ Differences Between the Textus Receptus and Nestle-Aland Texts* demonstrates the enormity of the problem. Here though we have limited ourselves to 356 passages where doctrine has been undermined in one way or another. Many others should have been included. Passages affecting

120 Early Manuscripts, Church Fathers, & the Authorized Version

a range of doctrines are listed, but the emphasis is upon those that affect the Person and Work of Christ.

AV, NIV ... The evidence is divided between the Authorized Version and New International Version, with the passage quoted from each. In some cases the passage cited on the NIV side may be the reading from it's footnote, or the New American Standard Version. This is always stated.

P66, Aleph, B, Theta, 056 ... The first lines of evidence present the Papyri (where available) and Uncial manuscripts. See Summaries 1-4.

B*, B-1, B-2, B-c, B-mg, D-gr ... The original reading of B*, where there are also corrections. The first correction to B. A second correction to B, or a scribe who is known to be the 2nd corrector. A "c" may stand for a correction in general, without reference to the particular corrector, while "mg" is a reading in the margin, which may be the same as a correction. "gr" the Greek reading of a bi-lingual manuscript which is at variance with the Latin on the facing pages.

MAJORITY, pm, al, pc ... The second lines present the cursive manuscripts according to their approximate numbers: MOST, many, some, a few or none. See Summary 5.

na, ubs, hf, legg ... The editions of Nestle Aland-26th, United Bible Societies-3rd, Hodges Farstad (Majority Text Edition), Legg's edition on Matthew and Mark. The hf estimate is used when one is not available from na.

fam 1,13 ... Two cursive "families", containing a total of about 18 MSS. These diverge somewhat from the Traditional majority. The designation is used only in the Gospels. See Summary 6.

a, aur, Vulg ... The third lines present the Old Latin and Vulgate evidence. See Summaries 5 and 6.

( ), pt, ms, mss ... The witness supports the reading, but with some divergence. Part of the witnesses support the reading. An early manuscript or manuscripts support the reading.

Syr, Cop ... The fourth lines present the Syriac and Coptic evidence. See Summaries 9 and 10.

Syr: pesh, sin, cur, philox, harc, pal ... Six versions of the Syriac: Peshitta, Sinaitic, Curetonian, Philoxenian, Harclean, Palestinian.

Section Three--A Manuscript Digest of 356 Doctrinal Passages

Cop: sa, bo, pbo, mae, fay ach, ach-2 ... Seven versions of the Coptic: Sahidic, Bohairic, Proto-Bohairic, Middle Egyptian, Fayyumic, Achmimic, Sub-Achmimic.

Goth, Arm, Eth ... The fifth lines present the Gothic, Armenian and Ethiopic evidence. See Summary 11.

Arm-usc, zoh ... The Armenian editions of Uscan and Zohrab, when they disagree.

Eth-rom, ppl ... The Rome and Platt-Praetorius editions of the Ethiopic, when they disagree.

Also extant in Y 047 0233? ... The final lines list uncial manuscripts which apparently contain the passage, though not cited in the editions consulted. "?" indicates a greater amount of uncertainty. Given the readiness of the critical editors to list everything possible for the Aleph-B side, most of these can be assumed to support the AV.

Other Digest, KJVMT ... The Manuscript Digest in *When the KJV Departs from the 'Majority' Text*.

See the introduction to the Summaries for an account of the sources of current MS information.

122 Early Manuscripts, Church Fathers, & the Authorized Version

AV	NIV
MATTHEW 1:25	
And knew her not till she had brought forth her <u>firstborn</u> son	But he had no union with her until she gave birth to a son
C D (D2) E K L M S U V W Gamma Delta Pi Sigma Omega 087 Cursives: MAJORITY Old Latin: aur (d) f ff1 g2 q Vulg Syr: pesh harc pal-ms Arm Eth Also extant in 047 055 0133? 0211 0248?	Aleph B Z 071 pc fam 1, 13 a b c gl k cur pal-ms Cop: (sa) (bo) mae
MATTHEW 4:12	
When <u>Jesus</u> heard that John had been put in prison	(NASV) "Jesus" is removed from the prophecy of the great light (12-16)
C-2 E K L M P S U V W Gamma Delta Theta Sigma Omega 0233 Cursives: MAJORITY fam 1, 13 Old Latin: a aur b c gl h l Vulg-pt Syr: pesh cur harc Cop: bo-pt Arm Also extant in 047 055 0211	Aleph B C D Z pc ff1 k Vulg-pt sin bo-pt Eth

Section Three--A Manuscript Digest of 356 Doctrinal Passages

AV	NIV

MATTHEW 4:18

And <u>Jesus</u> walking by the sea	(NASV) "Jesus" is removed from the call to discipleship (18-22)
E L Delta Omega	Aleph B C D K M P S U V Gamma Pi Sigma
Cursives: al(legg)	MAJORITY (hf) fam 1
Old Latin: a c ff1? h m Vulg-pt	d l Vulg
	Syr: pesh harc Cop: sa bo
Arm	Eth
Also extant in 047 055 0211. See KJVMT p. 31 for additional material	

MATTHEW 4:23

And <u>Jesus</u> went about all Galilee	Codex B removes "Jesus" from the miracle working ministry of Galilee
Aleph* (Aleph-1) C* C-3 D E K M S U V W Gamma Delta Pi Sigma Omega	B
Cursives: MAJORITY fam 1,13	
Old Latin: a aur b c d f ff1 gl h l Vulg	pc (none cited in na, ubs, legg) k
Syr: pesh sin harc pal Cop: bo	cur sa mae
Arm Eth	
Also extant in 047 055 0211 0233?	

124 Early Manuscripts, Church Fathers, & the Authorized Version

AV	NIV
MATTHEW 5:22	
That whosoever is angry with his brother <u>without a cause</u> shall be in danger of the judgement Aleph-2 D E K L M S U V W Gamma Delta* Theta Pi Sigma Omega 0233 Cursives: MAJORITY fam 1,13 Old Latin: a aur b c d f ff1 g1 h k l q Syr: pesh sin cur harc Cop: sa bo Goth Arm Also extant in P86? 047 055 0133? 0211 0248? 0257? The world has never liked the thought of a righteous and just anger. Where would the NIV reading leave Christ after He drove out the money changers?	That anyone who is angry with his brother will be subject to judgement. P67 Aleph* B D-2 pc m r2 Vulg Eth

Section Three--A Manuscript Digest of 356 Doctrinal Passages   125

AV	NIV

MATTHEW 5:27

Ye have heard that it was said <u>by them of old time,</u> Thou shalt not commit adultery L M Delta Theta Cursives: pm fam 13 Old Latin: aur (c) ff1 g1,2 h l m r2 Vulg Syr: cur harc** Also extant in p64? 047 055 0133? 0211 0233? 0248? 0257? The command against adultery is an <u>old one.</u> See *KJVMT* p. 32.	You have heard that it was said, Do not commit adultery Aleph B D E K S U V W Gamma Pi Sigma Omega pm a b d f k m pesh Cop: bo Goth Arm Eth

MATTHEW 5:44

But I say unto you, Love your enemies, <u>bless them that curse you, do good to them that hate you</u> D E K L M S U W Delta Theta Pi Sigma Omega Cursives: MAJORITY fam 13 Old Latin: c d f h m Syr: (pesh) harc pal Goth Arm Eth Also extant in 047 055 0133? 0211 0233 0248? 0257? Other witnesses support a shorter reading. The persecuting Roman Church discovered this passage to have a double edge.	But I tell you: Love your enemies Aleph B pc fam 1 k sin cur Cop: sa bo

AV	NIV

MATTHEW 6:1

Take heed that ye do not your <u>alms</u> before men	Be careful not to do your <u>acts of righteousness</u> before men
E K L M S U W Z Delta Theta Pi Sigma Omega Cursives: MAJORITY fam 13 Old Latin: f k Syr: pesh harc Cop: mae Goth Arm Eth Also extant in Phi? 047 055 0211 0233? 0248? To many within Christendom "acts of righteousness" have meant acts which procure righteousness.	Aleph* Aleph-2 B D 0250 pc fam 1 Most OL Vulg.

MATTHEW 6:13

but deliver us from evil: <u>for thine is the kingdom, and the power and the glory, forever, Amen</u>	And lead us not into temptation, but deliver us from the *evil* one
E G K L M S U V W Delta Theta Pi Sigma Phi Omega Cursives: MAJORITY fam 13 Old Latin: f (delta) g1 (k)(q) Syr: pesh cur harc pal Cop: (sa) bo-pt (fay) Goth Arm Eth Also extant in 047 055 0211 0248? Any thought of a literal kingdom on earth as foretold in the O.T. has been banished from "mainline" religious thought since the 4th century.	Aleph B D Z 0170 pc fam 1 a aur b c ff1 g2 h 1 m Vulg bo-pt mae

AV	NIV

MATTHEW 6:33

But seek ye first the kingdom <u>of God</u> and his righteousness E G K L M S U V W Delta Theta Pi Sigma Omega Cursives: MAJORITY fam 1,13 Old Latin: a aur b c f ff1 g1 h Vulg Syr: pesh cur harc pal Cop: mae Arm Eth-ms Also extant in Phi? 047 055 0248	But seek first his kingdom and his righteousness Aleph (B) pc (ubs cites 1 cursive) g2 (k) 1 sa bo Eth?

MATTHEW 8:29

What have we to do with thee, <u>Jesus</u>, thou Son of God C-3 E K M S U V W X Delta Theta Pi Sigma Omega 0242 Cursives: MAJORITY fam 13 Old Latin: a aur b c d f g1 h 1 q Vulg-pt Syr: pesh harc Cop: sa bo-pt Goth Arm Eth Also extant in Phi? 047 055 0211 0233? 0242 0248? 0257?	What do you want with us, Son of God? Aleph B C* L al fam 1 ff1 k m Vulg bo-pt mae

128 Early Manuscripts, Church Fathers, & the Authorized Version

AV	NIV

MATTHEW 9:13	
for I am not come to call the righteous, but sinners to repentance C E G K L M S U V-mg X Y Gamma-mg Theta Pi Omega Cursives: MAJORITY fam 13 Old Latin: c g1,2 Syr: sin harc-mg Cop: sa bo-pt mae Also extant in 047 055 0211 0248? Certainly the modern gospel stops where the NIV does.	For I have not come to call the righteous but sinners Aleph B D N Y* W Gamma Delta Sigma Phi 0233 al fam 1 a aur b d f ff1 h k l q Vulg pesh harc bo-pt Goth Arm Eth

MATTHEW 12:6	
That in this place is one greater than the temple C L N Delta Phi 0233 Cursives: pm Old Latin: most incl. d Vulg Syr: pesh sin cur harc Arm Eth Also extant in Omega 047 055 0211 0257? Substituting "something" for Christ opens up all kinds of "possibilities" for those seeking to promote their own doctrines and practices.	(NASV) that something greater than the temple is here Aleph B D E G K M S U V W Gamma Theta Pi Sigma Psi pm ff1 q Cop: bo (? See legg)

Section Three--A Manuscript Digest of 356 Doctrinal Passages   129

AV	NIV

MATTHEW 12:25	
And <u>Jesus</u> knew their thoughts	(NASV) "Jesus" is removed from the healing of the demoniac (22-30)
C E G K L M S U V X Gamma Delta Theta Pi Sigma Phi Omega 0106 Cursives: MAJORITY fam 1, 13 Old Latin: a aur b c f ff1,2 g1 h l q Vulg Syr: pesh harc Cop: bo-mss mae Arm Eth Also extant in N 047 055 0211 0233? 0257?	P21 Aleph B D pc (legg, na, ubs cite 1 cursive) d k sin cur sa bo

MATTHEW 12:47	
<u>then one said unto him, behold thy mother and thy brethren stand without desiring to speak with thee.</u>	Footnote reads: "Some manuscripts do not have verse 47."
(Aleph-1) Aleph-2 C (D) E F G K M S U V W Y Z Delta Theta Pi Sigma Phi Omega Cursives: MAJORITY fam (1),13 Old Latin: a aur b c d f ff2 g1 h l q Syr: pesh harc Cop: bo mae Arm Eth Also extant in 047 055 0211 0233? 0257? Our Lord's family relations were common knowledge. This verse is a counter to those who denied His true humanity.	Aleph* B L Gamma pc ff1 k sin cur sa

130 Early Manuscripts, Church Fathers, & the Authorized Version

AV	NIV
MATTHEW 13:35	
I will utter things which have been kept secret from the foundation of the <u>world</u>	In NIV and NASV (no footnote), but omitted from some early manuscripts.
Aleph* Aleph-2 C D E F G K L M S U V W X Y Gamma Delta Theta Pi Sigma Phi Omega Cursives: Majority fam 13 Old Latin: a aur b c d ff1,2 g1,2 h 1 pi r2 q Vulg Syr: (pesh) harc Cop: sa bo fay Arm Also extant in 0? 047 055 0211 0233? 0242 0248? 0257	Aleph-1 B pc fam 1 e k sin cur Eth
MATTHEW 13:36	
Then <u>Jesus</u> sent the multitude away	"Jesus" is removed from the wheat and tares explanation (36-43).
C E F G K L M S U V W X Y Gamma Delta Theta Pi Sigma Phi Omega 0233 Cursives: MAJORITY fam 13 Old Latin: f h q Syr: pesh harc Arm Also extant in 0? 047 055 0106 0211 0242 0248? 0250 0257	Aleph B D pc (fam 1) Most OL Vulg sin cur Cop* sa bo Eth

Section Three--A Manuscript Digest of 356 Doctrinal Passages   131

AV	NIV

MATTHEW 13:51

Jesus saith unto them, Have ye understood all these things? They say unto him, Yea, <u>Lord</u> C E F G K L M S U V W X Y Gamma Delta Pi Sigma Phi Omega 0137 0233 Cursives: MAJORITY Old Latin: a b c e f g1,2 h q r2 Arm Eth-rom (apparently) Also extant in 0? 047 055 0106 0211 0248? 0257	Have you understood all these things? Jesus asked. Yes, they replied Aleph B D Theta pc fam 1,13 aur d ff1,2 k l Vulg Eth-pp1

MATTHEW 14:14

And <u>Jesus</u> went forth C E F G (L) K M S U V W X Y Gamma Delta Pi Sigma Phi Omega 067 0106 Cursives: MAJORITY Old Latin: f h q Syr: pesh harc Also extant in 0? Z 047 055 0211 0233? 0257?	(NASV) "Jesus" is removed from the account of a miracle. Aleph B D Theta pc fam 1,13 a b c ff1,2 g1 k cur Cop: sa bo Arm Eth

AV	NIV

MATTHEW 14:22

And straightway Jesus constrained his disciples to get into a ship	(NASV) "Jesus" is removed from much of the account of His walking on the sea
C-3 E F G K L M S U V X Y Gamma Theta-2 Pi Omega Cursives: MAJORITY (hf) fam 13 Old Latin: a b c ff2 h q Vulg-pt Also extant in 0 047 055 073 0211 0233? 0257?	Aleph B C* D P W Delta Theta* Sigma Phi 067 0106 al (legg, hf) fam 1 aur e ff1 l Vulg Syr: pesh cur harc Cop: bo Arm Eth

MATTHEW 14:25

Jesus went unto them, walking on the sea	(NASV) "Jesus" is removed from much of the account of His walking on the sea.
C-3 E F G K L M U X Y Theta Pi Phi Cursives: MAJORITY (hf) fam 13 Old Latin: a b c f ff2 Syr: pesh cur Cop: bo-ms Arm Also extant in N 0? 047 055 067 073 0211 0233? 0257?	Aleph B C* D P S V W Gamma Delta Sigma 047 084 0106 pc (legg, hf) ff1 g1 h q Vulg harc sa bo Eth

Section Three--A Manuscript Digest of 356 Doctrinal Passages   133

AV	NIV

MATTHEW 15:16	
And <u>Jesus</u> said C E F G K L M S U V W X Y Gamma Delta Theta Pi Sigma Phi Omega 0119 Cursives: MAJORITY fam 1,13 Old Latin: f q Syr: harc Arm also extant in 047 055 0106 0211 0233? 0248? 0257?	(NASV) Jesus is removed from the discourse on defilement (10-20) Aleph B D O Z pc a aur c d e ffl,2 g1 l m Vulg pesh sin cur Cop: sa bo Eth

MATTHEW 16:3	
<u>And in the morning, It will be foul weather to day: for the sky is red and lowering. O ye hypocrites ye can discern the face of the sky; but can ye not discern the signs of the times</u> C D E (F) G H K L M (N) S U W Delta Theta Pi Sigma Psi Cursives: MAJORITY fam 1 Old Latin: a aur b c d a e f ff1,2 g1 l q Vulg Syr: pesh harc Cop: bo-pt Arm-usc (apparently) Eth Also extant in 0? 047 055 0211 0233? 0248 0257?	Footnote: "some early manuscripts do not have the rest of verse 2 and all of verse 3." Aleph B V X Y Gamma Omega al fam 13 sin cur sa bo-pt mae Arm-zoh

134 Early Manuscripts, Church Fathers, & the Authorized Version

AV	NIV

MATTHEW 16:20	
Then charged he his disciples that they should tell no man that: he was <u>Jesus</u> the Christ	Then he warned his disciples not to tell anyone that he was the Christ
Aleph-2 C E F G H K M S U V W Y Sigma Omega Cursives: MAJORITY Old Latin: (c) d f (ff2) g2 l q Vulg Syr: harc Cop: bo mae Eth Also extant in 0? 047 055 0211 0233? 0248? 0257?	Aleph* B L X Gamma Delta Theta Pi Phi al a aur b e ff1 g1 r2 pesh cur sa Arm

MATTHEW 17:20	
Because of your <u>unbelief:</u> for... If ye had faith as a grain of mustard seed	Because you have <u>so little faith</u>.. if you have faith as small as a mustard seed
C D E F G H K L M S U V W X Y Gamma Delta Pi Sigma Phi Omega Cursives: MAJORITY Old Latin: a aur b c d a f ff1,2 g1 n q r1 Vulg Syr: pesh sin harc Arm-ms Also extant in 0? 047 055 0211. The NIV reading is pointless.	Aleph B Theta pc fam 1,13 cur pal Cop: sa bo Arm Eth

Section Three--A Manuscript Digest of 356 Doctrinal Passages

AV	NIV

MATTHEW 17:21

Howbeit this kind goeth not out but by prayer and fasting Aleph-2 C D E F G H K L M 0 S U V W X Y Gamma Delta Pi Sigma Phi Omega Cursives: MAJORITY fam 1,13 Old Latin: (a) aur (b) (c) d f ff2 g1 l (n) q r1,2 Vulg Syr: (pesh) (harc) Cop: bo-pt mae Arm Eth-pp1 Also extant in 047 055 0211	------- Aleph* B Theta pc e ff1 sin cur pa1 sa bo-pt Eth-rom, ms

MATTHEW 18:11

For the son of man is come to save that which was lost D E F G H I K L-c M N S U V W X Y Theta-c Sigma Phi Omega Cursives: MAJORITY Old Latin: (a) aur b (c) d f ff2 g1 l n q rl,2 Vulg Syr: pesh cur harc Cop:bo-pt Arm Eth Also extant in 0? 047 055 0211 0233? 0248?	_____ Aleph B L* Theta* pc fam 1,13 a ff1 sin pal sa bo-pt mae

AV	NIV

MATTHEW 18:15

if thy brother shall trespass <u>against</u> <u>thee,</u> go and tell him his fault	Footnote: "Some manuscripts do not have..."
D E FG H K L M S U V W X Y Gamma Delta Theta Pi Sigma Omega 067 078 Cursives: MAJORITY fam 13 Old Latin: a aur b c d e f ff1,2 h l n q Vulg Syr: pesh sin cur harc pal Cop: bo-pt mae Arm Eth Also extant in P44 N 0? Phi? 047 055 0211 0233? 0248? The "church" has long been involved in disputes which go far beyond this simple limit. See also Luke 17:3.	Aleph B pc fam 1 sa bo-pt

Section Three--A Manuscript Digest of 356 Doctrinal Passages 137

AV	NIV

MATTHEW 19:9

and shall marry another, committeth adultery :<u>and whoso marrieth her which is put away doth commit adultery</u>	and marries another woman commits adultery:
(P25) B C* E F G H K M N O U V W X Y Z Delta Theta Pi Sigma Phi 078 Cursives: MAJORITY fam 1,13 Old Latin: aur c f g2 Vulg Syr: pesh harc pal Cop: bo Arm Eth Also extant in Omega 047 055 0211 0233?	Aleph C-3 D L S pc a b d e ff1,2 g1 h l r1 sin cur sa bo-ms

AV	NIV

MATTHEW 19:16

AV	NIV
<u>Good</u> Master, what good thing shall 1 do, that I may have eternal life?	Teacher what good thing must I do to get eternal life?
C E F G H K M S U V W Y Gamma Delta Theta Sigma Omega Cursives: Majority fam 13 Old Latin: aur b c f ff2 g1,2 h l q (r1) Vulg. Syr: pesh sin cur harc pal Cop: sa bo-pt mae Arm Eth-ms Also extant in 0? Phi? 0116 0211 0233? If Christ is not God then He is not good. This point was missed by the rich young ruler, and it would seem purposely so by scribes of some early manuscripts.	Aleph B D L pc fam 1 a d e ff1

Section Three--A Manuscript Digest of 356 Doctrinal Passages

AV	NIV

MATTHEW 19:17

Why callest thou me good? There is none good but one, that is God C E F G H K M S U V (W) Y (Delta) Sigma Phi Omega Cursives: MAJORITY fam 13 Old Latin: f q Syr: pesh cur harc pal-ms Cop: sa bo-ms Eth-ms Also extant in P71? 0? 047 055 0116 0211 0233?	Why do you ask me about what is good? There is only One who is good Aleph (b*) B-2 (D) L Theta pc (fam 1) aur a b c d e ff(1),2 g1 h l m r1 Vulg (sin) (harc-mg) pal-mss bo mae Arm Eth

MATTHEW 20:16

So the last shall be first and the first last: for many be called but few chosen C D E F G H K M N S U V W X Y Gamma Delta Theta Pi Sigma Omega Cursives: MAJORITY fam 1,13 Old Latin: most Vulg Syr: pesh sin cur harc pal Cop: bo-pt mae Arm Eth extant in 0? Phi? 047 055 0211	so the last will be first, and the first will be last: Aleph B L Z 085 pc sa bo-pt Eth-ms

AV	NIV

MATTHEW 20:22

Are ye able to drink of the cup that I shall drink of, <u>and to be baptized with the baptism that I am baptized with</u>?	Can you drink the cup I am going to drink?
C E F G H K M N O S U V W X Y Gamma Delta Pi Sigma Phi Omega 0197 Cursives: MAJORITY Old Latin: (f) h q Syr: pesh harc Cop: bo-pt Arm Also extant in 047 055 0211	Aleph B D L Z Theta 085 pc fam 1,13 a b c d e ff1,2 g1,2 l m n r1,2 Vulg sin cur sa bo-pt Eth

MATTHEW 20:23

Ye shall drink indeed of my cup, <u>and be baptized with the baptism that I am baptized with</u>	You will indeed drink from my cup
C E F G H K M N O S U V W X Y Gamma Delta Pi Sigma Phi Omega 0197 Cursives: MAJORITY Old Latin: f h q Syr: pesh harc Cop: bo-pt Arm Also extant in P83? 047 055 0116 0211	Aleph B D L Z Theta 085 pc fam 1,13 Most OL Vulg sin cur sa bo-pt mae Eth

Section Three--A Manuscript Digest of 356 Doctrinal Passages

AV	NIV
MATTHEW 21:44	
And whosoever shall fall on this stone shall be broken: but on whomsoever it shall fall it will grind him to powder Aleph B C E F G H K L M S U V W X Y Z Gamma Delta Theta Pi Sigma Phi Omega 0138 Cursives: MAJORITY fam 1,13 Old Latin: aur c f gl,2 h l q Vulg Syr: pesh cur harc Cop: sa bo Arm Eth Also extant in 047 055 0102 0211 0233? 0248? 0257?	Footnote: "Some manuscripts do not have verse 44." D pc (legg ubs na cite 1 cursive) a b d e ff1,2 r1,2 sin
MATTHEW 22:30	
but are as the angels <u>of God</u> in heaven Aleph E F G H K L M S U V W Y Gamma Delta Theta-c Pi Sigma Phi Omega 0107 0138 0161 Cursives: MAJORITY fam 13 Old Latin: aur ff1 gl,2 l Vulg Syr: pesh harc pal Cop: bo Eth Also extant in 0? 047 055 0211 0233? 0257?	they will be like the angels in heaven B D Theta 0197 pc fam 1 (na ubs cite 1 cursive) a b c d e ff2 gig h r q r1,2 sin cur sa mae Arm

AV	NIV

MATTHEW 23:8

But be not ye called Rabbi: for one is your Master, <u>even Christ</u>; and all ye are brethren	But you are not to be called Rabbi, for you have only one Master and you are all brethren
E* F G H K M S U V Y Gamma Delta Sigma Omega 0138 Cursives: MAJORITY Old Latin: r2 Syr: cur harc** Also extant in Phi 047 055 0104 0107 0133? 0211 0233? 0257?	Aleph B D E-2 L W Theta-c Pi 0107 pc (legg cites 10 cursives) Most OL Vulg pesh harc-ms pal Cop: sa bo Arm Eth

MATTHEW 23:14

<u>Woe unto you, scribes and pharisees, hypocrites! for ye devour widows' houses, and for a pretense make long prayer: therefore ye shall receive the greater damnation</u>	-----------
E F G H K M O S U V W Y Gamma Delta-gr Theta-c Pi Sigma Omega 0104 Cursives: MAJORITY (fam 13) Old Latin: b c f ff2 h l r1,2 Vulg-pt Syr: pesh cur harc pal-mss Cop: bo-pt Arm-usc (apparently) Eth Many of the above interchange verses 13 and 14. Also extant in Phi 047 055 0211 0233? 0257? It has not only been Jewish scribes who have devoured widows' houses.	Aleph B D L Z Theta pc fam 1 a aur d e ff1 gl,2 q Vulg sin pal-ms sa bo-pt mae Arm-zoh

Section Three--A Manuscript Digest of 356 Doctrinal Passages

AV	NIV

MATTHEW 23:38

Behold, your house is left unto you <u>desolate</u>	NASV footnote: "Some manuscripts omit..."
P77 Aleph C D E F G H K M S U V W X Y Gamma. Delta Theta Pi Sigma Phi Omega 0138 Cursives: MAJORITY fam 1,13 Old Latin: a aur b c d e f ff1 g1 h l q r1 Vulg Syr: pesh harc pal Cop: bo-pt mae Arm Eth Also extant in 0? 047 055 0102 0133? 0211 0233? 0257	B L pc (no cursives cited in legg ubs na) ff2 sin sa bo-pt

MATTHEW 24:7

and there shall be famines, <u>and pestilences</u>	there will be famines
C E-2 F G H K (L) M O S U V (W) V Gamma Delta Theta Pi Sigma Phi Omega 0138 Cursives: MAJORITY fam 1,13 Old Latin: (aur c f ff1 g1,2) h (l)q (Vulg) Syr: pesh harc Cop: mae Arm Eth Also extant in 047 055 0102 0133 0211 0257?	Aleph B D E* pc a b d e ff2 r1,2 sin sa

144 Early Manuscripts, Church Fathers, & the Authorized Version

AV	NIV
MATTHEW 24:36	
But of that day and hour knoweth no man, no, not the angels of heaven, but my Father only	No one knows about that day or hour, not even the angels in heaven, nor the Son, but only the Father
Aleph-1 E F G H K L M S U V W Y Gamma Delta Pi Sigma Omega 0133 Cursives: MAJORITY fam 1 Old Latin: g1,2 l r2 Vulg Syr: pesh sin harc Cop: sa bo Also extant in 0? 047 055 0211 0257? It is in Mark, not Matthew (the Gospel of the King) that "the servant knoweth not what his lord doeth".	Aleph* Aleph-2 B D Theta Phi pc fam 13 a aur b c (e) f ff1,2 h l q r1 pal fay Arm Eth
MATTHEW 24:48	
that evil servant shall say in his heart, My lord delayeth his coming	NIV, NASV remove "his coming."
(C) (D) E F G H K (L) M S U V W Y Gamma Delta (Theta) Sigma Pi Phi Omega 067 0133 Cursives: MAJORITY fam (1),13 Old Latin: Most Vulg Syr: pesh sin harc Cop: bo-mss mae Arm Eth Also extant in 0? 047 055 067? 0204 0211 0257?	Aleph pc sa bo

Section Three--A Manuscript Digest of 356 Doctrinal Passages

AV	NIV

MATTHEW 25:13

ye know neither the day nor the hour <u>wherein the son of man cometh</u> C-3 E F G H K M S U V Gamma Pi-3 Omega Cursives: MAJORITY fam 13 Vulg-pt Syr: pal-mg Also extant in 055 067? 0133? 0211 0233? 0257?	you do not know the day or the hour P35 Aleph B C* D L X Y* Delta Theta Pi Sigma Phi 047 0136 al (legg cites 22 cursives) Old Latin: most Vulg pesh harc pal Cop: sa bo Arm Eth

MATTHEW 25:31

and all the <u>holy</u> angels with him A E F G H K M S U V W Y Gamma Delta Pi-2 Sigma Phi Omega Cursives: MAJORITY fam 13 Old Latin: f Syr: pesh harc Cop: bo-pt Also extant in 047 055 067? 074 0133? 0211 0233? 0257?	and all the angels with him Aleph B D L Theta Pi* 074 pc fam 1 Most OL Vulg pal bo-pt mae

AV	NIV

MATTHEW 26:28	
For this is my blood of the <u>new</u> testament	This is my blood of the covenant
A C D E F G H K M S U V W Y Gamma Delta Pi Sigma Omega 074 Cursives: MAJORITY fam 1,13 Old Latin: a aur c d f ff1,2 g1 h l q r1 Vulg Syr: pesh sin harc Cop: sa bo Arm Eth	P37 Aleph B L Z Theta pc bo-ms
Also extant in P45? 047 055 067? 0133? 0160 0211. Not merely a covenant but an entirely new dispensation was about to be sealed. The word is again omitted in Mark 14:24	

MATTHEW 26:42	
O my Father, if this <u>cup</u> may not pass away from me, except I drink it	(NASV) My Father, if this cannot pass away unless I drink it
D E F G H K M S U Y Gamma Theta Pi-2 Sigma Phi Omega Cursives: MAJORITY fam 13 Old Latin: a aur c f ff1 h Vulg Syr: pesh sin Cop: bo mae Arm Also extant in 047 055 067 0133? 0211? 0257?	P37 Aleph A B C L W Delta-c Pi* 067 pc fam 1 b ff2 q harc sa-mss Eth

Section Three--A Manuscript Digest of 356 Doctrinal Passages 147

AV	NIV
MATTHEW 27:34	
they gave him <u>vinegar</u> to drink mingled with gall A E F G H M N S U V W Y Delta Pi-2 Sigma Phi Omega 0250 Cursives: MAJORITY Old Latin: c f h q Syr: pesh harc Cop: bo-mss mae Also extant in 047 055 0133? 0211 0233? The concluding prophecy of our Lord's passion said that it must be vinegar, Psalm 69:21.	There they offered him <u>wine</u> to drink, mixed with gall Aleph B D K L Theta Pi: al fam 1,13 a b ff1,2 g1,2 l Vulg sin harc-mg pal sa bo Arm Eth

148 Early Manuscripts, Church Fathers, & the Authorized Version

AV	NIV

MATTHEW 27:35

AV	NIV
And they crucified him, and parted his garments, casting lots: <u>that it might be fulfilled which was spoken by the prophet, They parted my garments among them, and upon my vesture did they cast lots</u>	When they had crucified him, they divided up his clothes by casting lots
Delta Theta Phi 0250 Cursives: al (na) fam 1,13 (27 cursives sited in our other Digest) Old Latin: a aur b c delta g2 gig h q r1,2 Vulg-pt Syr: harc pal Cop: mae Arm Also extant in 047 055 064 0133? 0211 0233? This prophecy is given in John, but only Matthew among the synoptic Gospels records it. See *KJVMT* for further evidence , p 38.	Aleph A B D E F G H K L M S U V W Y Gamma Pi Sigma Omega MAJORITY (hf) d f ff1,2 gl l Vulg-pt pesh sin harc-mg sa bo Eth

MATTHEW 28:6

AV	NIV
Come, see the place where the <u>Lord</u> lay	Come and see the place where he lay
A C D E F G H K L M S U V W Y Gamma Delta Pi 0148 Cursives: MAJORITY fam 1,13 Old Latin: a aur b c d f ff1,2 g1 h l n q r1 Vulg Syr: pesh harc pal-mss Also extant in Phi 047? 0211	Aleph B Theta pc e sin pal-ms Cop: sa bo Arm Eth

Section Three--A Manuscript Digest of 356 Doctrinal Passages

AV	NIV

MARK 1:1

The beginning of the gospel of Jesus Christ, <u>the Son of God</u>	Footnote: "Some manuscripts do not have..."
Aleph-1 A B D E F G-suppl H K L M S U V W Y Gamma Delta Pi Sigma Phi Omega Cursives: Majority fam 1,13 Old Latin: a aur b c d f ff2 q r1 Vulg. Syr: pesh harc Cop: sa bo Goth Arm Eth Also extant in 047 055 0133? 0211 0233?	Aleph* Theta pc

MARK 1:2

As it is written <u>in the prophets</u>, Behold, I send my messenger before thy face	It is written <u>in Isaiah the prophet</u>: I will send my messenger ahead of you
A E F G-suppl H K M P S U V W Y Gamma Pi Sigma Phi Omega Cursives: Majority fam 13 Syr: harc Cop: bo-mss Arm Eth Also extant in 047 055 0133? 0211 0233? The next verse quotes Isaiah 40:3, but verse 2 is from Malachi 3:1, thus it can only be "in the prophets".	Aleph B D L Delta Theta al fam 1 Old Latin: a aur b c d f ff2 1 q Vulg pesh harc-mg pal sa bo Goth

150 Early Manuscripts, Church Fathers, & the Authorized Version

AV	NIV

MARK 1:14	
Jesus came into Galilee, preaching the gospel <u>of the kingdom</u> of God	Jesus went into Galilee, proclaiming the good news of God
A D E F G H K M S U V W Y Gamma, Delta Pi Sigma Phi Omega 074 Cursives: MAJORITY Old Latin: a f g1,2 l r1,2 Vulg Syr: pesh harc-mg Cop: bo-pt Goth Eth Also extant in 047 055 0133? 0135 0211 0233?	Aleph B L Theta pc fam 1,13 b c ff2 t sin harc sa bo-pt Arm

MARK 1:41	
And <u>Jesus</u> moved with compassion, put forth his hand	(NASV) "Jesus" is removed from this miracle.
A C E F G H K L M S U V W Y Gamma Delta Theta Pi Sigma Phi Omega 090 Cursives: MAJORITY fam 1,13 Old Latin: c f1 g2 q r2 Vulg Syr: pesh sin harc Cop: sa-ms bo-pt Goth Arm Eth Also extant in 047 055 064 0211 0233?	Aleph B D pc (legg, na cite 1 cursive) a b e ff2 r1 sa-mss bo-pt

Section Three--A Manuscript Digest of 356 Doctrinal Passages

AV	NIV

MARK 1:42

And as soon as he had spoken, immediately the leprosy departed from him A C E F G H K M S U V Y Gamma Theta Pi Sigma Phi Omega 090 0130 0133 Cursives: MAJORITY fam 1 Old Latin: f g2 l q r2 Vulg Syr: harc Goth Arm Eth Also extant in 047 055 064 0211 0233? "He sent his word and healed them," Psalms 107:20.	Immediately the leprosy left him Aleph B D L W pc fam 13 a b c e ff2 g1 pesh sin Cop: sa bo

MARK 2:17

I came not to call the righteous, but sinners <u>to repentance</u> C E F G H M S U V Y Gamma Omega Cursives: MAJORITY (hf) fam 13 Old Latin: a c g1 Cop: bo-pt Also extant in 047 055 0133? 0211	I have not come to call the righteous, but sinners P88 Aleph A B D K L W Delta Pi Sigma Phi al (legg) fam 1 b e f ff2 g2 i l q r2 Vulg Syr: pesh harc sa bo-pt Goth Arm Eth

152 Early Manuscripts, Church Fathers, & the Authorized Version

AV	NIV

MARK 3:15

And to have power to heal sickenesses and to cast out devils	and to have authority to drive out demons
A C-2 D E F G H K M P S U V W Y Gamma Theta Pi Sigma Phi Omega Cursives: MAJORITY (hf) Old Latin: most Vulg Syr: pesh sin harc Cop: bo-pt Goth Arm (Eth) Also extant in Psi 047 055 0133 0134 0211	Aleph B C* L Delta pc (legg cites 2 cursives) sa bo-pt

MARK 3:29

hath never forgiveness, but is in danger of eternal damnation	will never be forgiven; he is guilty of an eternal sin
A C-2 E F G H K M S U V Y Gamma Pi Sigma Phi Omega 074 0134 Cursives: MAJORITY fam 1 Old Latin: f r l Syr: pesh harc Cop: bo-pt Eth Also extant in Psi 047 055 064 0133 0211. The NIV reading will not cause the lost sinner so much alarm, but eternal damnation is another matter.	Aleph B C* D L W Delta Theta pc fam 13 (legg, na, ubs cite 4 cursives) a aur b c d e ff2 l q Vulg sin bo-pt Goth Arm

AV	NIV

MARK 4:11

Unto you it is given <u>to know</u> the mystery of the kingdom of God C-2 D E F G H M S U V Y Delta Theta Sigma Phi Omega Cursives: MAJORITY (hf) fam 1,13 Old Latin: most Vulg Syr: pesh harc Cop: bo-pt Goth Eth Also extant in 047 055 0133? 0211. The NASV reading takes us uncomfortably close to mysteries other than those of the Gospel.	(NASV) To you has been given the mystery of the kingdom of God Aleph A B C* K L W Pi al (legg cites 12 cursives) ff1 sin bo-pt

MARK 5:13

And forthwith <u>Jesus</u> gave them leave A D F G H K M S U V Y Pi Sigma Phi Omega 074 Cursives: MAJORITY fam 13 Old Latin: a c f ff2 g1,2 i l q rl Vulg Syr: harc Eth Some of the above include "Lord Jesus". Also extant in 047? 055 064 0133? 0211.	"Jesus" is removed from the immediate context of a miracle in the NASV and to a lesser extent in the NIV Aleph B C L W Delta Theta pc fam 1 (na cites 4 cursives) b e pesh sin Cop: bo Arm

AV	NIV

MARK 5:19	
Howbeit <u>Jesus</u>...tell them how great things the Lord D E F G H S U V Y Theta Omega Cursives: pm (legg) fam 13 Old Latin: b c e ff2 g2 i q r1 Vulg-pt Arm Eth Also extant in P45? 047? 055 064 0107 0132 0133? 0134 0211	(NASV) "Jesus" is removed from association with "Lord." Aleph A B C K L M W Delta Pi Sigma Phi 074 0107 pm (legg) fam 1 f 1 r2 Vulg-pt Syr: pesh sin harc Cop: sa bo Goth

MARK 6:11	
shake off the dust under your feet for a testimony against them. <u>Verily I say unto you, It shall be more tolerable for Sodom and Gomorrha in the day of judgement than for that city</u>	shake the dust off your feet when you leave, as a testimony against them
A E F G H K M N S U V Y Pi Sigma Phi Omega 0133 Cursives: Majority fam 1,13 Old Latin: a f g2 q Syr: pesh harc Cop: bo-pt Goth Eth Also extant in 047? 055 0167 0211 0257?	Aleph B C D L W Delta Theta pc b c ff2 g1 i l Vulg sin sa bo-pt

Section Three--A Manuscript Digest of 356 Doctrinal Passages   155

AV	NIV

MARK 6:34

And <u>Jesus</u> when he came out A D E F G H K M N S U V Y Delta Pi Sigma Phi Omega Cursives: MAJORITY (hf) Old Latin: a b c f ff2 i l q r1,2 Vulg Syr: pesh harc Eth Also extant in P84 047? 055 0133? 0144? 0187 0211 0257?	(NASV) "Jesus" is removed from the feeding of the 5000 (22-44). Aleph B L W Theta 0149 al (hf) fam 1 g1 Cop: sa bo Arm

MARK 7:27

And <u>Jesus</u> said unto her, Let the children first be filled A E F G H K M N S U V W X Y Gamma Pi Sigma Phi Omega Cursives: MAJORITY (hf) fam 13 Old Latin: f g2 q Syr: pesh sin harc Goth Arm (Eth) Also extant in P45? 047 055 0144? 0211 0257?	(NASV) "Jesus" is removed from the healing of the Syrophonician woman's daughter (24-30) Aleph B D L Delta Theta pc (legg cites 3 cursives) a b c d ff2 g1 i l r2 Vulg pal sa bo

AV	NIV

MARK 8:1

having nothing to eat, <u>Jesus</u> called his disciples E F G H S U V Y X Gamma Omega Cursives: MAJORITY (hf) fam 13 Old Latin: f g2 Also extant in P45? 047? 055 0131 0211 0233? 0257?	(NASV) "Jesus" is removed from the feeding of the 4000 (1-9). Aleph A B D K L M N W Delta Theta Pi Sigma Phi 0131 al (hf) fam 1 Most OL Vulg Syr: pesh sin harc Cop: sa bo Goth Arm Eth

MARK 8:17

And when <u>Jesus</u> knew it	"Jesus" is removed from the discourse about leaven (14-21) in a few early manuscripts.
Aleph* A C D E L G H K L M N S U V W X Y Gamma Delta-2 Theta Pi Sigma Phi Omega Cursives: MAJORITY fam 1,13 Old Latin: a b c f ff2 g2 l q Vulg Syr: pesh sin harc . Cop: sa-mss Goth Arm Eth Also extant in P45? 047? 055 0211 0233? 0257?	Aleph-1 B Delta* pc (legg, na cite 1 cursive) aur i sa-mss bo

Section Three--A Manuscript Digest of 356 Doctrinal Passages 157

AV	NIV

MARK 9:24	

<u>Lord</u>, I believe	I do believe
C-2 E F G H K M N S U V X Y Gamma Delta Pi Sigma Omega Cursives: Majority (hf) Old Latin: a aur b c f g2 (q) Vulg Cop: bo-pt Arm-usc Also extant in P45? 047 055 0211 0233? 0257?	Aleph A B C* D L W Theta Phi Psi pc (legg cites 2 cursives) g1 i k l r1,2 Syr: pesh harc pal sa bo-pt Goth Arm-zoh Eth

MARK 9:29	

This kind can come forth by nothing, but by prayer <u>and fasting</u>	This kind can come out only by prayer
P45 Aleph-2 C D E F G H K L M N S U V W X Y Gamma Delta Theta Pi Sigma Phi Psi Omega Cursives: MAJORITY fam 1,13 Old Latin: a aur b c d f f2 i l q r1 Vulg Syr: (pesh) (sin) harc (pal) Cop: sa bo Goth (Arm) (Eth) Also extant in 047? O55 0211 0233? 0257?	Aleph* B 0274 pc (no cursives cited by na, ubs) k

158 Early Manuscripts, Church Fathers, & the Authorized Version

AV	NIV

MARK 9:42

And whosoever shall offend one of these little ones that believe <u>in me</u>	(NASV) And whoever causes one of these little ones who believe to stumble
A B C-2 E F G H K L M N S U V W X Y Gamma Theta Pi Sigma Phi Psi Omega Cursives: MAJORITY fam 1,13 Old Latin: aur c f g1,2 l q r2 Vulg Syr: pesh sin harc Cop: sa bo-pt fay Goth Arm Eth Also extant in 047? 055 0143? 0211 0233? 0257? It is not "faith in faith" that saves, but rather the Object of faith.	Aleph C* D Delta pc (no cursives cited by legg, na, ubs) (a) b ff2i k

MARK 9:44

<u>Where their worm dieth not and the fire is not quenched</u>	----------
A D E F G H K M N S U V X Y Theta Pi Sigma Phi Omega Cursives: MAJORITY fam 13 Old Latin: a aur b c d ff2 g2 i l q r1 Vulg Syr: pesh harc Goth Arm-usc (apparently) Eth Also extant in 047? 055 0211 0233? 0257? 0274	Aleph B C L W Delta Psi pc fam 1 sin Cop: sa bo fay Arm-zoh, mss

Section Three--A Manuscript Digest of 356 Doctrinal Passages

AV	NIV

MARK 9:46

Where their worm dieth not, and the fire is not quenched A D E F G H K M N S U V X Y Gamma Theta Pi Sigma Phi Omega Cursives: MAJORITY fam 13 Old Latin: a aur b c d f ff2 i l q r1 Vulg Syr: pesh harc Goth (Eth) Also extant in 047? 055 0211 0233? 0257? 0274	---------- Aleph B C L W Delta Psi pc fam 1 k sin Cop: sa bo fay Arm

MARK 10:7

For this cause shall a man leave his father and mother, and cleave to his wife A C D E F G H K L M N S U V W X Y Gamma Delta Pi Sigma Omega Cursives: MAJORITY fam 1,13 Old Latin: a aur b c d f g2 (k) l r1 Vulg Syr: pesh harc Cop: sa bo fay Arm Eth Also extant in Phi 047 055 0133? 0154 0211 0233? 0257	Footnote: "Some early manuscripts do not have..." Aleph B Psi pc (legg, ubs, na, cite 1 cursive) sin Goth

160 Early Manuscripts, Church Fathers, & the Authorized Version

AV	NIV

MARK 10:21

and come <u>take up the cross</u>, and follow me	Then come, follow me
A (E) F (G) H K M N S U V W X Y Gamma Pi Sigma Phi Omega Cursives: MAJORITY fam 13 Old Latin: (a) q Syr: (pesh) sin harc Cop: (sa-mss) bo-mss Goth (Arm) (Eth) Also extant in 047 05 0133? 0211 0233? 0257. There has always been an attempt to take the cross out of discipleship.	Aleph B C D Delta Theta Psi 0274 pc b c f f2 g1,2 k l Vulg sa-ms bo

MARK 10:24

children how hard it is <u>for them that trust in riches</u> to enter into the kingdom of God	children, how hard it is to enter the kingdom of God
A C D E F G H K M N S U V X Y Gamma Theta Pi Sigma Phi Omega Cursives: MAJORITY Old Latin:(a) aur b d f ff2 (g1),2 l q Syr: pesh sin harc Cop: bo Goth Arm Eth Also extant in 047 055 0133? 0211? 0257. Christendom places great trust in its amassed wealth and properties. See II Peter 2:3	Aleph B Delta Psi pc (no cursives cited by na, ubs) k sa bo-mss

Section Three--A Manuscript Digest of 356 Doctrinal Passages

AV	NIV

MARK 10:43

But so <u>shall it not be</u> among you: but whosoever will be great.... A C-3 E F G H K M N S U V X Y Gamma Pi Sigma Phi Omega Cursives: MAJORITY fam 1,13 Old Latin: q Syr: pesh sin harc pal Cop: bo-ms Goth Arm (Eth) Also extant in 047 055 0133? 0146 0154? 0211 0233? 0257 There is a subtile difference here. A bishop exercising authority over an entire area was the first major error in the early church. It was not so at the time Christ spoke these words, but soon would be.	<u>Not so</u> with you, Instead, whoever wants to become great... Aleph B C* D L W Delta theta Psi pc a aur b c d f ff2 g1 i k l r1 Vulg sa bo

162 Early Manuscripts, Church Fathers, & the Authorized Version

AV	NIV
MARK 11:10	
Blessed be the kingdom of our father David, that cometh <u>in the name of the Lord</u>	Blessed is the coming kingdom of our father David
A E F G H K M N S V X Y Gamma Pi Sigma Phi Omega Cursives: MAJORITY (hf) Old Latin: q Syr: harc Goth Eth also extant in 047 055 0133? 0211 0233? 0257 Religion has long talked of a kingdom which somehow comes apart from the literal return of Christ.	Aleph B C D L U W Delta Theta Psi al fam 1,13 (10 cursives cited by legg) Most OL Vulg pesh sin Cop: sa bo Arm
MARK 11:14	
And <u>Jesus</u> answered and said unto it	(NASV) "Jesus" is removed from the cursing of the fig tree (12-14).
E G H S U V W X Y Gamma Pi-2 Omega 0188 Cursives: Majority (hf) Cop: sa Also extant in 047 055 0133? 0154? 0211 0233? 0257?	Aleph A B C D K L M N Delta Theta Pi* Sigma Phi Psi al (hf) fam 1,13 Old Latin: most (apparently) Vulg Syr: pesh harc bo Goth Arm Eth

Section Three--A Manuscript Digest of 356 Doctrinal Passages 163

AV	NIV
MARK 11:15	
and Jesus went into the temple A E F G H K M N S U V X Y Gamma Theta Pi Sigma Phi Omega Cursives: MAJORITY (hf) fam 13 Old Latin: f q Syr: pesh harc Goth Also extant in 047 055 0133? 0154? 0188 0211 0233? 0257?	(NASV) "Jesus" is removed from the cleansing of the temple. Aleph B C D L W Delta Psi 0188 al fam 1 (legg cites 10 cursives) a b c ff2 g1,2 i k l Vulg sin Cop: sa bo Arm Eth
MARK 11:26	
But if you do not forgive neither will your Father which is in heaven forgive your trespasses A C D E F G H K M N U V X Y Gamma Theta Pi Sigma Phi Omega Cursives: MAJORITY fam 1,13 Old Latin: a b c d f ff2 (i) m q r1 Vulg Syr: pesh harc Cop: bo-pt Goth Arm-usc Eth-ppl Also extant in 047 055 0133? 0154 0211 0233? 0257?	----------- Aleph B L S W Delta Psi pc sin pal sa bo-pt Arm-zoh Eth-rom

164 Early Manuscripts, Church Fathers, & the Authorized Version

AV	NIV

| **MARK 12:23** ||

| In the resurrection <u>therefore, when they shall rise</u> | At the resurrection |
| A E F G H K M S U V X Y Gamma Theta Pi Sigma Phi Omega
Cursives: MAJORITY fam 1,(13)
Old Latin: (a) aur (b) ff2 g2 (i) l q Vulg
Syr: sin harc Cop: bo-ms
Goth Arm
Also extant in 047 055 0211 0233? | Aleph B C* C-2 D L W Delta Psi

pc
c d k r1

pesh sa bo
Eth |

| **MARK 12:30** ||

| <u>this is the first commandment</u> | ---------- |
| A D F G H (K) M S (U) V (W) X Y Gamma (Theta) (Pi) Sigma Phi Omega
Cursives: MAJORITY fam 1,13
Old Latin: most incl b c i (k) Vulg
Syr: pesh sin harc Cop: bo-ms
Goth Arm Eth
Also extant in 047 055 0211 0233? 0257. Compare this verse with Exodus 20, and the way in which for example the Catholic Church begins its numbering of the Ten Commandments. | Aleph B E L Delta Phi

pc
(a)

sa bo |

Section Three--A Manuscript Digest of 356 Doctrinal Passages

AV	NIV
MARK 12:41	
And <u>Jesus</u> sat over against the treasury	(NASV) "Jesus" is removed from the account of the widow's mite (41-44)
A D E F G H K M S U V X Y Gamma Theta Pi Sigma Phi Omega Cursives: MAJORITY fam 1,13 Old Latin: aur b c ff2 g2 i l q r1 Vulg Syr: pesh sin harc pal Cop: sa-ms Arm Eth Also extant in 047 055 0211 0233?	Aleph B L Delta Psi pc a k sa-ms bo fay
MARK 13:14	
But when ye shall see the abomination of desolation <u>spoken of by Daniel the prophet</u> A E F G H K M S U V X Y Gamma Delta Theta Pi Sigma Phi Omega Cursives: MAJORITY (hf) fam 1,13 Old Latin: aur c k l n** Syr: pesh harc Eth Arm Also extant in 047 055 083 0104 0116 0211 0233? The attack against the authorship and prophecies of the Book of Daniel is an old one.	When you see the abomination that causes desolation Aleph B D L W Psi pc (legg cites 3 cursives) a ff2 g1,2 i n* q r2 Vulg sin Cop: sa bo

166 Early Manuscripts, Church Fathers, & the Authorized Version

AV	NIV

MARK 13:33	
Take ye heed, watch <u>and pray</u>	Be on guard! Be alert!
Aleph A C E F G H K L M S U V W X Y Gamma Delta Theta Pi Sigma Psi Omega 0104 0116 Cursives: MAJORITY fam 1,13 Old Latin: aur f ff2 g1,2 i l q r1 Vulg Syr: pesh (sin) harc Cop: sa bo Also extant in Phi 047 055 0211 0233?	B D pc a c k fay

MARK 14:22a	
And as they did eat, <u>Jesus</u> took bread	(Nasv) "Jesus" is removed from the account of the Last Supper (22-25).
Aleph* Aleph-2 A C E F G H K L M P S U V X Y Gamma Delta Theta Pi Sigma Phi Psi Omega 0116 Cursives: MAJORITY fam 1 Old Latin: b c f g1,2 l q Vulg Syr: pesh harc Cop: bo Arm Eth Also extant in 047 055 0103 0211 0223? 0257?	Aleph-1 B D W pc (legg, na, ubs cite 1 cursive) a ff2 i k r2 sin sa

Section Three--A Manuscript Digest of 356 Doctrinal Passages

AV	NIV

MARK 14:22b	
Take, <u>eat</u>: this is my body E F H M-2 S Y X Y Gamma Sigma Omega 0116 Cursives: MAJORITY fam 13 Old Latin: ff2 Cop: bo-ms Also extant in 047 055 083 0103 0116 0211 0233? 0257?	Take it; this is my body Aleph A B C D K L M* P U W Delta Theta Pi Phi Psi pc fam 1 (12 cursives cited by legg) a c f (k) (g1,2) i l q r1,2 Vulg Syr: pesh sin harc sa bo-mss Arm Eth

MARK 14:24	
This is my blood of the <u>new</u> testament A E F G H K M P S U V X Y W-c X Gamma Delta Pi Sigma Phi Omega Cursives: MAJORITY fam 1,13 Old Latin: a aur b c f (g1,2) i l q (ff2) r1 Vulg Syr: pesh sin harc Cop: sa-mss bo-pt Arm Eth Also extant in 047 055 083 0103 0116 0211 0233? 0257? Also omitted in Matt. 26:28.	This is my blood of the covenant Aleph B C D* D-c L W Theta Psi pc (na ubs cite 1 cursive) d k sa-ms bo

168 Early Manuscripts, Church Fathers, & the Authorized Version

AV	NIV
MARK 14:27	
All ye shall be offended <u>because of me this night</u>	You will fall away
A C-2 E F G K M (N) U W Y Theta Pi* Sigma Phi Cursives: pm fam 1,(13) Old Latin: a aur c e f g1,2 i k Vulg-pt Syr: pesh harc Cop: sa-mss bo-mss Arm Eth Other manuscripts have a shorter wording. Also extant in 047 055 0211 0233? 0257?	Aleph B C* D H L S V X Gamma Delta Pi-2 Psi* Omega 0116 pm b ff2 q sa-ms bo-pt
MARK 15:28	
<u>And the Scripture was fulfilled which saith, And he was numbered with the transgressors.</u>	----------
E F G H K L M P S U V Y-mg Gamma Delta Theta Pi Sigma Omega 0112 0250 Cursives: MAJORITY fam 1,13 Old Latin: aur c ff2 g1 l n r1 Vulg Syr: pesh harc pal Cop: (bo-pt) Goth Arm Eth Also extant in 047 055 083 0233? 0250 0257	Aleph A B C D X Y-txt Psi pc d k sin sa bo-pt fay

AV	NIV
MARK 15:39	
And when the centurion...saw <u>that he so cried out,</u> and gave up the ghost	And when the centurion...saw how he died
A C (D) E G H K M N S U V (W) X Y Gamma Delta (Theta) Pi Sigma Omega 0112 Cursives: MAJORITY fam 1,13 Old Latin: aur c (d) ff2 (i) l n q Vulg Syr: pesh (sin) harc Goth (Arm) Eth Also extant in 047 055 083 0211 0233? 0257. It was the manner of the cry which so convinced the centurion.	Aleph B L Psi pc Cop: sa (bo) fay

170 Early Manuscripts, Church Fathers, & the Authorized Version

AV	NIV
MARK 16:9-20	
Now when Jesus was risen...confirming the word with signs following. Amen	Footnote: "The two most reliable early manuscripts do not have Mark 16:9-20".
A C D E F G (H) K (L) M S U V (W) X Y Gamma Delta Theta Pi Sigma (Psi) Omega (099) (0112) Cursives: MAJORITY fam 1,13	Aleph B pc (na, ubs cite 1 cursive, and say that some others make reference to a shorter ending)
Old Latin: aur c d-suppl ff2 g1,2 l n o q r2 Vulg Syr: pesh cur harc pal Cop: sa bo fay Goth Arm Eth Also extant in 047 055 0211 0233? 0257. Early bishops who claimed to be direct successors of the apostles would find their inability to perform the works of the apostles (II Cor. 12:12) a matter of embarrassment. Are we really to believe that the Gospel of Mark would end in verse 8 with the words, "for they were afraid"? See Burgon's great work on this chapter.	(k) sin sa-ms Arm-mss

AV	NIV

LUKE 1:28

| The Lord is with thee: <u>blessed art thou among women</u>

A C D E F G H K M S U V X
Gamma Delta Theta Lambda Pi
053 0135
Cursives: MAJORITY fam 13
Old Latin: a aur b c d e f ff2 l q r1
Vulg
Syr: pesh harc   Cop: bo-mss
Goth Eth
Also extant in Y Xi Omega? 047 053 055 0130 0211 0233? | The Lord is with you

Aleph B L W Psi

pc   fam 1

pal   sa bo
Arm |

AV	NIV
LUKE 2:14	
Glory to God in the highest and on earth peace, <u>goodwill toward men</u>	Glory to God in the highest, and on earth peace <u>to men on whom his favor rests.</u>
Aleph-2 B-3 E G H K L M P S U V Gamma Delta Theta Lambda Xi Psi 053 Cursives: MAJORITY fam 1,13 Syr: pesh sin harc (pal) Cop: bo Arm Eth Also extant in Y Omega 047 055 0211 0233? As with the angel's pronouncement in Luke 1:32-33 this verse looks ultimately to Christ's reign <u>on earth</u> at His Second Coming. That there will be complete peace *on earth*, though taught everywhere in Scripture, runs counter to "official" church teaching.	Aleph* A B* D W pc Old Latin: a aur b beta c d e f (ff2) l q rl Vulg sa Goth

Section Three--A Manuscript Digest of 356 Doctrinal Passages 173

AV	NIV

LUKE 2:22

AV	NIV
And when the days of <u>her</u> purification according to the law of Moses were accomplished, they brought him to Jerusalem	When the time of <u>their</u> purification according to the Law had been completed, Joseph and Mary took him to Jerusalem
Cursives: pc Old Latin: l f1 (a aur b beta c d e ff2 l r1 Vulg. The Latin "eius" can mean either "her" or "his" depending on the contest. As it could not mean Joseph's or the Child's purification it must be "her". An early vulgate manuscript reads: "...the days of Mary's purification.")	Aleph A B K L W X Delta Theta Xi Pi Psi 053 Majority fam 1,13 q
	Syr: pesh harc pal Cop: sal bo-pt Goth Arm-zoh Eth
Also extant in R Y 047 055 0211 0233? The Law in Leviticus 12 required purification only for the mother - not the child, not the father. This for the birth of a son lasted 40 days. Despite the manuscript support for "their purification" the reading is clearly wrong. It contradicts Scripture and brings dishonour to Christ.	

174 Early Manuscripts, Church Fathers, & the Authorized Version

AV	NIV

LUKE 2:33

And <u>Joseph</u> and his mother marvelled at those things which were spoken of him	The childs <u>father</u> and mother marvelled at what was said about him
A E G H K M S U Y X Gamma Delta Theta Lambda Pi Psi 053 Cursives: MAJORITY fam13 Old Latin: a aur b beta c e f ff2 g1 l q (r1) Syr: pesh harc pal-ms Cop: bo-pt Goth Also extant in Y Xi Omega 045 055 0130 0211 0233? Here and in 2:43 the virgin birth is attacked.	Aleph B D L W pc fam 1 d g2 Vulg sin harc-mg sa bo-pt Arm Eth

LUKE 2:40

And the child grew, and waxed strong <u>in spirit</u>	And the child grew and became strong
A E F G H K M S U V Gamma Delta Theta Lambda Pi Psi 053 Cursives: MAJORITY Old Latin: f q Syr: pesh harc Cop: bo-mss Goth (Eth) Also extant in Y Omega 047 055 0130 0211 0233?	Aleph B D L N W pc a b c e ff2 g1,2 l Vulg sin pal sa bo Arm

Section Three--A Manuscript Digest of 356 Doctrinal Passages 175

AV	NIV
LUKE 2:43	
THE CHILD Jesus tarried behind in Jerusalem; and Joseph and his mother knew not of it A C E F G H K M S U V X Gamma Delta Lambda Pi Psi 0130 Cursives: MAJORITY fam 13 Old Latin: b c f ff2 g1 l q Syr: pesh harc Cop: bo-pt Goth Eth Also extant in Y Omega 047 055 0211 0233? See on verse 33.	While his parents were returning home... Aleph B D L W Theta pc fam 1 a e Vulg sin harc-mg pal sa bo-pt Arm
LUKE 4:4	
It is written, That man shall not live by bread alone, but by every word of God A D E F G H K M S U V Gamma Delta Theta Lambda Pi Psi 0102 0116 Cursives: MAJORITY fam 1,13 Old Latin: a aur b c d e f ff2 l q r1 Vulg Syr: pesh harc Cop: (bo-pt) Goth Arm (Eth) Also extant in Y Omega 047 055 0211 0233?	It is written: Man does not live on bread alone Aleph B L W pc sin sa bo-pt

AV	NIV

| LUKE 4:8 ||

| And Jesus answered <u>and said unto him, Get thee behind me, Satan:</u> for it is written | Jesus answered, It is written |
| A E F G H K M S U V Gamma Delta Theta Lambda Pi Psi 0102 0116
Cursives: MAJORITY fam 13
Old Latin: b e l q
Syr: harc Cop: (bo-pt)
Eth-ms
Also extant in Y Omega 047 055 0211 0233? | Aleph B D L Xi

pc fam 1
a c f ff2 g1,2 Vulg
pesh sin sa bo-pt
Goth Arm Eth |

| LUKE 4:41 ||

| And devils...saying, Thou art <u>Christ</u> the Son of God | Moreover demons...shouting, you are the Son of God |
| A E G H K M Q S U V Gamma Delta Theta Lambda Pi Psi 0102
Cursives: MAJORITY fam 1,13
Old Latin: f q
Syr: pesh harc Cop: bo-pt
Goth Eth
Also extant in P25 Q R Y Omega 047 055 0211 0233? | Aleph B C D F L R W X Xi

pc
Most OL Vulg
sin sa bo-pt
Arm |

Section Three--A Manuscript Digest of 356 Doctrinal Passages

AV	NIV
LUKE 7:22	
Then <u>Jesus</u> answering...Go your way, and tell John A E F G H K L M R S U V X Gamma Delta Lambda Pi Cursives: MAJORITY (hf) Old Latin: c f q Syr: pesh harc pal Goth Eth Also extant in Y Theta Psi Omega 047 055 0211	"Jesus" is removed from His witness of miracles to John (19-23) in some early manuscripts. P75 Aleph B D Xi pc (hf) a b e ff2 g1,2 l Vulg Cop: bo Arm
LUKE 7:31	
<u>And the Lord said,</u> Whereunto... M-mg Cursives: pc (hf) Old Latin: f g1 Vulg-pt Also extant in P75 W Y Theta Xi Psi Omega 047 055 0211 see *KJVMT* p. 45. There, g2 should be g1.	To what... Aleph A B D E F G H K L M S U V X Gamma Delta Lamba Pi MAJORITY (hf) a b c e ff2 g2 l q Vulg Syr: pesh harc Cop: bo Goth Arm Eth

178 Early Manuscripts, Church Fathers, & the Authorized Version

AV	NIV

LUKE 9:35

This is my <u>beloved</u> Son	this is my Son, whom I have <u>chosen</u>
A C* (C-3) (D) E F G H K M P R S U Y W X Gamma Delta Lambda Pi (Psi) Cursives: MAJORITY fam 13 Old Latin: b c (d) e f g Vulg Syr: pesh cur harc pal Cop: (bo-ms) Goth Also extant in Y Omega 047 055 0115 0211. Chosen from among whom?	P45, 75 Aleph B L Theta Xi pc fam 1 a aur ff2 l sa-bo Arm Eth-ppl

LUKE 9:43

They were all amazed...at all things which <u>Jesus</u> did	(NASV) "Jesus" is removed from an account of his miracles and coming crucifixion (43-45).
A C E F G H K M S U V W X Gamma Delta Theta Lambda Pi Psi 0115 0135 Cursives: MAJORITY fam 13 Old Latin: f q rl Syr: pesh harc Goth Eth Also extant in R Y Omega 047 055 0181? 0211	P75 Aleph B D L Xi pc fam 1 a b c e ff2 g1,2 l Vulg sin cur sa bo Arm

Section Three--A Manuscript Digest of 356 Doctrinal Passages

AV	NIV

LUKE 9:55

But he turned and rebuked them, and said, Ye know not what manner of spirit ye are of	But Jesus turned and rebuked them
D F K M U Gamma Theta Lamba Pi Cursives: pm fam 1,13 Old Latin: a aur b c d e f q r1 Vulg Syr: pesh cur harc Goth Eth-ms Also extant in Y Omega 047 055 0211	P45, 75 Aleph A B C E G H L S V W X Delta Xi Psi pm g1 1 sa bo-pt Eth

LUKE 9:56

For the Son of man is not come to destroy men's lives, but to save them. And they went to another village	and they went to another village
F K M U Gamma Lambda Pi Cursives: pm fam 1,13 Old Latin: a aur b c e f q r1 Vulg Syr: pesh cur harc Cop: bo-pt Goth Arm Eth-ms Also extant in Y Omega 047 055 0211	P45, 75 Aleph A B C D E G H L S V E X Delta Xi Psi pm g1,2 1 sin sa bo-pt Eth

180 Early Manuscripts, Church Fathers, & the Authorized Version

AV	NIV

LUKE 9:57

<u>Lord,</u> I will follow thee withersoever thou goest	I will follow you wherever you go
A C E F G H K M S U V W X Gamma Delta Theta Lambda Pi Psi Cursives: MAJORITY fam 13 Old Latin: (b) f q Syr: pesh harc pal Cop: bo-ms Goth Eth Also extant in Omega 047 055 0211	P45, 75 Aleph B D L Xi pc fam 1 a c e g1,2 l Vulg sin cur sa bo Arm

LUKE 9:59

<u>Lord</u>, suffer me first	(NASV) Permit me first
P45, 75 Aleph A B-3 C E F G H K L M S U V W X Gamma Delta Theta Lambda Xi Pi Psi 0181 Cursives: MAJORITY fam 1,13 Old Latin: a aur b c e f l q r1 Vulg Syr: pesh cur harc Cop: sa bo Goth Arm Eth Also extant in Y Omega 047 055 0211	B* D V pc d sin

Section Three--A Manuscript Digest of 356 Doctrinal Passages 181

AV	NIV
LUKE 9:60	
Jesus said...(connect with above) A C E F G H K M S U V X Gamma Delta Lambda Pi Cursives: MAJORITY (hf) Old Latin: most Vulg Syr: pesh cur harc pal Goth Arm Eth Also extant in P75 W Y Theta Psi Omega 047 055 0181 0211	(NASV) But he said... P45 Aleph B D L Xi pc (hf) a Cop: bo
LUKE 10:21	
Jesus rejoiced... I thank thee O Father A C E F G H K L M S U V X W Gamma Delta Lambda Pi 0115 0253 Cursives: MAJORITY fam 1,13 Old Latin: c e f ff2 g q rl Syr: pesh harc pal Cop: bo-pt Goth Arm Eth Also extant in Y Theta Psi Omega 047 055 070 0211 0233?	(NASV) "Jesus" is removed from a declaration of union with His Father. P45, 75 Aleph B D Xi pc a aur b i l Vulg sin cur Cop: sa bo-pt

AV	NIV

LUKE 10:41, 42

thou art careful and troubled about many things: But <u>one thing is needful</u>: and Mary hat chosen that good part	you are worried and bothered about so many things; <u>but only a few things are necessary really only one</u>: for Mary has chosen the good part
P45, 75 A C* C-3 E F G H K M P S U V W Gamma Delta Theta Lambda Pi Psi Cursives: MAJORITY fam 13 Old Latin: aur f g1 q Vulg Syr: pesh cur harc Cop: sa bo-ms Also extant in Y Omega 047 055 0211 0233? Christ in the altered text is made to speak about food rather than single-hearted devotion to Himself.	P3 (Aleph*) Aleph-c B C-2 L pc fam 1 harc-mg pal bo (Arm) Eth

LUKE 11:2a

When ye pray, say, Our Father <u>which art in heaven</u>	When you pray, say: Father
A C D E F G H K M P S U V W X Gamma Delta Theta Lambda Pi Psi Cursives: MAJORITY fam 13 Old Latin: (a) b (c) d e f (ff2) (i) l q r1 Syr: pesh cur harc Cop: sa bo Eth Also extant in Y Xi Omega 047 055 0211 0233?	P75 Aleph B L pc fam 1 aur g1,2? Vulg sin Arm

Section Three--A Manuscript Digest of 356 Doctrinal Passages

AV	NIV
LUKE 11:2b	
Thy Kingdom come. <u>Thy will be done, as in heaven, so in earth</u> Aleph* Aleph-c A C D E F G H K M P S U V W X Gamma Delta Theta Lamba Pi Psi Cursives: MAJORITY fam 13 Old Latin: aur b c e f ff2 i l q r1 Syr: pesh harc Cop: bo Eth Also extant in Y Xi Omega 047 055 0211 0233?	Your kingdom come P75 B L pc fam 1 Vulg sin cur Arm
LUKE 12:31	
But rather seek ye the kingdom <u>of God</u> P45 A D-1 E F G H K M Q S U V W X Gamma Delta Theta Lambda Pi 070 Cursives: MAJORITY fam 1,13 Old Latin: aur b d e f ff2 i l q r1 Vulg Syr: pesh sin cur harc Arm Also extant in Y Omega 047 055 0211 0233?	But seek his kingdom (P75) Aleph B D-gr L Psi pc a c Cop: sa bo Eth

184 Early Manuscripts, Church Fathers, & the Authorized Version

AV	NIV

LUKE 12:39

that if the goodman of the house had known what hour the thief would come, <u>he would have watched</u>	If the owner of the house had known at what hour the thief was coming
Aleph-1 (A) B E F G H K L M P (Q) S U V W X Gamma Delta Theta Lamba Pi Psi (070) Cursives: MAJORITY fam 1,13 Old Latin: (aur) b c (f) ff2 (l) (q) r1 (Vulg) Syr: pesh harc Cop: sa bo Arm-usc Eth Also extant in Y Omega 047 055 0211 0233?	P75 Aleph* (D) pc (No cursives cited by na, ubs) (d) e i sin cur sa-mss ach

LUKE 13:2

And <u>Jesus</u> answering said unto them	(NASV) "Jesus" is removed from this exhortation to repent (1-5).
A D E F G H K M S U V W X Delta Theta Lambda Pi Psi Cursives: MAJORITY fam 1,13 Old Latin: c f ff2 q Syr: pesh sin cur harc Cop: sa-ms bo-pt Also extant in N Y Omega 047 055 070 0211 0233?	P75 Aleph B L pc a b e i l (g1,2 ?) Vulg sa-mss bo-pt

Section Three--A Manuscript Digest of 356 Doctrinal Passages

AV	NIV

LUKE 13:25

Lord <u>Lord</u> open to us	Sir, open the door for us
A D E F G H K M S U V W X Gamma Delta Theta Lambda Pi Psi 070 Cursives: MAJORITY fam 1,13 Old Latin: h f i q Syr: pesh sin cur harc Cop: sa-ms bo-pt Arm Eth Also extant in Y Omega 047 055 0211 0233? Verse 26 shows that it is Christ who is being addressed.	P75 Aleph B L pc a c e ff2 g1,2 l Vulg sin sa bo-pt

LUKE 13:35

Behold your house is left unto you <u>desolate</u>	(NASV) places in italics.
D E G H M N U X Delta Theta Psi Cursives: pm fam 13 Old Latin: a b c f gl l q Vulg-pt Syr: pesh cur harc Eth Also extant in Y Omega 047 055 0211 0233?	P45, 75 Aleph A B K L P S V W Gamma Lambda Pi pm fam 1 e ff2 g2 i Vulg sin sa Arm

AV	NIV

LUKE 14:5

AV	NIV
Which of you shall have an <u>ass</u> or an ox fallen into a pit Aleph K L X Pi Psi Cursives: al fam 1,13 (51 cursives cited in our other Digest) Old Latin: a aur b c ff2 g1,2? i l rl Vulg Syr: (sin) pal Cop: bo fay Arm (Eth) Also extant in N? Y Omega 047 055 0211 0233? See *KJVMT*, p. 48 for further evidence.	If one of you has a <u>son</u> or an ox that falls into a well P45,75 (A) B E G H M S U V W Gamma Delta Lambda MAJORITY e f g pesh harc sa

LUKE 17:3

AV	NIV
If thy brother trespass <u>against thee</u>, rebuke him D E F G H K M S U V X Gamma Delta Lambda Pi Psi 063 0135 Cursives: MAJORITY fam 13 Old Latin: c e q rl Vulg-pt Syr: harc-mg Cop: bo-mss Arm-usc Also extant in P75? N Y Omega 047 055 0211 0272. See on Matt. 18:15.	If your brother sins, rebuke him Aleph A B L W Theta pc fam 1 a b f ff2 g1,2 i l m Vulg pesh sin harc pal sa bo Goth Arm-zoh

Section Three--A Manuscript Digest of 356 Doctrinal Passages

AV	NIV
LUKE 17:24	
So shall also the Son of man be <u>in his day</u> Aleph A E F G H K L M R S U V W X Gamma Delta Theta Lambda Pi Psi 063 Cursives: MAJORITY fam 1,13 Old Latin: aur q r1 Vulg Syr: pesh (sin) cur harc Cop:bo Goth Arm Also extant in N Omega 047 055 0211 0272	Footnote: "Some manuscripts do not have..." P75 B D pc (no cursives cited by na, ubs) a b d e i sa Eth
LUKE 17:36	
Two men shall be in the field; the one shall be taken, and the other left. DU Cursives: al fam 13 (41 cursives cited in our other Digest) Old Latin: a aur c d (e) f ff2 i l q (r1) Vulg Syr: pesh cur harc Arm Also extant in N Y Omega 047 055 0211 0272. See *KJVMT*, p. 49.	---------- P75 Aleph A B E F G K L M Q R S V W X Gamma Delta Theta Lambda Pi Psi 063 MAJORITY fam 1 g1 sa bo Goth Eth

188   Early Manuscripts, Church Fathers, & the Authorized Version

AV	NIV

LUKE 18:28

Lo, we have left <u>all</u>, and followed thee	(Literal) Lo, we have left <u>our own</u>, and followed thee
Aleph* A E F G H K M P R S U V W X Gamma Delta Lambda Pi Psi Cursives: MAJORITY Old Latin: f Vulg Syr: pesh harc Goth Eth Also extant in Q Y Omega 047 055 0211 0233? The "successors" of Peter and the apostles have left considerably less than "all".	Aleph-2 B (D) L pc b ff2 rl harc-mg Cop: sa-mss bo Arm

LUKE 20:23

but he perceived their craftiness, and said unto them, <u>Why tempt ye me</u>?	He saw through their duplicity and said to them
A (C) D E F G H K M P S U V W Gamma Delta Theta Lambda Pi Psi Cursives: MAJORITY fam 13 Old Latin: most Vulg Syr: pesh sin cur harc Goth Eth Also extant in Y Omega 047 055 063 0211 0233? 0266	Aleph B L 0266 pc fam 1 e Cop: sa bo Arm

Section Three--A Manuscript Digest of 356 Doctrinal Passages   189

AV	NIV

LUKE 21:36

and pray always, that ye <u>may be accounted worthy</u> to escape all these things that shall come to pass A C D E F G H K M R S U V Gamma Delta Theta Lambda Pi Cursives: MAJORITY fam 13 Old Latin: Most Vulg Syr: pesh sin cur harc Arm Also extant in T Y Omega 047 055 070 0211 0233? The NASV reading in effect rules out the pre-tribulational rapture.	(NASV) at all times, praying in order that you <u>may have strength</u> to escape all these things that are about to take place Aleph B L (W) X Psi 0113 0179 pc fam 1 pal Cop: sa bo Eth

LUKE 22:19, 20

This is my body <u>which is given for you: this do in remembrance of me. Likewise the cup after supper saying. This cup is the new testament in my blood, which is shed for you.</u> P75 Aleph A B D E F G H K L M S T U V W X Gamma Delta Theta Pi Psi 063 Cursives: MAJORITY fam 1,13 Old Latin: aur c f q r1 Vulg Syr: pesh harc pal Cop: sa bo Arm Eth? Also extant in Y Omega 047 055 0135 0211 0233?	NASV Footnote: "Some ancient manuscripts omit the remainder of verse 19 and all of verse 20." D pc (no cursive cited by na, ubs) a d ff2 i l cur

AV	NIV

LUKE 22:19, 20 continued
There are eight passages at the end of Luke (22:19,20; 24:3,6,12,36,40,51,52) which appear in the AV and practically all other witnesses including Aleph (exc. 24:5) and B. These are, however, missing from the early western manuscript D and certain of the Old Latin. Hort felt it likely that they should in fact be omitted as D characteristically expanded the text, and any shortening in that manuscript was a matter for special notice. In the end Westcott and Hort placed the passages in their 1881 edition, but within double brackets indicating they were probably interpolations. Therefore, in these eight places W/H were led to believe that their B-Aleph text could be wrong. But as they could not bring themselves to speak of "B-Aleph interpolations" they gave to them the question-begging title "Western non-interpolations." While the evidence for their inclusion is overwhelming, doubt is still expressed in the NASV and some other modern versions. These passages proclaim some of the most important doctrinal truths in the Bible

LUKE 22:31

AV	NIV
And the Lord said Simon, Simon, behold, Satan...	Simon, Simon, Satan...
Aleph A D E F G H K M Q S U V W X Gamma Delta Theta Lambda Pi Psi	P75 B L T
Cursives: MAJORITY fam 1,13	pc (na cites 1 cursive)
Old Latin: (a) b f (ff2 g1 i l) Vulg	
Syr: (pesh cur) harc (pal)	sin
Cop: bo-ms)	sa bo
Arm-Eth (apparently)	
Also extant in Y Omega 047 055 0211 0233?	

Section Three--A Manuscript Digest of 356 Doctrinal Passages

AV	NIV
LUKE 22:43,44	
And there appeared an angel unto him from heaven strenthening him. And being in an agony he prayed more earnestly: and his sweat was as it were great drops of blood falling down to the ground.	Footnote: "Some early manuscripts do not have verses 43 and 44."
Aleph* Aleph-2 D E F G H K L M Q S U V X Delta* Theta Lambda Pi* Psi 0171 Cursives: MAJORITY fam 1,13 (misplaces) Old Latin: a aur b c d e ff2 q1,2 i l r1 Vulg Syr: pesh cur harc pal Arm Eth Also extant in Y Omega 047 055 0211 0233? Probably removed by early heretics who denied Christ's true humanity ("great drops of blood") and also by the more orthodox who wrongly felt the passage conflicted with Christ's Deity ("an angel strengthening him").	P 69,75 Aleph-1 A B R T W pc f sin sa bo-pt

192   Early Manuscripts, Church Fathers, & the Authorized Version

AV	NIV

LUKE 22:64	
And when they had blindfolded him, they struck him on the face A D E F G H S U V W X Gamma Delta Theta Lambda Psi 0135 Cursives: MAJORITY fam 13 Old Latin: f Vulg Syr: pesh harc Arm Eth Also extant in Y 047 055 070 0171 0211 0233?	They blindfolded him P75 (Aleph) B K L M T Pi al ff2 i Cop: bo

LUKE 22:68	
And if I also ask you, ye will not answer me, nor let me go A D E F G H K M S U V W X Gamma Delta Lambda Pi Psi 063 Cursives: MAJORITY fam 13 Old Latin: (a) aur b c d f ff2 (i) (l) q r1 Vulg Syr: pesh sin cur harc Arm Also extant in Y Omega 047 055 0211 0233?	and if I asked you, you would not answer P75 Aleph B L T (Theta) pc (fam 1) Cop: sa bo

Section Three--A Manuscript Digest of 356 Doctrinal Passages

AV	NIV

LUKE 23:34

AV	NIV
Then said Jesus, Father, forgive them; for they know not what they do	Footnote: "Some early manuscripts not have this sentence."
Aleph* Aleph-2 (A) C D-gr,2 E F G H K L M Q S U V X Gamma Delta Lambda Pi Psi 0117 0250 Cursives: MAJORITY fam 1,13 Old Latin: aur b c e f ff2 l r1 Vulg Syr: pesh cur harc pal Cop: (bo-pt) Arm Eth Also extant in Y Omega 047 055 0211. Then, as in this day there would be those who would not want to see the Jews forgiven for their part in the crucifixion of Christ.	P75 Aleph-1 B D* W Theta 0124 pc a d sin Cop: sa bo-pt

AV	NIV

LUKE 23:38	
And a superscription also was written over him in letters of Greek, and Latin, and Hebrew, THIS IS THE KING OF THE JEWS	There was a written notice above him, written over him which read: THIS IS THE KING OF THE JEWS
Aleph* Aleph-2 A C-3 D E F G H K M Q R S U V W X Gamma Delta Theta Pi (Psi) 0117 0135 0250 Cursives: MAJORITY fam 1,13 Old Latin: aur (c) e f ff2 1 r1 Vulg Syr: pesh harc Cop: (bo-pt) Arm Eth Also extant in Y Omega 047 055 0211	P75 Aleph-1 B L 0124 pc (na, ubs cite 1 cursive) a Syr: sin cur Cop: sa bo-pt

Section Three--A Manuscript Digest of 356 Doctrinal Passages

AV	NIV
LUKE 23:42	
And he said unto Jesus, <u>Lord</u>, remember me	Then he said, Jesus, remember me
A C-2 (D) E F G H K M-2(Q) S U V R W X Gamma Delta Theta Lambda Pi Psi (0124) 0135 Cursives: MAJORITY Old Latin: b © e f ff2 l) q Vulg Syr: pesh sin (cur) harc Cop: bo-pt Arm Eth Also extant in R Y Omega 047 055 0117 0211 0212. This would be the only time in Scripture where Christ is addressed by his personal name.	P75 Aleph B C* L M* pc (no cursives cited by na) a pal sa-mss bo-pt

196 Early Manuscripts, Church Fathers, & the Authorized Version

AV	NIV

LUKE 23:45	
And the sun was <u>darkened</u> A C-3 D E F G H K M Q R S U Y W X Gamma Delta Theta Lambda Pi Psi 0117 0135 Cursives: MAJORITY fam 1,13 Old Latin: (a) aur (b) (c) d (e) f ff2 l q Vulg Syr: pesh sin cur harc pal (Arm) Eth Also extant in P Y Omega 047 055 063 070 0211. "This rationalistic explanation of the supernatural darkness at the crucifixion is ascribed to the Jews in the Acts of Pilate and to a heathen historian Thallus by Julius Africanus, but as Julius noted, it was impossible because at Passover time the moon was full." (Hills, *KJVD*, p 127).	(NASV) the sun being <u>obscured</u> (lit. eclipsed) P75 75-c Aleph B C* L 0124 pc harc-mg

Section Three--A Manuscript Digest of 356 Doctrinal Passages 197

AV	NIV
LUKE 24:6	
He is not here, but is risen P75 Aleph A B (C) C-3 E F G H K L M S U V W X Gamma Delta Theta Lambda Pi Psi 063 0124 Cursives: MAJORITY fam 1,13 Old Latin: aur f q Vulg Syr: (pesh) sin cur harc pal Cop: sa bo Arm (Eth) Also extant in Y Omega 047 055 070 0211 0250. See concerning the "Western non-interpolations" in 22:19, 20. Notice in these how the NASV casts doubt upon this primary witness to the Resurrection (6,12,36,40), Ascension (51), and Deity (52) of Christ. Yet there are many fundamentalists today who praise the "doctrinal integrity" of the NASV.	NASV Footnote: "Some ancient manuscripts omit." D pc (no cursives cited by na, ubs) a b d e ff2 l rl

198   Early Manuscripts, Church Fathers, & the Authorized Version

AV	NIV
LUKE 24:12	
Then arose Peter, and ran unto the sepulchre;.and stooping down, he: beheld the linen clothes laid by themselves, and departed, wondering in himself at that which was come to pass:	NASV places in brackets with a footnote: "Some ancient manuscripts omit verse 12."
P75 Aleph A B E F G H K L M S U V W X Gamma Delta Theta Lambda Pi Psi 063 079 0124 Cursives: MAJORITY fam 1,13 Old Latin: aur c ff2 Vulg Syr: pesh sin cur harc pal-mss Cop: sa bo Arm Eth Also extant in Y Omega 047 055 070 079 0211 0250?	D pc (no cursives cited by na, ubs) a b d e l rl pal-mss
LUKE 24:36a	
Jesus himself stood in the midst of them	(NASV) "Jesus" is removed from the upper room appearance (36-53).
A E G K M P S U V W X Gamma Delta Theta Lambda Psi 0135 Cursives: MAJORITY fam 1,13 Old Latin: f ff2 Vulg Syr: pesh harc pal Cop: bo-pt Arm Also extant in Y Omega 047 055 0135 0211	P75 Aleph B D L pc (na cites 1 cursive) a b e sin cur sa bo-mss

Section Three--A Manuscript Digest of 356 Doctrinal Passages   199

AV	NIV
LUKE 24:36b	
and saith unto them, peace be unto you P75 Aleph A B E F G H K L M P D S U V W X Gamma Delta Theta Lambda Pi Psi Cursives: MAJORITY fam 1,13 Old Latin: aur c f g1,2 Vulg Syr: pesh sin cur harc pal Cop: sa bo Arm Eth Some of the above add "be not afraid." Also extant in Y Omega 047 055 0135 0211	NASV omits. D pc (no cursives cited by na, ubs) a b d e ff2 1 rl
LUKE 24:40	
And when he had thus spoken he shewed them his hands and his feet P75 Aleph A B E F G H K L M N S U V W X Gamma Delta Theta Lambda Pi Psi Cursives: MAJORITY fam 1,13 Old Latin: aur c f g Vulg Syr: pesh harc pal Cop: sa bo Arm Eth (apparently) Also extant in Y Omega 047 055 0135 0211	NASV omits from text and places in footnote. D pc (no cursives cited by na, ubs) a b e ff2 1 rl sin cur

200 Early Manuscripts, Church Fathers, & the Authorized Version

AV	NIV

LUKE 24:46

Thus it is written, and thus it behoved Christ to suffer	This is what is written: The Christ will suffer
A C-2 E F G H K M N S U V W Gamma Delta Theta Lambda Pi Psi 063 0135 Cursive: MAJORITY fam 1,13 Old Latin: f q Vulg Syr: pesh harc Cop: sa-ms Also extant in Y Omega 047 055 0211	P75 Aleph B C* D L pc a b c e ff1 1 pal sa-mss bo Eth

LUKE 24:47

And that repentance and remission off sins should be preached	(Literal) And that repentance unto remission of sins should be preached
A C D E F G H K M N S U V W X Gamma Delta Theta Lambda Pi Psi 063 Cursive: MAJORITY fam 1,13 Old Latin: a aur b c d e f ff2 q r1 Vulg Syr: harc pal Arm Eth Also extant in Y Omega 047 055 0211. The revised reading lends support to the teaching that "acts of penance" will lead to salvation.	P75 Aleph B pc (no cursives cited by na, ubs) pesh Cop: sa bo

Section Three--A Manuscript Digest of 356 Doctrinal Passages   201

AV	NIV

LUKE 24:51

and carried up into heaven	NASV omits from text and places in footnote.
P75 Aleph-c A B C G H K L M S U V W X Gamma Delta Theta Lambda Pi Psi 063 Cursives: MAJORITY fam 1,13 Old Latin: aur c f q (r1) Vulg Syr: pesh harc pal Cop: sa bo Arm Eth (apparently) Also extant in Y Omega 047 055 0211	Aleph* D pc (no cursives cited by na, ubs) a b d e ff2 1

LUKE 24:52

And they worshipped him	NASV omits from text and places in footnote.
P75 Aleph A B C E F G H K L M S U V W X Gamma Delta Theta Lambda Pi Psi 063 Cursives: MAJORITY fam 1, 13 Old Latin: aur (c) f q (Vulg) Syr: pesh harc pal Cop: sa bo Arm Eth (apparently) Also extant in Y Omega 047 055 0211	D pc (no cursives cited by na, ubs) a b d e ff2 1 sin

AV	NIV

JOHN 1:18

No man hath seen God at any time; the only begotten <u>Son</u> which is in the bosom of the Father, he hath declared him	(NASV) No man has seen God at any time; the only begotten <u>God</u>, who is in the bosom of the father, he has explained Him.
A C-3 E F G H K M S U V W-suppl X Gamma Delta Theta Lambda Pi Psi 063 Cursives: MAJORITY fam 1,13 Old Latin: a aur b c e f ff2 l q Vulg Syr: cur harc pal Arm Eth-ppl Also extant in Y Omega 047 055 0141 0211 0233? This is the classic Gnostic perversion with its doctrine of "intermediary gods." It is the trademark of corruption in the early Egyptian manuscripts which unfortunately spread to some others.	P66, 75 Aleph* Aleph-1 B C* L pc pesh harc-mg Cop: bo Eth-rom

JOHN 1:27

He it is, who coming after me <u>is preferred before me</u>	He is the one who comes after me
A C-3 E F G H K M S U V X Gamma Delta Theta Lambda Pi Cursives: MAJORITY fam 13 Old Latin: a c e f ff2 q l Vulg Syr: (pesh) harc pal Cop: bo-ms Arm-usc Eth-ppl Also extant in N Y Omega 047 055 083 0141 0211 0233?	P5, 66, 75 Aleph B C* L N* W-suppl Psi 083 0113 al fam 1 b l sin cur sa bo Arm-zoh Eth-rom

Section Three--A Manuscript Digest of 356 Doctrinal Passages

AV	NIV

JOHN 1:51

<u>Hereafter</u> ye shall see heaven open A E F G H K M S U V X Gamma Delta Theta Lambda Pi Psi Cursives: MAJORITY fam 1,13 Old Latin: e q r1 Syr: pesh harc Also extant in P59? Y Omega 047 055 063 0141 0211 0233? The omission obscures the connection of this verse with Dan. 7:13.	you shall see heaven open P66,75 Aleph B L W* pc a b c f ff2 1 Vulg Arm Eth

JOHN 3:2

the same came to <u>Jesus</u> by night E F G H M Gamma Cursives: pm (hf) Old Latin: a e f Vulg-pt Syr: pesh pal Cop: bo Also extant in W Y Theta Psi 047 050 055 063 0141 0211 0233? 0273	(NASV) "Jesus" is removed from this acknowledgment of his miracles. P66,75 Aleph A B K L S U V Delta Lambda Pi 083 pm (hf) b c 1 q Vulg harc Arm Eth

AV	NIV
JOHN 3:13	
And no man hath ascended up to heaven, but he that came down from heaven, even the Son of man which is in heaven	No one has ever gone into heaven except the one who came from heaven - the Son of man
A* A-c E F G H K M S U V Gamma Delta Theta Pi Psi 050 (063) Cursives: MAJORITY fam 1,13 Old Latin: a aur b c f ff2 j l q r1 Vulg Syr: pesh cur harc pal? Cop: bo-pt Arm Also extant in Y Omega 047 055 0141 0211 0233? A statement of the Son of God's omnipresence which though veiled during the days of His humiliation was nevertheless a glorious fact.	P66,75 Aleph B L W-suppl 083 086 0113 pc bo-pt ach2 fay Eth

Section Three--A Manuscript Digest of 356 Doctrinal Passages

AV	NIV

JOHN 3:15

That whosoever believeth in him <u>should not perish</u> but have eternal life	that everyone who believes in him may have eternal life
P63 A E F G H K M S U V Gamma Delta Theta Lambda Pi Psi 063 Cursives: MAJORITY fam 13 Old Latin: b c e ff2 g1 l q Vulg Syr: pesh sin harc Cop: bo-ms Arm-usc Eth-ppl Also extant in Y Omega 047 055 0141 0211 0233?	P36,66,75 Aleph B L W-suppl 083 086 0113 pc fam 1 a f-c cur pal sa bo Arm-zoh Eth-rom

JOHN 4:42

and know that this is indeed <u>the Christ</u>, the Saviour of world	and we know that this man really is the Saviour of the world
A C-3 D E F G H K L M S U V Gamma Delta Theta Lambda Pi Psi Cursives: MAJORITY fam 1,13 Old Latin: e f q (delta) Syr: pesh hare pal Also extant in Y Omega 047 0141 0211 0233?	P66,75 Aleph B C* W-suppl 083 pc a b (c) ff2 l Vulg cur pal-mss Arm Eth

206 Early Manuscripts, Church Fathers, & the Authorized Version

AV	NIV

JOHN 5:3, 4

In these lay a great multitude of impotent folk, of blind, halt, withered, waiting for the moving of the water. for an angel went down at a certain season into the pool and troubled the water: Whosoever then first after the troubling of the water stepped in was made whole of whatsoever disease he had	Here a great number of disabled people used to lie - the blind, the lame the paralyzed
A C-3 E F G H K L M (S) U V X-comm Gamma Delta Theta Lambda Psi 047 063 078 Cursives: MAJORITY fam 1,13 Old Latin: a aur b c e ff2 g1 j r1 Vulg Syr: pesh harc pal Cop: bo-pt Arm Eth Also extant in Y Omega 055 0211 0233? Verse 7 pre-supposes a miraculous moving of the water. Tertullian © 200) refers to the passage and Tatian (c. 175) placed it in his Diatessaron. The account illustrates the "long time" (verse 6) that men with misplaced faith (angels, water) will have to wait.	P66,75 Aleph B C* D W-suppl 0125 0141 pc d f l q Vulg-pt cur sa bo-pt ach2 Arm-mss

Section Three--A Manuscript Digest of 356 Doctrinal Passages

AV	NIV

JOHN 5:16

And therefore did the Jews persecute Jesus, <u>and sought to</u> <u>slay</u> <u>him</u>	so, because Jesus...the Jews persecuted him
A E F G H K M S U V Gamma Delta Theta Lambda Pi Psi 063 Cursives: MAJORITY (fam 13) Old Latin: e f q Syr: pesh harc Eth Also extant in Y Omega 047 055 0141 0211 0233?	P66,75 Aleph B C D L W al (fam 1) a b c ff2 g l Vulg sin cur Arm

JOHN 5:17

And <u>Jesus</u> answered them My Father worketh hitherto, and I work	NASV "Jesus" is removed from this declaration of union with the Father
P66 A C D E F G H K L M S U V X-com M Gamma Delta Theta Lambda Pi Psi 063 Cursives: MAJORITY fam 1,13 Old Latin: a aur b c d e f ff2 l q Vulg Syr: pesh cur harc (pal) Cop: sa bo ach2 Arm Also extant in Y Omega 047 055 0141 0211 0233?	P75 Aleph B W pc bo-ms pbo

208 Early Manuscripts, Church Fathers, & the Authorized Version

AV	NIV

JOHN 5:19	
Then answered Jesus...The Son...	"Jesus" is removed from the entire discourse of union with the Father (17-47) in two early manuscripts.
P66 Aleph A D E F G H K L M S U V X Gamma Delta Lambda Pi Cursives: MAJORITY fam 1,13 Old Latin: most Vulg Syr: pesh harc pal Cop: sa bo Arm Eth Also extant in W Y Theta Psi Omega 047 055 063 0141 0211 0233?	P75 B. pc

JOHN 5:30	
because I seek not mine own will, but the will of the Father which hath sent me	for I seek not to please myself but him who sent me
E G H M S U V Gamma Theta 063 Cursives: MAJORITY fam 13 Old Latin: most Also extant in P66 P75? W Y Psi Omega 047 055 070 0141 0211 0233?	Aleph A B D K L Delta Lambda Pi al (hf) a e f ff2 g1 l q Vulg Syr: pesh cur harc pal Cop: bo Arm Eth

Section Three--A Manuscript Digest of 356 Doctrinal Passages

AV	NIV
JOHN 6:14	
When they had seen the miracle that <u>Jesus</u> did	(NASV) "Jesus" is removed from immediate association with "that prophet".
A E F G H K L M S U V Gamma Delta Theta Lambda Pi Psi 063 Cursives: MAJORITY fam 1,13 Old Latin: f q Vulg-pt Goth Eth Also extant in Y Omega 047 055 0141 0211 0233?	P75 Aleph B D W 091 pc a aur b c d ff2 g1 l Vulg Arm
JOHN 6:39	
And this is the <u>Father's</u> will which hath sent me	And this is the will of him who sent me
E F G H K S U V Gamma Delta Theta Lambda Pi Cursives: MAJORITY fam 13 Old Latin: a c (ff2 g) Vulg Syr: harc pal Arm Eth Also extant in T Y Omega 047 055 0141 0211 0233?	P66,75 Aleph-1 A B D L T W Psi al fam 1 be f q pesh (?) sin cur Goth

AV	NIV

JOHN 6:47

Verily, verily, I say unto you, He that believeth on me hath everlasting life	I tell you the truth, he who believes has everlasting life
A C-2 D E F G H K M S U V Gamma Delta Lambda Pi Psi Cursives: Majority fam 1,13 Old Latin: a aur b c d e f ff2 q r1 Vulg Syr: pesh harc Cop: sa bo pbo Goth Arm-usc Eth Also extant in T Y Omega 047 055 0141 0211 0233?	P66 Aleph B C* D L T W Theta pc j ach2 Arm-zoh

JOHN 6:65

except it were given unto him of my Father	unless the Father has enabled him
C-3 E F G H K M S U V Gamma Delta Lambda Pi Psi 0250 Cursives: MAJORITY fam 1,13 Old Latin: c e f q Vulg Syr: pesh harc Cop: sa-mss ach2 Goth Arm Also extant in T Y Omega 047 055 0141 0211 0233?	P66 Aleph B C* D L T W Theta al a b ff2 l sin cur pal sa-mss bo pbo fay Eth

Section Three--A Manuscript Digest of 356 Doctrinal Passages

AV	NIV
JOHN 6:69	
...that Chrst, the son of the living god C-3 E F G H K M S U V Gamma Delta Theta* Theta-c Pi Psi 0250 Cursives: MAJORITY fam 1,13 Old Latin: a (b) aur c e f* ff2 l q r1 Vulg Syr: pesh (sin) (cur) harc pal bo—mss Goth Arm Eth Some of the above omit "living." Also extant in T Y Omega 047 055 0141 0233?	...the Holy One of God P75 Aleph B C* D L W pc (no cursives cited by na, ubs) d Cop: sa-ms bo-ms
JOHN 7:8	
I go not up <u>yet</u> unto this feast P66,75 B E F G H K L S T U V W X Gamma Delta Theta Lambda Psi 0105 0180 0250 Cursives: MAJORITY fam 1,13 Old Latin: f g1 q Vulg-mss Syr: pesh harc-mg pal Cop: sa bo-ms pbo ach2 Goth Also extant in N Y Psi Omega 047 055 070 0141 0211 0233? The removal of "yet" makes our Lord to speak an untruth.	"Some early manuscripts do not have..." Aleph D K M Pi al a aur b c d a (ff2) l-c Vulg sin cur bo Arm Eth

212 Early Manuscripts, Church Fathers, & the Authorized Version

AV	NIV

JOHN 7:53 - 8:11	

And every man went unto his own house...go and sin no more D E (F) G H K M S T U Gamma Lambda Pi Cursives: MAJORITY (fam 1,13 both misplace) Old Latin: aur b* c d e ff2 j g1 l-mg r1 Vulg Syr: harc-mg pal Cop: bo-pt Arm-usc Eth Also extant in Omega 047 055 0233?	Footnote: "the earliest and most reliable manuscripts do not have 7:53 - 8:11." P66,75 Aleph A B C L N T W X Y Delta Theta Psi 0141 0211 al a b-c f l* q pesh sin cur sa bo-pt pbo ach2 Goth Arm

JOHN 7:53 -8:11 continued
 If 7:53 - 8:11 is removed, the narrative abruptly switches from a dispute involving Nicodemus in a Sanhedrin council chamber to Christ openly declaring in the Temple that He is the Light of the World. Thus, we go from "out of Galilee ariseth no prophet" to "I am the Light of the World" without the barest connective or explanation. The passage has substantial external support. The statement of Augustine (c. 400) is well known: "Certain persons of little faith, or rather enemies of the true faith, fearing, I suppose, lest their wives should be given impunity in sinning, removed from their manuscripts the Lord's act of forgiveness toward the adulteress, as if He who had said 'sin no more' had granted permission to sin."
 In the reading of Scripture, faith is always put to the test. Is Christ such a sufficient Saviour, and is His work on the cross so utterly "Finished" that He can and does forgive even the scarlet sin? For a full defense see the works of Burgon and Hills.

Section Three--A Manuscript Digest of 356 Doctrinal Passages

AV	NIV

JOHN 8:28

I do nothing of myself; but as <u>my</u> Father hath taught me, I speak these things B E F G H K M S U V Gamma Delta Lambda 0250 Cursives: MAJORITY fam 1 Old Latin: f q Syr: pesh harc Cop: sa bo Goth Arm Also extant in Y Omega 047 055 0141 0211 0233?	I do nothing on my own but speak just what the Father has taught me P66,75 Aleph B D L N T (W) X Theta Psi al fam 13 a b c e ff 1 Vulg sin pal bo-mss Eth

JOHN 8:29

And he that sent me is with me: the <u>Father</u> hath not left me alone E F G H K M S U V Gamma Delta Lambda 0250 Cursives: MAJORITY Old Latin: f q Syr: (pesh) harc Cop: (bo pt) Goth Also extant in Y Omega 047 055 0141 0211 0233?	The one who sent me is with me; he has not left me alone P66,75 Aleph B D H L N* T W X Theta Psi al fam 13 Most OL Vulg sin pal sa bo-pt Arm Eth

214 Early Manuscripts, Church Fathers, & the Authorized Version

AV	NIV

JOHN 8:38	
I speak that which I have seen with my Father: and ye do that which ye have seen with your father	I am telling you what I have seen in the Father's presence, and you do what you have heard from your father
Aleph (D) E F G H K M S U V (W) Gamma Delta Theta Lambda Psi 0250 Cursives: MAJORITY fam 1,13 Old Latin: a aur b c d e f ff2 m q Vulg-pt Syr: pesh sin harc Goth Arm Eth-ppl Also extant In Y Omega 047 055 0141 0211 0233?	P66,75 B C L T X 070 pc gl l Vulg-pt pal Eth-rom

John 8:59	
but Jesus hid himself, and went out of the temple going through the midst of them, and so passed by	but Jesus hid himself, slipping away from the temple grounds
(Aleph-1 Aleph-2) A (C) E F G H K (L)*M (N) S U V X Gamma Delta Theta-c Lambda Pi (Psi) (0124) Cursives: MAJORITY fam 1,13 Old Latin: f q Syr: (pesh) harc (pal) Cop: bo Goth Eth Also extant in Y Omega 047 055 0141 0211	P66,75 Aleph* B D W Theta pc a aur b c d e ff2 gl l rl Vulg sin sa bo-ms pbo ach2 Arm

Section Three--A Manuscript Digest of 356 Doctrinal Passages 215

AV	NIV
JOHN 9:4	
I must work the works of him that sent me	we must do the works of him who sent me
Aleph-1 A C E F G H K M S U V X Gamma Delta Theta Lambda P1 Psi Cursives: MAJORITY fam 1,13 Old Latin: a aur b c e f ff2 l q r1 Vulg Syr: pesh sin harc Cop: bo-ms ach2 Goth Arm Eth-ppl Eth-ppl Also extant in P44 Y Omega 047 055 070 0141 0211 0233	P66,75 Aleph* B D L W 0124 pc d pal-ms sa bo pbo Eth-rom
JOHN 9:35	
Dost thou believe on the Son of God?	do you believe in the Son of man?
A E F G K L M S U V X Gamma Delta Theta Lambda Psi 0124 0250 Cursives: MAJORITY fam 1,13 Old Latin: a aur b c e f ff2 l q r1 Vulg Syr: pesh harc pal Cop: bo Goth Arm Eth-ppl Also extant in Y Omega 047 055 0141 0211 0233	P66,75 Aleph B D W pc d sin sa bo-ms ach2 fay Eth-rom

AV	NIV

JOHN 9:38, 39

And he said, Lord, I believe, And he worshipped Him. And	Omitted from several early manuscripts.
P66 A B D E F G K L M S U V X Y Gamma Delta Theta Lambda Psi Omega 0124 Cursives: MAJORITY fam 1,13 Old Latin: most Vulg Syr: pesh sin harc pal Cop: sa bo Goth Arm Eth Also extant in 047 055 0141 0211 0233	P75 Aleph D W pc b (l)

JOHN 10:29

My Father, which gave them me, is greater than all	Footnote: "What my Father has given me is greater than all."
(P66) A B-2 E F G H K M S U V X Delta Theta (Lambda) Pi Cursives: MAJORITY fam 1,13 Old Latin: d Syr: pesh sin harc pal Cop: sa bo-ms ach2 Arm Eth Also extant in P75? Y Omega 047 055 0141 0211 0233?	Aleph B* D L W Psi pc a b c e f ff2 g1 l r1 Vulg bo Goth

JOHN 10:29 Of this verse Hills writes: "This alteration is of great doctrinal importance, since it makes the preservation of the saints depend on the church rather than on God. So Westcott expounds it, 'The faithful, regarded in their unity, are stronger than every opposing power'" *KJVD*, p 128.

Section Three--A Manuscript Digest of 356 Doctrinal Passages

AV	NIV

JOHN 10:32

AV	NIV
Many good works have I shewed you from <u>my</u> Father P66. Aleph-2 A E F G H K L M S U V W X Gamma Delta Lambda Pi Psi Cursives: MAJORITY fam 1,13 Old Latin: a aur b c f ff2 l rl Vulg Syr: pesh harc Cop: sa bo pbo Goth Arm Eth (apparently) Also extant in P75 Y Omega 047 055 0141 0211 0233?	I have shown you many great miracles from the Father P45 Aleph* B D Theta pc d e sin pal

JOHN 13:3

AV	NIV
<u>Jesus</u> knowing that the Father had given all things into his hands A E F G H K M S U V Gamma Delta Theta Lambda Pi Psi 0214 Cursives: MAJORITY fam 1 Old Latin: b f m q Syr: pesh sin harc** Cop: sa bo Goth-Arm (apparently) Also extant in Y Omega 047 055 070 0141 0211 0233?	Italicized in NASV P66 Aleph B D L W X pc (fam 13) a c e ff2 pbo Eth

AV	NIV

JOHN 13:32	
If God be glorified in him, God shall also glorify him in himself	Footnote: "Many early manuscripts do not have..."
Aleph-c A C-2 E F G H K M S U V Gamma Delta Theta Lambda Psi Cursives: MAJORITY fam 13 Old Latin: aur-mg e f l-c q r1 Vulg Syr: pesh pal Cop: sa bo-pt Goth Arm Eth Also extant in Y Omega 047 055 0141 0211 0233?	P66 Aleph* B C* D L W X Pi al fam 1 a aur* b c d ff2 g1 l* sin harc bo-pt ach2 fay Eth-mss

JOHN 14:17	
For he dwelleth with you, and shall be in you.	Footnote: "Some early manuscripts read 'and is'".
P66-c,75 Aleph A D-2 E F G H K L M Q S U V X Gamma Delta Theta Lambda Pi Psi Cursives: MAJORITY fam 13 Old Latin: aur g1 r1 Syr: sin harc Cop: sa bo ach2 Arm Eth Also extant in Y Omega 047? 055 060 0141 0211 0233? The indwelling ministry of the Holy Spirit was still future.	P66* B* B-3 W pc fam 1 a b c d e ff2 q pesh cur pal Goth

Section Three--A Manuscript Digest of 356 Doctrinal Passages

AV	NIV

JOHN 14:28

I go unto the Father: for <u>my</u> Father is greater than I Aleph* Aleph-2 D-2 E G H K S U V Gamma Delta Theta Lambda Pi 0250 Cursives: MAJORITY fam 13 Old Latin: a f q Syr: pesh harc Cop: sa-mss bo ach2 Goth Arm Also extant in P75? Y Omega 047? 055 060 0141 0211 0233?	I am going to the Father, for the Father is greater than I Aleph-1 A B D* L X Psi pc b c e ff2 gl 1 Vulg Eth

JOHN 16:10

Of righteousness, because I go to <u>my</u> Father A E G H K M S U V Y Gamma Delta Theta Lambda Pi 054 Cursives: MAJORITY fam 13 Old Latin: c f q Syr: pesh sin harc Cop: sa-mss ach2 pbo Goth Arm Also extant in Y Omega 047 055 0141 0211 0233?	...in regard to righteousness, because I am going to the Father Aleph B D L W (Psi) al a b e ff2 gl 1 Vulg pal sa bo Eth

Early Manuscripts, Church Fathers, & the Authorized Version

AV	NIV
JOHN 16:16	
and again, a little while and ye shall see me, <u>because I go to the Father</u>	and then after a little while you will see me
A E F G H K M S U V Gamma Delta Theta Lambda Pi (Psi) 054 068 Cursives: MAJORITY fam 1,13 Old Latin: c f g1 q Vulg Syr: pesh sin harc pal Cop: bo-pt pbo Goth Arm Eth-ppl Also extant in Y Omega 047 055 0141 0211 0233?	P5,66 Aleph B D L W 025O pc a b e ff2 sa bo-pt ach2 Eth-rom
JOHN 17:12	
While I was with them in <u>the world</u>, I kept them	While I was with them, I protected them
AC-3 E G H K M S U V X Y Gamma Delta Theta Lambda Pi Psi 054 Cursives: MAJORITY fam 13 Old Latin: (a) f q Syr: pesh sin harc pal Cop: bo-ms Goth Arm Eth Also extant in N Y 047 055 0141 0211. Christ is with us whether He is physically present on earth or not.	P60,66 Aleph B C* D L W pc b c e ff2 g1 Vulg sa bo

Section Three--A Manuscript Digest of 356 Doctrinal Passages

AV	NIV

JOHN 17:17	
Sanctify them through <u>thy</u> truth	Sanctify them by the truth
Aleph-2 C-3 E F G H K M S U V X Y Gamma Delta Pi* Psi 054 Cursives: MAJORITY Old Latin: q Syr: pesh sin harc Cop: bo-pt Arm Eth Also extant in N Y Omega 047 055 0141 0211. There are many claimants to truth.	P66 A B C* D L W Theta Pi-2 pc Most OL Vulg pal sa bo-pt Goth

JOHN 19:5	
<u>And he saith unto them, Behold the Man</u>	Omitted from a few early manuscripts.
Aleph A B D-suppl E G? H K L M N S U V W X Y Gamma Delta Theta Lambda Pi Omega Cursives: MAJORITY fam 1,13 Old Latin: ? Vulg Syr: pesh harc Cop: sa bo Arm Eth Also extant in P60 054 055 065 0141 0211	P66 pc a e ff2

AV	NIV

JOHN 19:26

he saith unto <u>his</u> mother, woman behold thy son	(Literal) he saith unto the mother, woman, behold thy son
A D-suppl E F G H K M S U V Y Gamma Theta Lambda Pi 054 Cursives: MAJORITY Old Latin: most Vulg Syr: pesh harc Cop: sa-bo (apparently) Eth (apparently) Also extant in P60 N Y Omega 055 0141 0211	P66 Aleph B L W X Psi pc b e Arm

JOHN 19:38

He came therefore, and took the body <u>of Jesus</u>	he came and took the body
(A) D-suppl E G K M S U V Y Gamma Delta Theta Pi 054 Cursives: MAJORITY fam (1),13 Old Latin: f g1 q Vulg Syr: pesh harc Cop: bo Eth-ppl Also extant in N Omega 055 0141 0211 0212	P66, 66-2 B L W X Lambda Psi al a b c e ff2 sa pbo Arm Eth-rom

Section Three--A Manuscript Digest of 356 Doctrinal Passages 223

AV	NIV

JOHN 20:17

for I am not yet ascended to my Father P66 A E G K L M S U V X Delta Theta Lambda Pi Psi 050 Cursives: MAJORITY fam 1,13 Old Latin: a aur c f ff2 g1 q r1 Vulg Syr: pesh sin harc Cop: sa bo Arm Eth Also extant in P5? Y? Omega 055 078 0114 0211?	for I have not yet returned to the Father Aleph B D W pc b d e pal

ACTS 2:1

They were all <u>with one accord</u> one place C-3 E-gr Psi Cursives: MAJORITY Also extant in 049 056 0142. "Coming together" is one thing but "one accord in the faith" is quite another.	they wore all <u>together</u> in one place Aleph A B C pc Old Latin: most (incl e) Vulg Syr: pesh harc Cop: sa bo

AV	NIV

ACTS 2:30		

that of the fruit of his loins, according to the flesh, he would raise up Christ to sit on his throne	that he would place one of his descendants on his throne
D P Psi 049 056 0142 Cursives: MAJORITY Old Latin: d Syr: harc Cop: mae No further uncials are known to be extant. That Christ came in the flesh, was raised in the flesh, and will return in the flesh is the great controversy between light and darkness.	Aleph A B C D-c pc ar gig r Vulg pesh pal sa bo Arm Eth

ACTS 2:47		

And the Lord added to the church daily	And the Lord added to their number daily
A D E P X Psi 049 056 0142 Cursives: MAJORITY Old Latin: d e p Syr: (pesh) harc Cop: mae	P74 Aleph A B C 095 pc ar gig Vulg sa bo Arm Eth

Section Three--A Manuscript Digest of 356 Doctrinal Passages

AV	NIV

ACTS 3:20

And he shall send Jesus Christ which <u>before was preached</u> unto you Cursives: pc Vulg Cop: bo Also extant in P74 Psi 049 056 0142. At issue is the Jews rejection of the previously preached message (3:18), as well as O.T. prediction generally. See *KJVMT*, p. 59.	(NASV) and that He may send Jesus the Christ <u>appointed</u> for you Aleph A B C D E P MAJORITY (hf) Old Latin: d e Syr: pesh harc sa Arm Eth

ACTS 3:26

God, having raised up his Son <u>Jesus</u>, sent him to bless you Cursives: MAJORITY (hf) Also extant in P74 Psi 049 056 0142 0165	....God raised up his servant, he sent him first to bless you Aleph B C D E pc (hf) Old Latin: p Vulg Syr: pesh harc Cop: sa bo Arm Eth

226 Early Manuscripts, Church Fathers, & the Authorized Version

AV	NIV

ACTS 6:8

And Stephen, full of faith and power	(NASV) And Stephen, full of grace and power
H P Cursives: MAJORITY Syr: harc Also extant in 049 056 0142. The New Testament speaks of grace that is great, abundant, exceeding, riches of, multiplied, manifold, and growth in; but only of Christ is it said that one was full of grace (John 1:14).	P8,45,74 Aleph A B D 0175 al Vulg pesh Cop: sa bo Arm Eth

ACTS 7:30

There appeared to him. ...an angel of the Lord in a flame	an angel appeared to Moses in the flames
D E H P Psi Cursives: MAJORITY Old Latin: p w Syr: pesh harc Cop: bo-ms mae Arm Eth Also extant in 049 056 0142	P74 Aleph A B C pc gig Vulg sa bo

AV	NIV
ACTS 7:37	
A prophet shall the Lord your God raise up...<u>him shall ye hear</u>	God will send you a prophet
C D E Cursives: al Old Latin: (e*) gig Vulg Syr: pesh harc Cop: bo mae Arm Eth Also extant in P74 049 056 0142	P45 Aleph A B H P Psi MAJORITY Vulg-pt sa

AV	NIV

ACTS 8:37

AV	NIV
And Philip said, if thou believest with all thine heart, thou mayest. And he answered and said, I believe that Jesus Christ is the Son of God E Cursives: pc (27 are cited in our other Digest) Old Latin: ar c e l (m) ph r Vulg-pt Syr: harc** Cop: mae Arm The verse is cited by Irenaeus (178), Tertullian (220), and Cyprian (258). J. A. Alexander suggested that the verse was omitted by many scribes "as unfriendly to the practice of delaying baptism, which had become common, if not prevalent, before the end of the 3rd century" (*KJVD*, p. 201). See *KJVMT*, p. 60 for further evidence.	---------- P45,74 Aleph A B C H L P psi 049 056 0142 Cursives: MAJORITY Vulg-pt pesh harc sa bo Eth

Section Three--A Manuscript Digest of 356 Doctrinal Passages 229

AV	NIV
ACTS 9:25	
Then the disciples took him by night E K L P Psi Cursives: MAJORITY Old Latin: gig Vulg-pt Syr: pesh harc Cap: sa bo Arm Eth Also extant in 049 056 0142. John the Baptist had disciples (Matt 9:14), but thereafter the term is used exclusively of the disciples of Christ.	(NASV) but his disciples took him by night P74 Aleph A B C pc Vulg-pt
ACTS 9:29	
he spoke boldly in the name of the Lord Jesus Aleph-c H L P Cursives: MAJORITY (hf) Eth-ppl The Peshitta has "Jesus" without "Lord." Also extant in P74 Psi 049 056 0142.	speaking boldly in the name of the Lord Aleph* A B E al (hf) Vulg Syr: harc Cop: sa bo Arm Eth-rom

AV	NIV

ACTS 10:30

AV	NIV
Four days ago' I was <u>fasting</u> until this hour	Four days ago I was...at this hour
P50 A-2 (D) E H (L) P Psi 049 056 0142 Cursives: MAJORITY Old Latin: ar d e gig l p ph Syr: pesh harc Cop: sa mae	P74 Aleph A* B C pc Vulg bo Arm Eth

ACTS 13:33

AV	NIV
...unto the fathers, God hath fulfilled the same <u>unto us their</u> children	NASV...to the fathers, that God has fulfilled this promise <u>to our</u> children
C-3 E H L P 049 056 0142 Cursives: MAJORITY Old Latin: e Syr: pesh harc Arm	P74 Aleph A B C* D (Psi) pc Vulg Eth

AV	NIV

ACTS 15:11

through the grace of the Lord Jesus <u>Christ</u> we shall be saved C D Psi Cursives: pc (16 Cited in our other Digest) Old Latin: most Vulg-pt Syr: pesh Cop: bo-pt Arm Eth-ppl Also extant in P74 049 056 0142. See *KJVMT*, p. 63.	through the grace of our Lord Jesus that we are saved Aleph A B E H L P MAJORITY Vulg-pt harc sa bo-pt Eth-rom

ACTS 15:18

Known <u>unto God are all his works</u> from the beginning of the world E H L P 049 056 0142 Old Latin: (d) e gig (l) Cursives: MAJORITY Syr: (pesh) harc "unto the Lord" in P74 A D d Vulg Syr: harc-mg and possibly several of the above.	that we have known from the ages Aleph B C Psi al Cop: sa bo Arm (Eth)

232 Early Manuscripts, Church Fathers, & the Authorized Version

AV	NIV

ACTS 16:31

Believe on the Lord Jesus <u>Christ</u> and thou shalt be saved C D E H L P Psi 0120 Cursives: MAJORITY Syr: pesh harc Cop: sa Arm Eth Also extant in 049 056 0142	Believe in the Lord Jesus and you will be saved P74 Aleph A B pc Old Latin: gig Vulg bo

ACTS 17:26

And hath made of one <u>blood</u> all nations D E H L P 049 056 0142 Cursives: MAJORITY Old Latin: ar d e gig Syr: pesh harc Arm	(NASV) and He made from one every nation P74 Aleph A B pc Vulg Cop: sa bo Eth-ppl

ACTS 17:30

God...now <u>commandeth</u> all men every where to repent P41,74 Aleph-c A D-gr E-gr H L P Psi 049 056 0142 Cursives: MAJORITY Old Latin: m Syr: pesh harc Cop: sa Arm	(NASV) God is now <u>declaring</u> to men that all...should repent Aleph B pc (no cursives cited by na, ubs) ar d e gig ph Vulg bo?

Section Three--A Manuscript Digest of 356 Doctrinal Passages 233

AV	NIV

ACTS 19:4

that they should believe on him which should come after him, that is, on <u>Christ</u> Jesus H L P Cursives: MAJORITY "Jesus Christ" in Psi gig pesh sa-mss Arm Eth-ppl. "Christ" in D. Also extant in P41 049 056 0142.	to believe in the one coming after him that is, in Jesus P38,74 Aleph A B E pc Vulg Syr: harc Cop: sa-mss bo Eth-rom

ACTS 19:10

all....heard the word of the Lord <u>Jesus</u> H L P Cursives: MAJORITY (hf) Also extant in P74 Psi 049 056 0142	all...heard the word of the Lord Aleph A B D E al (hf) Vulg Syr: pesh harc Cop: sa bo Arm Eth

AV	NIV

ACTS 20:21

repentance toward God, and faith toward our Lord Jesus Christ	...turn to God in repentance and have faith in our Lord Jesus
P74 Aleph A C D E 049 Cursives: pm Old Latin: ar d e ph Vulg Syr: pesh Cop: bo Arm Eth-ppl	B H L P Psi 056 0142 pm gig harc sa Eth-rom

ACTS 20:25

I have gone preaching the kingdom of God	I have gone about preaching the kingdom
E H L P Cursives: MAJORITY Vulg Syr: pesh Cop: bo-pt Eth "kingdom of Jesus" in D. "of Lord Jesus" in gig. Also extant in 049 056 0142.	P74 Aleph A B C Psi pc harc bo-pt

Section Three--A Manuscript Digest of 356 Doctrinal Passages

AV	NIV
ACTS 20:28	
to feed the church <u>of God</u> which he hath purchased with his own blood Aleph B 056 0142 Cursives: al Old Latin: ar c Vulg Syr: pesh harc Cop: ba-ms Also extant in P41 049. This verse has been a battleground between faith and unbelief. Two great issues are at stake. Is Christ God? Is His blood divine? Acts 20:28 answers both in the affirmative. See *KJVMT*, p. 64.	Footnote: "Many manuscripts have 'of the Lord.'" P74 A C* D E Psi al d e gig p harc-mg sa bo Arm
ACTS 21:25	
<u>that they observe no such things</u> C D E H L P Psi 049 056 0142 Cursives: MAJORITY Old Latin: d e gig Syr: harc Arm Eth	---------- P74 Aleph A B pc ar Vulg pesh Cop: sa bo

236 Early Manuscripts, Church Fathers, & the Authorized Version

AV	NIV

ACTS 22:16

calling on the name of the Lord Cursives: MAJORITY (hf) Also extant in P41,74 Psi 049 056 0142. The context, with Acts 9:5,6 shows that the "Lord" is Christ.	calling on his name Aleph A B E al (hf) Old Latin: d Vulg Syr: pesh harc Cop: sa bo Arm Eth

ACTS 24:15

that there shall be a resurrection of the dead both of the just and unjust E H L P Psi 049 056 0142 Cursives: MAJORITY Old Latin: ar* e Syr: pesh harc Eth Christendom has always been uneasy about a literal resurrection of the dead.	that there will be a resurrection of both the righteous and the wicked P74 Aleph A B C pc ar-c gig s Vulg Cop: sa bo Arm

Section Three--A Manuscript Digest of 356 Doctrinal Passages

AV	NIV
ROMANS 1:16	
For I am not ashamed of the gospel of Christ D-c K L P Psi Cursives: MAJORITY "Gospel of Jesus" in Eth. Also extant in 049 056 0142 0151.	For I am not ashamed of the gospel P26 Aleph A B C D* Dabs G pc Old Latin: d e g Vulg Syr: pesh harc Cop: sa bo Arm
ROMANS 5:1	
Therefore being justified by faith, we have peace with God Aleph-1 B-2 F-gr P Psi 0220 Cursives: pm Old Latin: ar? z Syr: harc Cop: sa Also extant in 049 056 0142 0151. Christ secured our peace on the Cross (Col. 1:20). The revised reading contorts the entire Biblical plan of salvation.	Footnote: "Or, 'let us have'". Aleph* A B* C D Dabs K L pm d dem e f g t x Vulg pesh pal bo Arm Eth

AV	NIV

ROMANS 5:6

For when we were yet without strength	"If indeed" in Codex B
Aleph A C D*-gr Dabs K P Psi Cursives: MAJORITY Syr: harc Also extant in 049 056 0142 0151, much of the Latin supports a variant. There were no "ifs' in this matter.	B pc (na cites 2 cursives) pesh Cop: sa bo

ROMANS 6:11

alive unto God through Jesus Christ our Lord	alive to God in Christ Jesus
Aleph C K L P Cursives: MAJORITY Vulg-pt Syr: (pesh) Cop: bo Arm Also extant in 049 056 0142 0151	P46 A B D Dabs F G Psi pc Old Latin: ar d e f g m x z Vulg harc Eth

Section Three--A Manuscript Digest of 356 Doctrinal Passages 239

AV	NIV

ROMANS 8:1

There is therefore now no condemnation to them which are in Christ Jesus, who walk not after the flesh, but after the Spirit Aleph-2 D-2 Dabs K L P Cursives: MAJORITY Old Latin: ar (d-c) e Syr: harc A number of other witnesses omit "but after the Spirit." Also extant in 049 056 0142 0151. By their fruits ye shall know them.	Therefore, there is now no condemnation for those who are in Christ Jesus Aleph* B C D* F G pc d* g Cop: sa bo Eth

ROMANS 9:32

Because they sought it not by faith, but as it were by the works of the law Aleph-2 D Dabs K L P Psi Cursives: MAJORITY Old Latin: d e Syr: pesh harc pal Goth Arm Also extant in P46 049 056 0142 0151	Because they pursued it not by faith but as if it were by works Aleph* A B F G pc ar dem f g x z Vulg Cop: bo

AV	NIV

ROMANS 10:15

How beautiful are the feet of them that <u>preach the gospel of peace</u>, and bring glad tidings of good things	How beautiful are the feet of those who bring good news
Aleph-2 D Dabs F G K L P Psi Cursives: MAJORITY Old Latin: d dem e f g x z Vulg Syr: pesh harc Goth Arm Also extant in 049 056 0142 0151. The Bible emphasis is on <u>preaching.</u> See 1 Cor1:21.	P46 Aleph* A B C pc ar Cop: sa bo Eth

ROMANS 11:6

And if by grace, then is it no more of works: otherwise grace is no more grace, <u>But if it be of works, then is it no more grace: otherwise work is no more work</u>	And if by grace, then it is no longer by works; if it were, grace would no longer be grace
Aleph-2 (B) L Psi Cursives: MAJORITY Syr: pesh harc (Eth) Also extant in 049 056 0142 0151, This is the Bible's strongest statement showing that in the saving of the soul grace and works cannot be mingled.	P46 Aleph* A C D Dabs F G P Old Latin: ar d dem e f g x z Vulg Cop: sa bo Arm

Section Three--A Manuscript Digest of 356 Doctrinal Passages

AV	NIV

ROMANS 13:9		
Thou shalt not steal, <u>Thou shalt not bear false witness</u>, Thou shalt not covet	Do not steal, do not covet
Aleph (P) 048 Cursives: pm Old Latin: ar c dem gig z Vulg-pt Syr: (harc) Cop: bo Arm Eth Also extant in 049 056 0142 0150? 0151. Ponder the false witness of the persecuting Roman Church.	P46 A B D Dabs F G L Psi pm d e f g x Vulg-pt pesh sa Goth

ROMANS 14:10		
for we must all stand before the judgement seat <u>of Christ</u>	For we will all stand before <u>God's</u> judgement seat
Aleph-c C-2 L P Psi 048 0209 Cursives: MAJORITY Old Latin: dem gue r1 Vulg-pt Syr: pesh harc Goth Arm Eth Also extent in P46? 049 056 0142 0150 0151. "The Father judgeth no man but hath committed all judgement unto the Son," (John 5:20).	Aleph* A B C* D Dabs F G pc ar d e f g x z Vulg Cop: sa bo

242 Early Manuscripts, Church Fathers, & the Authorized Version

AV	NIV
ROMANS 15:8	
Now I say that <u>Jesus</u> Christ was a minister of the circumcision D Dabs F C Cursives: pc (hf, 11 cited in our other Digest) Old Latin: d e f g Syr: pesh harc "Christ Jesus" in L P MAJORITY Vulg Goth. Also extant in Psi 048 049 056 0142 0150 0151. See *KJVMT*, p. 67.	"Jesus" is removed from association with the title "Christ". Aleph A B C pc (hf) Cop: bo Arm Eth
ROMANS 15:19	
wonders, by the power of' the spirit <u>of God</u> P46 Aleph D-1 L P Psi Cursives: MAJORITY Syr: pesh harc Eth Also extant in 049 056 0142 0150 0151.	miracles, through the power of the Spirit B pc (no cursives cited by na,ubs) Arm "Holy Spirit" in Old Latin and Vulg.

Section Three--A Manuscript Digest of 356 Doctrinal Passages

AV	NIV
ROMANS 15:29	
I shall come in the fulness of the blessing <u>of the gospel</u> of Christ Aleph-2 L Psi Cursives: MAJORITY Vulg-pt Syr: pesh harc Arm-mss Also extant in 049 056 0142 0150 0151	I will come in the full measure of the blessing of Christ P46 Aleph* A B C D Dabs F G P pc Old Latin: a r d e f g x z Vulg Cop: sa bo Arm
ROMANS 16:18	
For they that are such serve not our Lord <u>Jesus</u> Christ L Cursives: pm (hf) Syr: pesh Cop: bo Arm-mss Eth-pp Also extant in P46 Psi 049 056 0142 0150 0151	"Jesus" is removed from the titles "Lord" and "Christ". Aleph A B C D Dabs P pm (hf) Old Latin: d-c m f g Vulg harc Arm Eth-rom

AV	NIV

| ROMANS 16:20 ||

AV	NIV
The grace of our Lord Jesus Christ be with you A C L P Psi Cursives: MAJORITY Old Latin: ar c d-c dem t z Vulg Syr: pesh harc Cop: sa bo Arm Eth	The grace of our Lord Jesus be with you P46 Aleph B pc

| I CORINTHIANS 5:4a ||

AV	NIV
In the name of our Lord Jesus Christ P46 Aleph D-2 Dabs F G L P Cursives: MAJORITY Old Latin: ar e f g x z Vulg Syr: pesh harc** Cop: sa bo Goth Arm Eth-ppl Also extant in P11? 049? 056 0142 0150 0151	...in the name of our Lord Jesus A B D* Psi pc d Syr: harc Eth-rom

Section Three--A Manuscript Digest of 356 Doctrinal Passages

AV	NIV

I CORINTHIANS 5:4b

with the power of our Lord Jesus <u>Christ</u> D-c Dabs F G L P Cursives: MAJORITY (hf) Old Latin: e f g Vulg-pt Syr: pesh harc** Cop; bo Goth Arm Eth-ppl Also extant in P11? 049? 056 0142 0150 0151	and the power of our Lord Jesus P46 Aleph A B D* P Psi pc (hf) d Vulg-pt Syr: harc Eth-rom

I CORINTHIANS 5:5

that the spirit may be saved in the day of the Lord <u>Jesus</u> Aleph L Psi Cursives: MAJORITY Vulg-pt Syr: harc Goth Eth "Lord Jesus Christ" in a number of other witnesses. Also extant in P11?,61? 049? 056 0142 0150 0151	and his spirit saved on the day of the Lord P46 B pc

246 Early Manuscripts, Church Fathers, & the Authorized Version

AV	NIV

I CORINTHIANS 5:7

Christ...is sacrificed <u>for us</u> Aleph-2 C-3 L (P) Psi Cursives: MAJORITY Syr: pesh harc Cop: sa bo-ms Goth Also extant in 049? 056 0142 0150 0151	Christ... has been sacrificed P11 Aleph* A B C* D Dabs F G pc Old Latin: most Vulg bo Arm Eth

I CORINTHIANS 6:20

glorify God in your body <u>and in your spirit, which are God's</u> C-3 D-2 K L P Psi Cursives: MAJORITY Syr: pesh harc Arm-usc Also extant in 056 0142 0150 0151	honour God with your body P46 Aleph A B C* D* Dabs F G pc Old Latin ar d e f g m rl t x z Vulg Cop: sa bo fay Eth

Section Three--A Manuscript Digest of 356 Doctrinal Passages

AV	NIV

I CORINTHIANS 7:5

AV	NIV
that ye may give yourselves <u>to fastings and</u> prayer Aleph-2 K L Cursives: MAJORITY Syr: pesh harc Goth Also extant in 056 0142 0150 0151	so that you may devote yourselves to prayer P11, 46 Aleph* A B C D Dabs F G P Psi al Old Latin: ar d dem e f g rl t x z Vulg Cop: sa bo fay Arm Eth

I CORINTHIANS 7:39

AV	NIV
The wife is bound <u>by the law</u> as long as her husband liveth Aleph-2 D-1 Dabs F G L P Psi Cursives: MAJORITY Old Latin: a f g Vulg-pt Syr: pesh harc Also extant in 056 0142 0150 0151	A woman is bound to her husband as long as he lives P15,46 Aleph* A B D* pc d e Vulg Cop: sa-mss Arm Eth

AV	NIV

I CORINTHIANS 9:1	
have I not seen Jesus Christ our Lord? D Dabs K L P Cursives: MAJORITY (hf) Old Latin: d e Syr: pesh harc-mg Cop: bo Goth Arm Eth-ppl "Christ Jesus" in other witnesses. Also extant in P46? Psi 056 0142 0150 0151.	Have I not seen Jesus our Lord? Aleph A B pc (hf) Vulg-pt harc sa Eth-rom

I CORINTHIANS 9:18	
I may make the gospel of Christ without charge D-2 Dabs F G K L P Cursives: MAJORITY Old Latin: f g Syr: pesh harc Also extant in 056 0142 0150 0151	the gospel I may offer it free of charge P46 Aleph A B C D* Psi al d e Vulg Cop: sa bo Arm Eth

Section Three--A Manuscript Digest of 356 Doctrinal Passages 249

AV	NIV

I CORINTHIANS 9:22

AV	NIV
To the weak became I <u>as</u> weak	to the weak I became weak
Aleph-2 C D-gr Dabs F G K L P Psi Cursives: MAJORITY Old Latin: f g Vulg-ms Syr: pesh harc Cop: sa bo Goth Arm Eth Also extant in 056 0142 0150 0151. What a difference!	P46 Aleph* A B pc d e Vulg

250 Early Manuscripts, Church Fathers, & the Authorized Version

AV	NIV

I CORINTHIANS 9:23

And <u>this</u> I do for the gospel's sake	(NASV) I do <u>all things</u> for the sake of the gospel
K L Psi Cursives: MAJORITY Syr: pesh harc Goth Also extant in 056 0142 0150 0151 0202? The revised reading opens up a "Pandoras Box" of unscriptural practices.	P46 Aleph* A B C D Dabs F G P al Old Latin: most Vulg Cop: sa bo Arm Eth

I CORINTHIANS 10:20

the things which <u>the Gentiles</u> sacrifice, they sacrifice to devils	Omitted from some early manuscripts
P46 Aleph A C K L Psi Cursives: MAJORITY Old Latin: ar dem f g t x z Vulg Syr: pesh harc Cop: sa bo Goth Arm Eth Also extant in 056 0142 0150 0151	B D Dabs F G-gr pc (no cursives cited by na, ubs) d e m

Section Three--A Manuscript Digest of 356 Doctrinal Passages 251

AV	NIV
I CORINTHIANS 11:24a	
And when he had given thanks, he brake it and said, <u>Take eat</u> C-3 K L P Psi Cursives: MAJORITY Vulg-pt Syr: pesh harc Goth Arm-usc Eth Also extant in 056 0142 0150 0151	And when he had given thanks, he broke it and said... P46 Aleph A B C* D Dabs F G 0199 pc Old Latin: d e f g Vulg Cop: sa bo Arm-zoh
I CORINTHIANS 11:24b	
this is my body, which is <u>broken</u> for you: this do in remembrance of me Aleph-c C-3 (D*) D-2 Dabs F G K L P Psi Cursives: MAJORITY Old Latin: d e g Syr: pesh harc Cop: (sa bo) Goth Arm-(usc) Also extant in 056 0142 0150 0151 0199	this is my body which is for you, do this in remembrance of me P46 Aleph* A B C* pc Vulg-pt Arm-zoh

AV	NIV

I CORINTHIANS 11:29	
For he that eateth and. drinketh unworthily...	For anyone who eats and drinks
Aleph-2 C-3 D Dabs F G K L P Psi Cursives: MAJORITY Old Latin: ar d dem e f g t x z Vulg Syr: pesh harc Goth Arm Eth-ppl Also extant in 056 0142 0150 0151. Thus the doctrine of the Lord's Table is diminished in these three successive passages.	P46 Aleph* A B C pc Cop: sa bo Eth-rom

I CORINTHIANS 15:47	
The first man is of the earth earthy: the second man is <u>the Lord</u> from heaven	The first man was of the dust of earth, the second man from heaven
Aleph-2 A D-1 K L P Psi 075 Cursives: MAJORITY Syr: pesh harc pal Goth Arm Also extant in 049 056 0142 0150 0151. This is a well-known attempt to remove the Deity of Christ from the text. But what is not so known is the Gnostic twist that Papyrus 46 gives to the passage; "The second man is <u>the spirit from heaven</u>." This was the corruption of 2nd/3rd century Egypt!	Aleph* B C D* Dabs F G 0245 pc Old Latin: ar d dem e f g x z Vulg Cop: bo Eth

Section Three--A Manuscript Digest of 356 Doctrinal Passages

AV	NIV

I CORINTHIANS 15:54

So when this corruptible shall have put on incorruption, and this mortal shall have put on immortality Aleph-c (A) B C-2 D Dabs K L P Psi Cursives: MAJORITY Old Latin: d e Syr: pesh harc Cop: sa-ms (Arm) Also extant in 049 056 075? 0142 0150 0151	Omitted from some early manuscripts P46 Aleph* C F I G 088 0121a 0243 pc ar dem f g x z Vulg bo Goth Eth

I CORINTHIANS 16:22

If any man love not the Lord Jesus Christ Aleph-c C-c Dabs F G K L P Cursives: MAJORITY (hf) Old Latin: d e f g Vulg Syr: pesh harc Cop: bo Goth Eth Also extant in Psi 049 056 075 0142 0150 0151 0243	If anyone does not love the Lord Aleph* A B C* 0121a pc (hf)

AV	NIV

I CORINTHIANS 16:23

The grace of our Lord Jesus <u>Christ</u> be with you Aleph-2 A C D Dabs F G K L P 075 0121a 0243 Cursives: MAJORITY Old Latin: d e g r Vulg-pt Syr: pesh harc Cop: bo Arm Eth Also extant in 049 056 0142 0151	The grace of the Lord Jesus be with you Aleph* B Psi pc f Vulg-pt sa Goth

II CORINTHIANS 4:10

Always bearing about in the body the dying of <u>the Lord</u> Jesus K L Cursives: MAJORITY (hf) Old Latin: m Syr: harc Goth Also extant in P46? Psi 048 049 056 075 0142 0150 0151 0186 0209 0243	We always carry around in our body the death of Jesus Aleph A B C D Dabs F G P pc (hf) d e f g r Vulg pesh Cop: bo Arm Eth

AV	NIV

| II CORINTHIANS 4:14 |

AV	NIV
shall raise up us also <u>by</u> Jesus	will also raise us <u>with</u> Jesus
Aleph-2 D-1 K L Psi	P46 Aleph* B C D* Dabs F G P 0243
Cursives: MAJORITY	pc
	Old Latin: d e f g r Vulg
	Cop: bo
Syr: pesh harc	
Goth	Arm Eth
Also extant in 048 049 056 075 0142 0150 0151. This "slight" difference opens the way for a spiritual rather than bodily resurrection for both the believer and Christ.	

256 Early Manuscripts, Church Fathers, & the Authorized Version

AV	NIV

II CORINTHIANS 5:17

Therefore if any man be in Christ, he is a new creature: old things are passed away; behold, all things are become new	Therefore, if anyone is in Christ, he is a new creation: the old has gone, the new has come
D-2 Dabs K L P Psi Cursives: MAJORITY Old Latin: ar (dem) Vulg-pt Syr: harc Goth Arm-mss, usc? Eth-ppl Also extant in I 049 056 075 0142 0150 0151. "All things" tests the believer's faith and Scriptural perception as to his present standing in Christ and his future glory with Christ.	P46 Aleph B C D* F G 048 0243 pc d e f g rl x z Vulg-pt (pesh) pal Cop: bo Arm-zoh Eth-rom

II CORINTHIANS 5:18

Who hath reconciled us to himself by Jesus Christ	"Jesus" is removed from association with the title "Christ."
D-c Dabs K L Cursives: MAJORITY (hf)	Aleph B C D* F G P pc (hf) Old Latin: most Vulg Syr: pesh harc Cop: bo Goth Arm Eth
Also extant in P34 P46? I Psi 048 049 056 075 0142 0150 0151 0243	

Section Three--A Manuscript Digest of 356 Doctrinal Passages

AV	NIV
II CORINTHIANS 11:31	
The God and Father of our Lord Jesus <u>Christ</u> D Dabs K L P 0121b Cursives: MAJORITY (hf) Old Latin: d e f Vulg Syr: pesh Cop: bo Eth. Also extant in P46? I Psi 049 056 075 0121b 0142 0150 0151 0243	The God and Father of the Lord Jesus Aleph B F-gr G pc (hf) g harc Goth Arm
II CORINTHIANS 12:9	
for <u>my</u> strength is made perfect in weakness Aleph-2 A D-2 Dabs K I P Psi 0243 Cursives: MAJORITY Syr: pesh harc Cop: bo-pt Also extant in 049 056 075 0142 0150 0151	(NASV) for power is perfected in weakness P46 Aleph* B D* F G pc (no cursives cited by na) Old Latin: d e f g Vulg sa bo-pt Goth Arm Eth

258 Early Manuscripts, Church Fathers, & the Authorized Version

AV	NIV

GALATIANS 3:1	
O foolish Galatians, who hath bewitched you, that ye should not obey the truth	you foolish Galatians! Who has bewitched you?
C D-2 Dabs K L P Psi Cursives: MAJORITY Vulg-pt Syr: harc Goth Arm-usc Eth Also extant in 049 056 075 0142 0150 0151. The great object of Satan's wiles - to separate a believer from Scriptural truth.	Aleph A B D* F G pc Old Latin: d e f g r Vulg-pt pesh Cop: sa bo Arm-zoh mss

GALATIANS 3:17	
the covenant, that was confirmed before of God in Christ	the covenant previously established by God
D* Dabs F G-gr I K L 0176 Cursives: MAJORITY Old Latin: ar d e g Syr: pesh harc Arm Also extant in 049 056 075 0142 0150 0151	P46 Aleph A B C P Psi pc dem f rl x z Vulg Cop: sa bo Eth

Section Three--A Manuscript Digest of 356 Doctrinal Passages 259

AV	NIV

| GALATIANS 4:7 |||

| and if a son, then an heir of God <u>through Christ</u>

Aleph-2 C-3 D Dabs K L
Cursives: MAJORITY

"God through Jesus Christ" in a number of other witnesses, including P Syr: pesh harc Eth-pt. Also extant in 049 056 075 0142 0150 0151. | and since you are a son, God has made you also an heir

P46 Aleph* A B C* F G-gr
pc (na,ubs cite 3 cursives)
Old Latin: dem f q r3 x z Vulg
Cop: bo
Arm Eth-rom |

| GALATIANS 5:19 |||

| Now the works of the flesh are manifest, which are these:
<u>Adultery</u>

Aleph-2 D Dabs (F) (G) K L
Psi 0121b
Cursives: MAJORITY
Old Latin: (b) d e (f) (g)
Syr: harc
Goth Arm
Also extant in 049 056 075 0142 0150 0151 | The acts of the sinful nature are obvious

Aleph* A B C P

pc
a   Vulg
pesh   Cop: sa   bo
Eth |

260 Early Manuscripts, Church Fathers, & the Authorized Version

AV	NIV
GALATIANS 6:15	
For in Christ Jesus neither circumcision availeth anything nor uncircumcision	Neither circumcision nor uncircumcision means anything
Aleph A C D Dabs F G K L P Cursives: MAJORITY Old Latin: d e f g Vulg Syr: harc** Cop: sa-mss bo Arm-usc? Eth-ppl Also extant in 049 056 075 0142 0150 0151.	P46 B Psi pc (na cites 3 cursives) r (pesh) harc sa-mss Goth Arm-zoh Eth-rom
GALATIANS 6:17	
for I bear in my body the marks of the Lord Jesus	for I bear on my body the marks of Jesus
C-3 D-2 Dabs K L Cursives: MAJORITY Vulg-pt Syr: (pesh) harc Goth Eth-ppl "Lord Jesus Christ" in Aleph D* F G, Old Latin. Also extant in 049 056 075 0142 0150 0151.	P46 A B C* pc Old Latin: f t Vulg-pt Cop: sa-ms

Section Three--A Manuscript Digest of 356 Doctrinal Passages 261

AV	NIV

EPHESIANS 1:1

AV	NIV
to the saints which are <u>at Ephesus</u>...."	Footnote:. "Some early manuscripts do not have." Thus it is said to be a circular letter where names of other cities could be added.
Aleph-2 A B-2 D Dabs F G K L P Psi Cursives: MAJORITY Old Latin: ar c d dem e f q rl x z Vulg Syr: pesh harc Cop: sa bo Goth Arm Eth (apparently) Also extant in 049? 056 075 0142 0150 0151. No city other than Ephesus is inserted in the manuscripts.	P46 Aleph* B* pc (2 cursives cited by na,ubs)

EPHESIANS 1:18

AV	NIV
The eyes of your <u>understanding</u> being enlightened	the eyes of your <u>heart</u> may be enlightened
Cursives: pc (hf)	Aleph A B D Dabs F G K L P MAJORITY (hf) Old Latin: most Vulg Syr: pesh harc Cop: bo
Also extant in Psi 049? 056 075 0142 0150 0151. "Eyes of your heart" is not found elsewhere in the Bible, but it is found in the mystical writings of the early heathen philosophers. See *KJVMT*, p. 71 for a fuller discussion.	

AV	NIV

EPHESIANS 3:9	
God, who created all things <u>by Jesus Christ</u> D-1 Dabs K L Cursives: MAJORITY Syr: harc** Also extant in 049 056 078 0142 0150 0151. Another wicked attempt to remove the Deity of Christ from Scripture.	God, who created all things P46 Aleph A B C D* F G P Psi pc Old Latin: most Vulg pesh Cop: sa bo Goth Arm Eth

EPHESIANS 3:14	
For this cause I bow my knees unto the Father <u>of our Lord Jesus Christ</u> Aleph-2 D Dabs F G K L Psi Cursives: MAJORITY Old Latin: ar c d e f g t x z Vulg Syr: pesh harc Goth Arm Also extent in 049 056 075 0142 0150 0151	For this reason I kneel before the Father P46 Aleph* A B C P pc pal Cop: sa bo Eth

Section Three--A Manuscript Digest of 356 Doctrinal Passages 263

AV	NIV

EPHESIANS 5:9	
For the fruit of the Spirit is in all goodness P46 D-2 Dabs-c K L Psi Cursives: MAJORITY Syr: harc Also extant in I 048 056 075 0142 0150 0151	for the fruit of the light consists in all goodness P49 Aleph A B D* Dabs* F G P pc Old Latin: ar c d dem e f g mon x. z Vulg pesh pal Cop: sa bo Goth Arm Eth

EPHESIANS 5:30	
For we are members of his body, of his flesh, and of his bones Aleph-2 D Dabs F G (K) L P Psi Cursives: MAJORITY Old Latin: ar c d dem e f g mon x z Vulg Syr: pesh harc Arm Also extant in 049 056 075 0142 0150 0151. Offensive to scribes influenced by the Gnostic view of Christ's humanity.	For we are members of his body P46 Aleph* A B 048 pc Cop: sa bo Eth

AV	NIV

| EPHESIANS 6:12 ||

| against the rulers of the darkness of this world

Aleph-2 D-2 Dabs K L P Psi
Cursives: MAJORITY

Syr: harc**

Also extant in I 048 056 075 0142 0150 0151 0230. The A/Post Millennial philosophy tries to maintain a more optimistic view of this world, it's course, and future. | Omitted in some early manuscripts.

P46 Aleph* A B D* F G
pc
Old Latin: d a f g m Vulg
pesh   Cop: sa bo
Goth Eth Arm |

| PHILIPPIANS 3:3 ||

| Which worship God in the spirit

Aleph-2 D* P Psi
Cursives: pc (9 cited in our other Digest)
Old Latin: ar c d dem div e f m x z Vulg
Syr: pesh   harc
Goth Eth
Also extant in 049? 056 075 0142 0150 0151.   See *KJVMT*, p.72. | Who worship by the Spirit of God

Aleph* A B C D-2 Dabs F G K L
MAJORITY

g   Vulg-pt
harc-mg   Cop: sa bo |

AV	NIV

PHILIPPIANS 4:13

I can do all things through Christ which strengtheneth me Aleph-2 D-2 Dabs-gr (F-gr) (G) K L P Psi Cursives: MAJORITY Old Latin: g Syr: pesh harc Also extant in 049 056 075 0142 0150 0151	I can do everything through him who gives me strength Aleph* A B D* I pc d e f r Vulg Cop: sa bo Arm Eth

COLOSSIANS 1:2

peace, from God our Father and the Lord Jesus Christ Aleph A C F G I (P) Cursives: MAJORITY Old Latin: c (dem) f g Vulg-pt Syr: (harc**) Cop: (bo) Arm Eth-ppl Also extant in P46? 049 056 075 0142 0150 0151	peace to you from God the Father B D Dabs K L Psi al ar d div e mon x z Vulg-pt pesh herc sa Eth-rom

AV	NIV

COLOSSIANS 1:14

| In whom. we have redemption through his blood, even the forgiveness of sins | In whom we have redemption, the forgiveness of sins |
| Cursives: pm (hf, na has "al")
 Vulg-pt
 Syr: harc
 Arm
 Also extant in 049 056 0142 0150 0151. It can be argued that in each N.T. instance where redemption (in the sense of forgiveness of sin) is expounded, blood is always in the context - Rom. 3:24,25; Eph. 1:7; Heb 9:12-15; I Pet. 1:18; Rev. 5:9. There was no redemption until it was through his blood | Aleph A B C D Dabs F G K L P <br> pm (hf)
 Old Latin: d e f g m   Vulg-pt <br> pesh   Cop: sa bo
 Goth Eth |

COLOSSIANS 1:28

| That we may present every man perfect in Christ Jesus | "Jesus" is removed from association with the title "Christ." |
| Aleph-2 D-2 Dabs H K L P Psi
 Cursives: MAJORITY
 Old Latin: a f Vulg
 Syr: (pesh) harc   Cop: sa bo-mss
 Goth Arm Eth
 Also extant in I 048 049 056 075 0142 0150 0151 | P46 Aleph* A B C D* F-gr G <br> pc

 b d e g m*
 bo |

Section Three--A Manuscript Digest of 356 Doctrinal Passages

AV	NIV
COLOSSIANS 2:18	
and worshipping of angels, intruding into those things which he hath <u>not</u> seen	and the worship of angels...goes into great detail about what he has seen
Aleph-2 C D-2 F G K L P Psi Cursives: MAJORITY Old Latin: ar c dem div f g mon x z Vulg Syr: pesh harc Goth Arm Also extant in 049 056 075 0142 0150 0151	P46 Aleph* A B D* I pc d e m Vulg-pt Cop: sa bo Eth
COLOSSIANS 3:6	
For which things' sake the wrath of God cometh <u>on the children of disobedience</u>	Because of these, the wrath of God is coming
Aleph A C D-1 Dabs F G H I K L P Psi Cursives: MAJORITY Old Latin: ar c d dem div f g mon t x z Vulg Syr: pesh harc Cop: bo Goth Arm Eth-ppl Also extant in 049 056 075 0142 0150 0151	P46 B D* pc (no cursives cited by na, ubs) sa Eth-rom

AV	NIV

I THESSALONIANS 1:1	
Grace be unto you, and peace, <u>from God the Father, and the Lord Jesus Christ</u>	Grace and peace to you
Aleph A (D) Dabs K L P Cursives: MAJORITY Old Latin: (d) (e) mon Vulg-pt Syr: harc** pal-ms Cop: bo Eth-ppl Also extant in P46 048 049 056 075 0142 0150 0151	B F G Psi pc ar c dem div f g r2 x z Vulg pesh pal-ms Cop: sa fay Arm Eth-rom

I THESSALONIANS 2:15	
Who both killed the Lord Jesus, and <u>their own</u> prophets	Who killed the Lord Jesus and the prophets
D-1 Dabs-c K L Psi Cursives: MAJORITY Syr: pesh harc Goth Also extant in 049 056 075 0142 0150 0151	Aleph A B D* Dabs* F G I P 0208 pc Old Latin: a r c d dem div e f g mon x z Vulg Cop: sa bo fay Arm Eth

Section Three--A Manuscript Digest of 356 Doctrinal Passages

AV	NIV

I THESSALONIANS 2:19

AV	NIV
in the presence of our Lord Jesus <u>Christ</u> at his coming F G L Cursives: pm (hf) Vulg. Cop: sa bo fay Goth Arm Eth also extant in 049 056 075 0142 0150 0208	in the presence of our Lord Jesus when he comes? Aleph A B D Dabs K P pm (hf) Old Latin: d e Vulg-pt Syr: pesh harc

I THESSALONIANS 3:11

AV	NIV
Now God himself and our Father, and our Lord Jesus <u>Christ</u>, direct our way unto you D-c Dabs F G K L Cursives: MAJORITY (hf) Old Latin: f g Vulg Syr: pesh harc Cop: bo Goth Arm Also extant in I Psi 049 056 075 0142 0150 0151	Now may our God and Father himself, and our Lord Jesus clear the way for us to come to you Aleph A B D* pc (hf) d e Vulg-pt Eth

AV	NIV

I THESSALONIANS 3:13	
at the coming of our Lord Jesus Christ	when our Lord Jesus comes
F G L Cursives: pm (hf) Old Latin: f g Vulg Syr: pesh harc Cop: bo Goth Arm Eth-ppl Also extant in I Psi 049 056 075 0142 0150 0151	Aleph A B D Dabs K pm (hf) d e Eth-rom (apparently)

II THESSALONIANS 1:8	
that obey not the gospel of our Lord Jesus Christ	and do not obey the gospel of our Lord Jesus
Aleph A F G Cursives: pm (hf) Old Latin: d e f g Vulg Syr: pesh Goth Arm-usc Also extant in Psi 056 075 0111 0142 0150 0151	B D-gr Dabs-gr K L P pm (hf) harc Cop: bo Arm-zoh Eth

AV	NIV

II THESSALONIANS 1:12

that the name of our Lord Jesus <u>Christ</u> may be glorified in you be glorified in you A F G P Cursives: pm Old Latin: f g Vulg Syr: pesh harc Cop: bo-pt Arm Eth-ppl Also extant in 056 075 0142 0150 0151	that the name of our Lord Jesus may be glorified in you Aleph B D Dabs K L Psi 0111 pm b d e sa bo-pt Goth Eth-rom

II THESSALONIANS 2:13

God hath <u>from the beginning</u> chosen you to salvation Aleph D Dabs K L Psi Cursives: MAJORITY Old Latin: ar d e g mon Syr: pesh Cop: sa Arm Eth Also extant in 056 075 0142 0150 0151	Footnote* Some manuscripts read "God chose you as his firstfruits." B F G-gr P al c dem div f x z Vulg harc bo

AV	NIV
I TIMOTHY 1:1	
by the commandment of God our Saviour and <u>Lord</u> Jesus Christ Aleph D-c K L Cursives: MAJORITY (hf) Also extant in I Psi 056 075 0142 0150 0151	by the commandment of God our Saviour and of Christ Jesus A D* F G P al (hf) Old Latin: d f g Vulg Syr: pesh harc Cop: sa bo Goth Arm Eth
1 TIMOTHY 1:17	
immortal, invisible, the only <u>wise</u> God Aleph-2 D-1 H-c K L P Psi Cursives: MAJORITY Syr: harc Goth Also extant in 056 075 0142 0150 0151 0262	immortal, invisible, the only God Aleph* A D* F C H* pc Old Latin: d f g Vulg pesh Cop: sa bo Arm Eth

Section Three--A Manuscript Digest of 356 Doctrinal Passages

AV	NIV

I TIMOTHY 2:7

I speak the truth in Christ Aleph* D-1 H K L Cursives: MAJORITY Old Latin: ar Goth Arm Also extant in 056 075 0142 0150 0151	I am telling the truth Aleph-2 A D* F G P Psi pc e d dem div f g mon r1 x z Vulg Syr: pesh harc Cop: sa bo Eth

I TIMOTHY 3:16

great is the mystery of godliness: God was manifest in the flesh Aleph-c A-c C-2 D-2 K L P Psi Cursives: MAJORITY Vulg-ms Also extant in 056 061 075 0142 0150 0151 0241	the mystery of godliness is great: He appeared in a body Aleph* (A* C*??) D* G-gr F-gr pc Old Latin: ar c d dem div f g mon x z Vulg Syr: pesh harc Cop: sa bo Goth Arm Eth

We have placed A and C on the revised side only because textual criticism insists in telling us that this is where they belong. In fact, that most careful of scholars, H. Hoskier believed the first hand of Palimpsest C read "God", and of Codex A, Scrivener wrote during the latter nineteenth century: "Cod. A, however, I have examined at least twenty times within as many years...seeing (as every one must see for himself) with Berriman and the earlier collators that Cod A read THEOS... the evidence of Young, of Huish, of Mill, of Berriman and his friends, when the page was comparatively unworn, cannot thus be disposed of." (*Plain Introduction*, pp 639, 640 note)." There is no mystery about "*He* appeared in a body". The same can be said for everyone ! It is only such if the one manifested in the flesh is stated to be God. In fact, despite the NIV, NASV translation, it is not even "he" but rather *hos* - "*who* was manifested in the flesh." *He* is not in the text! This leaves the textual critic with an incomplete sentence. To counter this, it is suggested (without evidence) that Paul was quoting from the fragment of an early hymn from which the "he" was missing. Accordingly the entire sentence would be: "he who was manifest in the flesh." It is then indented as a quotation in modern versions, including (though using *God*), the *New KJV*. What webs they weave!

The passage is perhaps the strongest in Scripture on the Deity of Christ and we are not surprised that it is the object of Satan's attack. According to Scrivener, it is quoted by some of the very earliest fathers as Ignatius (110) and Hippolytus (235). Of the more than 250 cursive manuscripts containing I Timothy, Theos is found in all but two or three.

Section Three--A Manuscript Digest of 356 Doctrinal Passages 275

AV	NIV
I TIMOTHY 4:10	
For therefore we both labour and suffer reproach	for this we labour and <u>strive</u>
Aleph-2 D L P 0241 Cursives: MAJORITY Old Latin: ar c (d) dem div f (g) mon x z Vulg Syr: pesh harc Cop: sa bo Goth Arm Eth Also extant in I 056 075 0142 0150 0151	Aleph* A C F-gr G-gr K Psi al
I TIMOTHY 4:12	
be thou an example... in charity, <u>in spirit</u>, in faith, in purity	set an example...in love, in faith and purity
K L P Cursives: MAJORITY Also extant in 056 075 0142 0150 0151	Aleph A C D F G I Psi pc Old Latin: d f g Vulg Syr: pesh harc Cop: sa bo Goth Arm Eth

AV	NIV

| I TIMOTHY 5:16 ||

If any <u>man or</u> woman that believeth have widows, let them relieve them	If any woman who is a believer has widows in her family, she should help them
D K L Psi Cursives: MAJORITY Old Latin: ar c d Vulg-pt Syr: pesh harc Also extant in I 056 075 0142 0150 0151	Aleph A C F-gr G-gr P 048 pc mon x z Vulg Cop: sa bo Eth-ppl

| I TIMOTHY 5:21 ||

I charge thee before God, and the <u>Lord</u> Jesus Christ, and the elect angels	I charge you, in the sight of God and Christ Jesus angels and the elect
D-2 K L P Cursives: MAJORITY Syr: pesh harc Goth Also extant in 056 075 0142 0150 0151	Aleph A D* (F) G Psi pc Old Latin: d f g Vulg Cop: sa bo Arm Eth

Section Three--A Manuscript Digest of 356 Doctrinal Passages

AV	NIV

I TIMOTHY 6:5

AV	NIV
destitute of the truth, supposing that gain is godliness: <u>from such withdraw thyself</u> D-gr2 K L P Psi 061 Cursives: MAJORITY Old Latin: ar m mon Vulg -pt Syr: pesh harc Goth-pt Arm Eth-ppl Also extant in 056 075 0142 0150 0151? The depth of truth among possible contributors has not been the Church's main concern.	robbed of the truth and who think that godliness is a means of financial gain Aleph A D* F G 048 pc c d dem div f g rl Vulg Cop: sa bo Goth-pt Eth-rom

I TIMOTHY 6:7

AV	NIV
For we brought nothing into this world, and <u>it is certain</u>, we can carry nothing out Aleph-2 (D*) D-2 K L P Psi Cursives: MAJORITY Old Latin: ar (a) c d dem div f m mon x z Vulg Syr: pesh harc (Goth) Also extant in 056 075 0142 0250 0151?	For we brought nothing into the this world, and we can take nothing out of it Aleph* A F G 048 061 pc g rl Vulg-mss Cop: sa bo Arm Eth

AV	NIV

I TIMOTHY 6:19

that they may lay hold <u>on eternal life</u>	(Literal) that they may lay hold <u>on life that is</u>
D-2 Dabs-c K L P Cursives: MAJORITY bo-ms Also extant in I 056 075 0142 0150 0151?	Aleph A D* Dabs F G H Psi pc Old Latin: ar c d dem div e f g m mon x z Vulg Syr: pesh harc Cop: sa bo Arm Eth

II TIMOTHY 1:11

I am appointed a...teacher <u>of the Gentiles</u>	I was appointed a...teacher
Aleph-2 C D Dabs F G K L P Psi Cursives: MAJORITY Old Latin: ar c d dem div e f g mon x z Vulg Syr: pesh harc Cop: sa bo Goth Arm Eth Also extant in 056 075 0142 0150	Aleph* A I pc pal

Section Three--A Manuscript Digest of 356 Doctrinal Passages 279

AV	NIV
II TIMOTHY 2:19	
Let everyone that nameth the name of Christ	Everyone who confesses the name of the Lord
Cursives: pc (hf)	Aleph A C D Dabs F G K L P MAJORITY (hf) Old Latin: d e f g Vulg Syr: pesh harc Cop: sa bo Goth Arm Eth
Also extant in Psi 048 056 075 0142 0150. The name of the *Lord* in this instance is not specific; *Christ* is. See the comments in *KJVMT*, p. 74.	
II TIMOTHY 4:1a	
before God and the Lord Jesus Christ	In the presence of God and of Christ Jesus
D-c Dabs K L Cursives: MAJORITY	Aleph A C D* F G P pc Old Latin: d e f g Vulg harc Cop: bo Arm Eth
Syr: pesh harc** Goth Also extant in I Psi 056 075 0142 0150	

Early Manuscripts, Church Fathers, & the Authorized Version

AV	NIV

II TIMOTHY 4:1b

Jesus Christ, who shall judge the quick and the dead <u>at</u> his appearing	(NASV) Christ Jesus who is to judge the living and the dead <u>and</u> <u>by</u> his appearing
Aleph-2 D-2 Dabs K L P Psi Cursives: MAJORITY Old Latin: (dem) Syr: pesh harc Cop: sa Goth Arm Eth Also extant in I 056 075 0142 0150. One of many alterations which diminishes and confuses a clear statement of the Lord's return.	Aleph* A C D* F G pc ar c d div e f g t x z Vulg bo

II TIMOTHY 4:22

The Lord <u>Jesus Christ</u> be with thy spirit	"Jesus Christ" is removed from association with the title "Lord."
Aleph-2 C D Dabs K L P Psi Cursives: MAJORITY Old Latin: a b d e f Vulg Syr: pesh harc Cop: bo Arm Also extant in 056 075 0142 0150	Aleph* F-gr G pc g sa Eth

Section Three--A Manuscript Digest of 356 Doctrinal Passages 281

AV	NIV
TITUS 1:4	
from God the Father and the <u>Lord</u> Jesus Christ our Saviour	from God the Father and Christ Jesus our Saviour
D-2 Dabs F G K L P Cursives: MAJORITY Old Latin: f g Syr: pesh harc Also extant in 056 075 0142 0150	Aleph A C D* Psi 088 0240 pc d e Vulg Cop: bo
HEBREWS 1:3	
When he had <u>by himself</u> purged our sins	After he had provided purfication for sins
(P46) (D*) Dabs H-c K L 0121b Cursives: MAJORITY Old Latin: a r d e Syr: pesh harc Cop: sa-mss bo fay (Eth) Also extant in I 056 075 0142 0150 0151. It was not long till early Christendom began to bring something or someone else into that work which belonged wholly to Christ.	Aleph A B H* P Psi al c dem div f t v x z Vulg pal Arm

282 Early Manuscripts, Church Fathers, & the Authorized Version

AV	NIV

HEBREWS 2:7

thou crownest him with glory and honour <u>and didst set him over the works of thy hands</u>	you crowned him with glory and honour
Aleph A C D* Dabs P Psi 0121b-c Cursives: al Old Latin: ar c dem div e f v x z Vulg Syr: pesh harc** Cop: sa bo fay Arm Eth Also extant in I 056 075 0142 0150 0151	P46 B D-2 Dabs-c K L MAJORITY Vulg-ms harc

HEBREWS 3:1

Consider the Apostle and High Priest of our profession, <u>Christ</u> Jesus	fix your thoughts on Jesus, the apostle and high priest whom we confess
Cursives: pc (hf)	Aleph A B C* D P 0121b pc (hf) Old Latin: d e f Vulg Cop: sa bo
Arm "Jesus Christ" in: C-2 Dc E K L, MAJORITY, Syr: pesh harc, Arm. Also extant in P13 P46? Psi 056 075 0142 0150 0151. See *KJVMT*, p. 74.	Eth

Section Three--A Manuscript Digest of 356 Doctrinal Passages

AV	NIV

HEBREWS 3:6

if we hold fast the confidence and the rejoicing of the hope <u>firm unto the end</u>	if we hold on to our courage and the hope of which we boast
Aleph A C D Dabs K L P Psi 0121- b,c Cursives: MAJORITY Old Latin: ar c d dem div e f v (x) z Vulg Syr: (pesh) harc pal Cop: bo Arm Eth-ppl Also extant in I 056 075 0142 0150 0151	P13,46 B pc (no cursives cited na, ubs) sa Eth-rom

HEBREWS 7:21

Thou art a priest for ever <u>after the order of Melchisedec</u>	You are a priest forever
Aleph-2 A D Dabs K L P Psi Cursives: MAJORITY Old Latin: d e Syr: pesh harc Cop: bo-pt Eth Also extant in 056 075 0142 0150 0151	P46 (Aleph*) B C pc f Vulg sa bo-pt fay Arm

284 Early Manuscripts, Church Fathers, & the Authorized Version

AV	NIV

HEBREWS 9:28

So Christ was once offered	(NASV) So Christ <u>also</u>, having been offered once
Cursives: pc (hf) Also extant in P46 Psi 056 075 0142 0150 0151. The insertion of "also" should be viewed in the same light as the deletion of "by himself" in Heb 1:3. See *KJVMT*, p. 75.	Aleph A C D Dabs K L P MAJORITY (hf) Old Latin: d e f Vulg Syr: pesh harc Cop: sa bo fay Arm Eth

HEBREWS 10:30

for we know him that hath said, Vengence belongeth unto me, I will recompense, <u>saith the Lord</u>	For we know him who said, It is mine to avenge; I will repay
Aleph-2 A D-2 Dabs K L Cursives: MAJORITY Old Latin: b r Vulg-pt Syr: harc Cop: sa-mss Arm Eth-ppl Also extant in P79 056 0150 0151. Consider carefully the first part of this verse, as it identifies Christ with the Old Testament Jehovah.	P13,46 Aleph* D* P Psi pc d e f Vulg pesh sa-ms bo Eth-rom

Section Three--A Manuscript Digest of 356 Doctrinal Passages

AV	NIV

HEBREWS 10:34

knowing in yourselves that ye have <u>in heaven</u> a better and an enduring substance	because you knew that you yourselves had better and lasting possessions
Aleph-2 D-2 Dabs H-c K L P Psi Cursives: MAJORITY Vulg-ms Syr: pesh harc Arm Eth-ppl Also extant in 056 0142 0150 0151	P13,46 Aleph* A D* H* pc (na cites 1 cursive) Old Latin: d e f Vulg Cop: sa bo Eth-rom

JAMES 2:20

faith without works is <u>dead</u>?	faith without deeds is <u>useless</u>?
Aleph A C-3 K L P Psi 049 056 0142 Cursives: MAJORITY Old Latin: pt Vulg-pt Syr: pesh harc Cop: bo Arm-usc Eth Also extant in P20?	B C* pc ar c dem div ff s z Vulg-pt sa Arm-zoh

AV	NIV

JAMES 4:4	
Ye <u>adulterers and</u> adulteresses	(NASV) You adulteresses
Aleph-2 K L P Psi 049 056 0142 Cursives: MAJORITY Syr: harc Also extant in P24? 048	Aleph* A B pc Old Latin: ar c dem div ff p s t z Vulg pesh Cop: sa bo Arm Eth

JAMES 5:16	
Confess your <u>faults</u> one to another	confess your <u>sins</u> to each other
K L 049 Cursives: MAJORITY The versional evidence does not distinguish between the two readings. There is but a short step from this alteration to the "Confessional." Also extant in 056 0142.	Aleph A B P Psi 048 al

Section Three--A Manuscript Digest of 356 Doctrinal Passages

AV	NIV

I PETER 1:22

Seeing ye have purified your souls in obeying the truth <u>through the Spirit</u> K L P 049 056 0142 Cursives: MAJORITY Vulg-ms Arm-zoh	Now that you have purified yourselves by obeying the truth P72 Aleph A B C Psi al Old Latin: ar c dem div p z Vulg Syr: pesh harc Cop: sa bo Arm-usc

I PETER 2:2

desire the sincere milk of the word, that ye may <u>grow thereby</u> L Cursives: MAJORITY Also extant in 049 056 0142. A classic salvation by works alteration which despite its uncial and versional support, cannot possibly be right. The NIV/NASV translators did not translate literally here!!	(Literal)....that ye may <u>grow unto salvation</u> P72 Aleph A B C K P Psi al Old Latin: most Vulg Syr: pesh harc Cop: sa bo Arm Eth

288 Early Manuscripts, Church Fathers, & the Authorized Version

AV	NIV

I PETER 2:24

by <u>whose</u> stripes ye were healed Aleph* L P 049 Cursives: MAJORITY Old Latin: b2 f g h j k l Also extant in (P72,74,81??) 056 093 0142, other versional not known.	"whose" is omitted in some early manuscripts Aleph-c A B C K Psi al (hf) Some OL Vulg

I PETER 3:16

Whereas they speak evil of you, <u>as of evildoers</u> Aleph A C K L P 049 056 0142 Cursives: MAJORITY Old Latin: ar c p Vulg-pt Syr: pesh harc**-mg Cop: bo Eth And, so it has been throughout church history - the Roman Catholics were "orthodox", while groups as the Waldensians were the hunted and slaughtered "heretics".	So that those who speak maliciously against your... P72 Psi al dem div (m) (Vulg) (harc) sa (Arm)

Section Three--A Manuscript Digest of 356 Doctrinal Passages 289

AV	NIV

I PETER 4:1

Forasmuch then as Christ hath suffered <u>for us</u> in the flesh Aleph-2 A K L P 056 0142 Cursives: MAJORITY Syr: harc Cop: bo Arm Eth "for you" in Aleph 049-c pesh	Therefore, since Christ suffered in his body P72 B C Psi 049* pc Old Latin: ar c dem div p z Vulg sa?

I PETER 4:14

..Christ...<u>on their part he is evil spoken of, but on your part he is glorified</u> K L P Psi Cursives: MAJORITY Old Latin: ar p q t z Vulg-pt Syr: harc** Cop: sa bo-ms	...Christ... P72 Aleph* A B 049 056 0142 al c dem (gig) Vulg pesh harc bo Arm Eth

Early Manuscripts, Church Fathers, & the Authorized Version

AV	NIV

I PETER 5:2

Feed the flock of God which is among you, <u>taking the oversight thereof</u>	(NASV) Shepherd the flock of God among you
P72 Aleph-c A K L P Psi 049 056 0142 Cursives: MAJORITY Old Latin: ar c dem div h m p t Vulg Syr: (pesh) harc Cop: bo Arm Eth Early bishops began to exercise authority far beyond the flock <u>among</u> them.	Aleph* B pc (na cites 1 cursive) sa

I PETER 5:5

Yea, all of you <u>be subject</u> one to another	...toward one another
K L P Cursives: MAJORITY Syr: harc Eth Also extant in 049 056 0142 0206. Subjection was to some the domain of the Bishop only.	Aleph A B al Old Latin: m Vulg pesh Cop: sa bo Arm

Section Three--A Manuscript Digest of 356 Doctrinal Passages

AV	NIV

I PETER 5:10

Who hath called us unto his eternal glory by Christ <u>Jesus</u>	"Jesus" is removed from association with the title "Christ."
P72 A K L P Psi 049 056 0142 Cursives: MAJORITY Old Latin: c dem div h p q t z Vulg Syr: (pesh) harc** Cop: sa bo Arm Eth Also extant in 0206	Aleph B pc harc

I PETER 5:11

To him be <u>glory and</u> dominion for ever und over	To him be the power for ever and ever
Aleph L P Cursives: MAJORITY Old Latin: c dem div p z Vulg-pt Syr: (pesh) (harc) Cop: sa (bo) (Arm) Eth-ppl Also extant in 049 056 0142 0206	(P72) A B Psi pc ar Vulg-pt Eth-rom

Early Manuscripts, Church Fathers, & the Authorized Version

AV	NIV

| **I PETER 5:14** ||

AV	NIV
all that are in Christ <u>Jesus</u> Aleph K L P 049 056 0142 Cursives: MAJORITY Old Latin: div h p Vulg-pt Syr: harc Cop: sa-mss bo Arm Also extant in 0247	"Jesus" is removed from association with the title "Christ". A B Psi c dem (gig) q z Vulg-pt pesh sa-ms bo-mss Eth

| **II PETER 1:3** ||

AV	NIV
him that hath called us <u>to</u> glory and virtue P72 B K L 049 056 0142 0209 Cursives: MAJORITY	him who called us <u>by his own</u> glory and goodness Aleph A C P Psi al Old Latin: ar c dem div h (m) p q (z) Vulg Syr: philox harc pal Cop: sa bo Arm

Section Three--A Manuscript Digest of 356 Doctrinal Passages

AV	NIV

II PETER 1:21

but <u>holy</u> men of God spoke as they were moved by the Holy Ghost	but men spoke from God as they were carried along by the Holy Spirit
Aleph A C K L Psi 049 056 0142 Cursives: MAJORITY Old Latin: ar c div h p z Vulg Syr: philox Eth	P72 B P al dem harc bo Arm

II PETER 2:17

...darkness is reserved <u>for ever</u>	...darkness is reserved
A C L P 049 Cursives: MAJORITY Cop: bo-ms Eth-ppl Also extant in 056 0142 0209	P72 Aleph B Psi 048 pc Old Latin: most Vulg Syr: philox harc sa bo Eth-rom

AV	NIV

II PETER 3:2

and of the commandment of <u>us</u> the apostles	and the command given...through <u>your</u> apostles
Psi Cursives: al (36 cited in our other Digest)	P72 Aleph A B C K L P 048 MAJORITY Vulg Syr: philox harc Arm
Also extant in 049 056 0142. The altered reading would rule out Simon Peter as the author of this second epistle. See *KJVMT*, p. 78.	

II PETER 3:10a

But the day of the Lord will come as a thief <u>in the night</u>	But the day of the Lord will come like a thief
C K L Cursives: MAJORITY Vulg-pt Syr: harc Also extant in 049 0142	P72 Aleph A B P Psi 048 0156 al Old Latin: m Vulg philox Cop: sa bo Arm Eth

Section Three--A Manuscript Digest of 356 Doctrinal Passages 295

AV	NIV

II PETER 3:10b

The earth also and the works that are therein shall be <u>burned up</u>	and the earth and everything in it will be <u>laid bare</u>
A L 048 049 056 0142 Cursives: MAJORITY Old Latin: ar c dem p Vulg-pt Syr: harc Cop: bo Eth	Aleph B (C) K P (Psi) 0156 pc philox harc-mg Arm

I JOHN 1:7

and the blood of Jesus <u>Christ</u> his Son	and the blood of Jesus, his Son
A K L Cursives: MAJORITY Old Latin: t z Vulg-pt Syr: harc** Cop: bo Eth-ppl Also extant in 049 056 0142	Aleph B C P Psi pc l Vulg-pt pesh sa bo-ms Arm Eth-rom

AV	NIV

I JOHN 2:7

The old commandment is the word which ye have heard <u>from the beginning</u>	The old command is the message you have heard
K L Cursives: MAJORITY Also extant in P74? 049 056 0142 0157	Aleph A B C P Psi al Old Latin: most Vulg Syr: pesh harc Cop: sa bo Arm Eth

I JOHN 2:20

but ye have an unction from the Holy One, and <u>ye know all things</u>	(NASV) But you have an anointing from the Holy One, and <u>you all know</u>
A C K L (049) 056 0142 Cursives: MAJORITY Old Latin: ar c dem div h p z Vulg Syr: (pesh) harc Cop: bo Arm Eth	Aleph B P Psi pc sa

Section Three--A Manuscript Digest of 356 Doctrinal Passages 297

AV	NIV
I JOHN 2:28	
<u>when</u> he shall appear	(NASV) <u>if</u> he should appear
K L Cursives: MAJORITY Vulg (Alford) Syr: pesh harc What a difference! Also extant in 049 056 0142 0157?	Aleph A B C P Psi al Cop: sa bo Arm Eth
I JOHN 3:5	
he was manifested to take away <u>our</u> sins	He appeared in order to take away sins
Aleph C K L Psi 049 056 0142 Cursives: MAJORITY Vulg-pt Syr: pesh Cop: sa-ms	A B P al Old Latin: ar c dem div h p z Vulg-pt harc sa-ms bo Arm Eth

AV	NIV

I JOHN 4:3

| And every spirit that confesseth not that Jesus <u>Christ is come in the flesh</u> is not of God | But every spirit that does not acknowledge Jesus is not from God |
| K L 049 056 0142
Cursives: MAJORITY
Vulg-ms
Syr: pesh harc

Also extant in 0245. This passage strikes at the chief heresy concerning the Person of Christ, i.e. that a man named Jesus of Nazareth <u>became</u> the Christ at his baptism. He was not the Christ prior to that event. This *depth of Satan* has continued in varied forms down to our day, and is the root of what lays behind modern publications as *From Jesus to Christ* by Paula Fredrikson, (Yale University Press). It is the primary reason for the disassociation between "Jesus" and "Christ" in certain early manuscripts. | A B Psi
pc
Old Latin: ar c dem div p q Vulg
Cop: (sa) bo
(Eth) |

Section Three--A Manuscript Digest of 356 Doctrinal Passages 299

AV	NIV

I JOHN 5:7, 8

AV	NIV
For there are three that bear record in heaven, the Father, the Word, and the Holy Ghost: and these three are one. And there are three that bear witness in earth, the spirit, and the water, and the blood: and these agree in one. Cursives: pc (9 cited in our other Digest) Old Latin: c dem div 1 m p qr Vulg Removing these words leaves a gender mismatch in Greek. To the native Greek speaker this is highly unusual. Thus, though wrongly excised from the Greek MSS, it has left its *footprint*! For a defense of this key Trinitarian passage, see *KJVMT*, p. 115.	For there are three that testify: the Spirit, the water and the blood Aleph A B K L P Psi 048 049 056 0142 MAJORITY Vulg-pt Syr: pesh harc Cop: (sa) bo Arm Eth

AV	NIV

I JOHN 5:13

that ye may know that ye have eternal life, <u>and that ye may believe on the name of the Son of God</u>	so that you may know that you have eternal life
K L P (Psi) Cursives: MAJORITY Also extant in 048 049 056 0142	Aleph* A B pc Old Latin: r Vulg Syr: harc Arm Eth

II JOHN 3

from God the Father, and from <u>the Lord</u> Jesus Christ	from God the Father and from Jesus Christ
Aleph K L P 049 056 0142 Cursives: MAJORITY Vulg-pt Syr: philox harc Cop: bo Arm	A B Psi 048 0232 al Old Latin: ar c dem div p Vulg sa Eth

Section Three—A Manuscript Digest of 356 Doctrinal Passages 301

AV	NIV

II JOHN 9a

Whosoever <u>transgresseth</u>...hath not God K L P Psi Cursives: MAJORITY Syr: philox harc Arm Also extant in 048 049 056 0142	Anyone who <u>runs ahead</u> does not have God Aleph A B 0232 pc (na cites 1 cursive) Vulg Cop: sa bo Eth

II JOHN 9b

He that abideth in the doctrine <u>of Christ</u>, he hath both the Father and the Son Support for this warning passage is similar to the above.	Whoever continues in the teaching has both the Father and the Son

JUDE 1

to them that are <u>sanctified by</u> God the Father K L P 049 056 0142 Cursives: MAJORITY Also extant in 0251	(NASV) to these who are...<u>beloved</u> in God the Father P72 Aleph A B Psi al Vulg Syr: philox harc Cop: sa bo Arm (Eth)

302 Early Manuscripts, Church Fathers, & the Authorized Version

AV	NIV
JUDE 25	
To the only <u>wise</u> God our Saviour K L P Cursives: MAJORITY Also extant in 049 056 0142	To the only God our Saviour P72 Aleph A B C Psi al Old Latin: most Vulg Syr: philox harc Cop: sa bo Arm
REVELATION 1:8	
I am Alpha and Omega, <u>the beginning and the ending</u> Aleph* Aleph-2 Cursives: pm-Andreas Mss Old Latin: ar c dem div gig haf t z Vulg Cop: bo	I am the Alpha and the Omega Aleph-1 A C P 046 pm-046 Mss h Syr: philox harc Arm Eth

Section Three--A Manuscript Digest of 356 Doctrinal Passages

AV	NIV

REVELATION 1:9a

and in the kingdom and patience of Jesus <u>Christ</u> Cursives: pm-Andreas Mss Syr: harc Cop: (sa) "in Christ Jesus" in Aleph-2, 046 Mss, Vulg-pt, Arm	in the...kingdom and patient endurance that are ours in Jesus Aleph* C P pc Old Latin: gig Vulg-pt philox bo

REVELATION 1:9b

and for the testimony of Jesus <u>Christ</u> Aleph-2 046 Cursives: pm-046 Mss Old Latin: a Vulg-ms Syr: philox harc Cop: sa bo Arm Eth	and the testimony of Jesus Aleph* A C P al-part of Andreas Mss Vulg

REVELATION 1:11

<u>I am Alpha and Omega, the first and the last</u> P Cursives: pm-Andreas Mss See *KJVMT*, p. 80.	---------- Aleph A C 046 pm-046 Mss Vulg Syr: philox hare Cop: sa bo Arm Eth

304 Early Manuscripts, Church Fathers, & the Authorized Version

AV	NIV
REVELATION 2:15	
and to commit fornication, So hast thou also them that hold the doctrine of the Nicolaitanes, <u>which thing I hate</u>	and by committing sexual immorality <u>Likewise</u> you also have those who hold to the teaching of the Nicolaitanes
P Cursives: pm-Andreas Mss Arm This alteration may well have been an attempt to link Nicolaitanism with the sins of 2:14 and thus avoid any reference of the term to the rapidly expanding power of early bishops. See p. 79 in *KJVMT*.	Aleph A C O46 pm-046 Mss Vulg Syr: philox harc Cop: bo
REVELATION 5:14	
and worshipped <u>him that liveth for ever and ever</u>	and worshipped
Cursives: pc (3 cited in our other Digest) Vulg-pt Arm-usc? Further evidence is given on p. 90 in *KJVMT*.	Aleph A C P O46 MAJORITY - Andreas and 046 Mss Vulg-pt Syr: philox harc Cop: bo Arm-zoh Eth

Section Three--A Manuscript Digest of 356 Doctrinal Passages

AV	NIV

REVELATION 6:17

For the great day of <u>his</u> wrath is come	For the great day of <u>their</u> wrath has come
A P 046 Cursives: MAJORITY - Andreas and 046 Mss Cop: sa-ms bo Arm Eth	Aleph C pc Old Latin: ar c dem div gig haf z Vulg Syr: philox harc

REVELATION 8:13

an <u>angel</u>...saying with a loud voice	an <u>eagle</u>...call out in a loud voice
P Cursives: pm-Andreas Mss Arm	Aleph A 046 pm-046 Mss Vulg Syr: philox harc Cop: bo Eth

AV	NIV

REVELATION 11:15

The kingdoms of this world are become the <u>kingdoms</u> of our Lord	The kingdom of the world has become the <u>kingdom</u> of our Lord
Cursives: pm- Andreas Mss	P47 Aleph A C P 046 pm-046 Mss Vulg Syr: philox harc Cop: bo Arm Eth
Christ will reign over kingdom<u>s</u> and nation<u>s</u> (as there are kingdoms and nation<u>s</u> now). See Dan 2:44; Isa 2:2; Psa 67:4 etc. See also *KJVMT*, p. 96.	

REVELATION 11:17

which art, and wast, <u>and art to come</u>	who is and who was
051 Cursives: al (about 65 indicated in our other Digest) Vulg-pt Cop: (bo) Arm-usc See *KJVMT*, p. 97.	P47 Aleph* Aleph-2 A C P 046 MAJORITY - Andreas and 046 Mss Old Latin: ar c dem div gig h haf z Vulg-pt Syr: philox harc sa Arm-zoh

Section Three--A Manuscript Digest of 356 Doctrinal Passages

AV	NIV

REVELATION 12:17

and have the testimony of Jesus <u>Christ</u> Cursives: pc (3 cited in our other Digest) Vulg-pt See *KJVMT*, p. 98.	and hold to the testimony of Jesus P47 Aleph-c A C P 046-c MAJORITY-Andreas and 046 Mss Vulg Syr: philox harc Cop: bo Arm Eth (Lord Jesus)

REVELATION 14:5

for they are without fault <u>before the throne of God</u> Cursives: pc (3 cited in our other Digest) Vulg-pt Arm-usc Also extant in 051. See *KJVMT*, p. 99.	they are blameless P47 Aleph A C P 046 MAJORITY-Andreas and 046 Mss Vulg-pt Syr: philox harc Cop: bo Arm-zoh Eth

AV	NIV

REVELATION 16:5a	
Thou art righteous, <u>O Lord</u> Cursives: pc (2 cited in our other Digest) Vulg-pt Eth Also extant in 051. See *KJVMT*, p. 102.	you are just P47 Aleph A C P 046 MAJORITY-Andreas and 046 Mss Vulg-pt Syr: philox harc Cop: bo Arm

REVELATION 16:5b	
which art, and wast, <u>and shalt be</u> Cursives: pc Compare with 1:4; 1:8; 4:8; 11:17. Tischendorf's citation of Primasius, the well-known commentator on Revelation (died 552), has *fuiciti* in addition to "Holy One". Indeed Christ is the Holy One, but in the Scriptures of the Apostle John the title is found only once (I John 2:20), and there an entirely different Greek word is used. See *KJVMT*, p. 102.	you who are and who were, <u>the Holy One</u> P47 Aleph A C P 046 051 MAJORITY-Andreas and 046 Mss Vulg Cop: sa

Section Three--A Manuscript Digest of 356 Doctrinal Passages 309

AV	NIV
REVELATION 16:17	
and there came a great voice out of the temple of heaven	and out of the temple came a loud voice
046 051-c Cursives: MAJORITY- (Andreas) and 046 Mss (Arm) "out of heaven" in 051, Arm	P47 Aleph A 0163 al Vulg Syr Cop: bo Eth
REVELATION 18:20	
Rejoice...ye holy apostles and prophets	Rejoice...saints and apostles and and prophets
C 051 Cursives: pm-Andreas Mss Vulg-pt Arm Notice how the altered reading gives support to the idea of "saints" in the Roman Catholic sense. See *KJVMT*, p. 105.	Aleph A P 046 pm-046 Mss Vulg-pt Syr: philox harc Cop: bo Eth

AV	NIV

| REVELATION 20:9 |

AV	NIV
and fire came down from <u>God</u> <u>out of</u> heaven and devoured them	but fire came down from heaven and devoured them
Aleph-c P 046 051 Cursives: MAJORITY-Andreas and 046 Mss Old Latin: ar c dem div gig haf Vulg Syr: philox harc Cop: sa bo Arm (Eth)	A pc Vulg-ms bo-mss

| REVELATION 20:12 |

AV	NIV
And I saw the dead, small and great stand before <u>God</u>	And I saw the dead, great and small, standing before <u>the throne</u>
Cursives: al (16 cited in our other Digest, part of the Andreas Mss read "throne of God")	Aleph A P 046 MAJORITY- part of Andreas, and 046 Mss
Also extant in 051. As all judgement has been committed to Christ (John 5:22), the altered reading removes this declaration of His Deity. See *KJVMT*, p. 108.	Vulg Syr: philox harc Cop: sa bo Arm Eth

Section Three--A Manuscript Digest of 356 Doctrinal Passages 311

AV	NIV

REVELATION 21:24

And the nations <u>of them which are saved</u> shall walk in the light of it	The nations will walk by its light
Cursives: al-part of Andreas Mss	Aleph A P 046 MAJORITY- part of Andreas 046 Mss Vulg Syr: philox harc Cop: bo Arm Eth
Also extant in 051. See *KJVMT*, p. 112.	

REVELATION 22:14

Blessed are they <u>that do his commandments</u>, that they may have right to the tree of life	Blessed are those <u>who wash their robes</u>, that they may have the right to the tree of life
046 Cursives: MAJORITY-Andreas and 046 Mss Old Latin: gig Syr: philox harc Cop: bo Arm See "commandments" in John: 12:50; 13:34; 14:15,21; 15:10,12,14,17; I John 1:34,7,8; 3:22,23,24; 4:21; 5:2,3; II John 4,5,6; Rev 12:17; 14:12.	Aleph A pc ar c dem div haf Vulg sa Arm-usc-mg Eth

AV	NIV

REVELATION 22:19	
And if any man shall take away from the words of the book of this prophecy, God shall take away his part out of <u>the book of life</u>	And if anyone takes words away from the book of prophecy, God will take away from him his share in <u>the tree of life</u>
	Aleph A 046
Cursives: pc (3 cited in our other Digest) Vulg-pt	MAJORITY-Andreas and 046 Mss Vulg-pt Syr: philox harc Cop: bo Arm Eth
Also extant in 051. Each person has their own individual part in the book of life, but what are we to make of a man's "part" in the tree of life? See *KJVMT*, p. 114.	

REVELATION 22:21	
The grace of our Lord Jesus <u>Christ</u>	The grace of the Lord Jesus
046 051-suppl Cursives: MAJORITY-Andreas and 046 Mss Old Latin: ar c dem div gig haf Vulg Syr: philox harc Arm Eth	Aleph A pc Cop: sa

Know now that there shall fall unto the earth nothing of the word of the Lord....

II Kings 10:10

Early Church Fathers and the Authorized Version

A DEMONSTRATION !

INTRODUCTION

The Received Text of the Authorized Version has a doctrinal heart that is substantially diminished in the critical texts underlying Modern Versions. In the previous section, *Early Manuscripts and the Authorized Version,* a factual demonstration is given as to how substantial the witness of early manuscripts and versions is to 356 distinctive doctrinal passages of the AV. We now look at the witness of the Early Fathers to many of these same passages.

Here, by using unambiguous guidelines and by referencing the most respected and comprehensive edition of the Fathers available in English, *early* theological writers are shown to vote on the side of the Doctrinal Text against Aleph and B by a 2.3 to 1 margin. This is of course contrary to the "official position" of Textual Criticism.. Who is right?

THE FATHERS, ROME, AND THE BIBLE: A STRANGE TWIST!

A study of the Fathers is generally a study of the development of Romanism. It is a study of early "Christendom", rather than the little known and maligned remnant who remained true to the Word of God. Many of the early Fathers contributed to the evolving Roman system, and others who did not have been *claimed* and *sainted* by that church.

A survey of the Fathers, and especially the Western, opens up a fact that is not commonly understood, and provides a missing piece in a textual puzzle, that is: Why has Rome changed her Bible? In recent times she has formally recognized the Aleph-B Text, but this is markedly different than the Vulgate she used through the centuries.

The doctrinal corruption of the Text is not as much a product of Rome as it is of early Alexandria (and this despite Kurt Aland's recent "turn around" that the Alexandrian Text did not come from Alexandria! See below.). The Catholic New Testament of the earlier and Middle Ages, though showing serious corruption, was not as bad as that which is manifest in the key Alexandrian MSS (Aleph, B, P46,47,66,74,75). This latter was Satan's master-stroke, and was too radical for even Papal Rome to handle. Why else would she have kept the famous Vaticanus MS (B) under lock and key for so long, were it not for the fact that it contradicted her own New Testament almost as much as it did the Textus Receptus.

Early Church Fathers and the Authorized Version 315

It was only with the rapid spread of printed Reformation Bibles based on the TR that Rome in desperation turned to this Alexandrian "alternative" as the weapon to undermine Protestant faith in their *paper pope*. Soon, polyglot editions began to appear. These were designed to display conflicting authorities in the Biblical Text and were largely financed by Rome. The Catholic, Richard Simon (died 1712), is looked upon as the Father of Biblical Criticism and lit the fires of opposition, both Catholic and Protestant, to the Textus Receptus. The fact that the Roman Bibles were closer to the TR than to the text of Alexandra, mattered not to a system that keeps the Bible from it's people. Faith in the Bible must be destroyed and the bringing forth of the Alexandrian "alternative" will be the means.

Remarkably, Rome did not *officially* recognize the Aleph-B text until about 1966 when the UBS-1 was published. At this time, Carlo Martini, Archbishop of Milan and later Cardinal, was invited to serve on the United Bible Societies editorial committee.

In addition to what has already been presented in this volume concerning the Church Fathers, we now seek to further demonstrate the extent to which the *early* Fathers in both the Latin West and Greek East support the Doctrinal Text of the Authorized Version. It was only in the enclave of Alexandria that a clearly dissenting voice could be heard.

It is a strange fact that today: Fundamentalist, Liberal, and Roman Catholic unite in listening to that voice! Many of our conservative Bible Colleges use the AV "up front" for respectability, but in the Greek departments, future pastors and missionaries are initiated into the Text of Egypt - Satan's master-stroke for the end time!

CHAPTER ONE
TEXTUAL CRITICISM AND THE CHURCH FATHERS

Students in Bible Colleges are given to believe that a search of the voluminous works of early Fathers will show that they quote frequently from the Alexandrian and "Western" type of text, but very little from the fuller Doctrinal Text that underlies our Authorized Version. And, if any such quotations are found, it is only because of "adaptation" by a later editor to the Received Text.

Kenneth I. Brown, formerly of Detroit Baptist Divinity School, is typical:

> The Fathers clearly show that the Neutral, Western, and Caesarean text were in existence at least by early third century, if not before. However, the Syrian text arose at the beginning of the fourth century. Chrysostom shows the point of division, since he and many following him used the Syrian text but none of the Fathers used it before his time ... The absence of any Syrian text before the time of Chrysostom lends much support to the view of Westcott and Hort. *(The Church Fathers and the Text of the New Testament,* published by author, 1978, pp. 25,26).

Daniel B. Wallace (Dallas Theological Seminary) writes:

> There is no proof that the Byzantine text was in existence in the first three centuries. It is not found.. .in the early church fathers. ("The Majority Text and the Original Text," *Bibliotheca Sacra,* April-June 1991, p. 165).

No factual evidence is given, Wallace apparently feels the issue can be placed out of reach by quoting Gordon Fee:

> Fee, who is recognized as one of the leading patristic authorities today, wrote: "Over the past eight years I have been collecting the Greek patristic evidence for Luke and John for the International Greek New Testament Project. In all of this material I have found one invariable: a good critical edition of a Father's text,

or the discovery of early MSS, *always moves* the Father's text of the NT *away from* the TR and *closer* to the text of our modern critical editions." (p. 164. Cited in:"Modern Textual Criticism and the Revival of the Textus Receptus," *Journal of the Evangelical Theological Society,* No. 21, 1978, p.26).

Fee's statement (which we will come back to) is about as strong and sweeping as any that can be found for their position. Naturally, we would like to know *how much* "away from", or *how much* "closer to", or how many examples of adaptation can be produced. Certainly, the one or two examples Fee gives in his article are no more than a pinprick in the overall picture.

Can it be convincingly demonstrated that modern editions will yield results substantially different than shown in Burgon's Index, or for that matter, in this book? And, if or where they do differ, is it based on adequate manuscript evidence, or does a subjective aligning by modern editors of the Father's quotations to Aleph-B and the Hortian theory also play a part? I think we may well find that this latter will turn out to be a far greater cause for concern than that of medieval copyists adapting quotations to the Traditional Text. The very fact that Textual Criticism unites in telling us that we must use the modern editions is a tacit admission that the standard works are not favorable to their Aleph-B text!

A number of recent books have demonstrated how adept our opponents are in performing a "vanishing act" with the early manuscript and versional evidence for the TR. They have been no less adept with the Fathers, and their chief means has been to *tell* (!) us about "the modern critical editions."

THE SEARCH FOR A "GOOD CRITICAL EDITION"

Gordon Fee says that we must use a "good critical edition" of the Fathers, which of course means one that will align with Aleph and B . Now surely if this *is* the true and original text, then such editions should be reasonably easy to come by. But this has not been the case! As the following authorities show, this "good modern edition" always seems to be just beyond reach.

FREDERIC KENYON

In 1936 Frederic Kenyon took issue with several aspects of John Burgon's massive Index of patristic references. These had been placed in the library of which he was director and demonstrated a 3/2 advantage to the Traditional Text. Kenyon's verdict on Edward Miller's tabulation of the Index is both revealing and contradictory:

> In the first place, it is fairly certain that critical editions of the several Fathers, if such existed, would show that in many cases

Chapter One--Textual Criticism and the Church Fathers 319

the quotations have been assimilated in later MSS to the Traditional Text, whereas in the earlier they agree rather with the "Neutral" or "Western" witnesses. For this defect, however, Mr Miller cannot be held responsible. The critical editions of the Greek and Latin Fathers, now in course of production by the Academies of Berlin and Vienna, had covered very little of the ground at the time when his materials were compiled, and meanwhile he might legitimately use the materials accessible to him; and the errors arising from this source would hardly affect the general result to any very serious extent. *(Handbook to the Textual Criticism of the New Testament 2nd ed.* Grand Rapids: Eerdmans, 1951, pp. 322-3; Cited in, *The Identity of the New Testament Text,* by Wilbur Pickering, Nashville: Thomas Nelson, 1980, pp. 68,69).

Here, the director of the British Museum Library says that if <u>critical editions existed</u> they "would show that in many cases the quotations have been assimilated". But "errors arising from this source would hardly affect the general result"!! This is a contradiction! But It is also an admission from an astute scholar that in 1936 no critical editions existed which would overturn the conclusions of Burgon and Miller, and, if and when they do become available they "would hardly affect" the general result.

The statement reveals further a kind of "hoped for deliverance" in these new editions. The reason is obvious: if a substantial number of early patristic quotations are shown to support the Received Text, then with this one stroke the entire theory to which Textual Criticism is committed collapses. For Kenyon, the "deliverance" never came; later editions of his works (which he prefaced) allow the statement to stand.

The Berlin and Vienna editions to which he referred, as well as others, did not alter the picture presented by Burgon.

We repeat what Edward F. Hills said about this:

> In regard to my references to the Church Fathers, I am sure that if you examine the notes to my KING JAMES DEFENDED and my BELIEVING BIBLE STUDY you will see that I have taken care to look up all of Burgon's references in the most modern editions available. During the years 1950-55 I spent many weeks at this task. ..Whether Pickering looked up all Burgon's references or not, I do not know. At any rate, Fee's rebuttal is a very ancient one, rather out of date, namely, the attempt to invalidate Burgon's patristic references by alleging that the editions of the Church Fathers which he used were old and out of date. Fair-minded naturalistic scholars, however, like Rendel Harris (1909), have

recognized that Burgon's arguments cannot be so easily disposed of. In fact, the newer German editions of the Church Fathers differ little from those of the 17th and 18th centuries. Certainly not enough to affect Burgon's arguments. (Letter from Edward F. Hills to Theodore P. Letis, February 15, 1980, as quoted in Theodore P. Letis, *Edward Freer Hills Contribution to the Revival of the Ecclesiastical Text*).

The works to which Hills and Kenyon refer are given the abbreviations *Berlin* for the Greek Fathers and *Vienna* for the Latin. Their full titles are: *Die Griechischen Christlichen Schriftsteller, Preussisch. Akademie der Wissenschaften, (Berlin). Corpus Scriptorum Ecciesiasticorum Latinorum, Academia Litterarum Vindobonensis. (Vienna)*. These are described further below.

BRUCE METZGER

The second edition (1968) of Bruce Metzger's widely used manual *The Text of the New Testament*, while having a section dealing with the Fathers, offers no advice on critical editions. However, his statements on variants in the Fathers does betray the subjective approach:

> When the manuscripts of a Father differ in a given passage, it is usually safest to adopt the one which diverges from...the Textus Receptus... (p. 87).

In 1971, Metzger admitted in as many words that the "good critical edition" still is not generally available:

> There are difficulties, first of all, in obtaining the evidence, not only because of the labour of combing through the very extensive literary remains of the Fathers in search of quotations from the New Testament, but also because satisfactory editions of the works of many of the Fathers have not yet been produced. ("Patristic Evidence and the Textual Criticism of the New Testament," *New Testament Tools and Studies,* Leiden: E. J. Brill, 1980, p.167).

Metzger's admission should be compared with his description of the vast amounts of patristic labor performed over the previous seventy years.
...reference may also be made to indexes of biblical citations in the writings of the Fathers. During the past century Dean J. W .Burgon, that doughty defender of the Textus Receptus, combed through

Chapter One--Textual Criticism and the Church Fathers 321

many Greek and Latin folios of the Fathers, marking New Testament quotations in the margins. Then Burgon's assistants extracted the passages (some 86,439 quotations!), arranged them in scriptural sequence, and placed them in sixteen huge scrapbooks, which today are in the British Museum.

...For the past several generations the well-known Vetus Latina Institut at Beuron has been gathering citations of the pre-Hieronymian [Jerome] Latin text of both Old and New Testaments. Planned by Pfarrer Josef Denk and developed by Pater Alban Dold, today the project is under the capable direction of P. Bonifatius Fischer. The files. . .contain cards bearing citations of almost one million patristic quotations, arranged in scriptural sequence. During the past two decades several volumes of apparatus for selected Old and New Testament books have been coming from the press with gratifying regularity.

For the past score or more of years ... the American Committee of the International Greek New Testament Project has collected the Gospel citations made by all of the Greek Fathers through the fifth century. Thus far for the Gospel of Luke there are about 8,500 cards, each containing a verse or a portion of a verse cited by a Father.

... the microcard file being assembled by the Centre of Patristic Analysis and Documentation.., of the Faculty of Protestant Theology of Strasbourg.. .there are already (as of 1970) about 40,000 microcards from 112 works, chiefly of the first three centuries. The microcard consists of a photograph of the page of the patristic text on which the citation or allusion is found. (p. 171, 2).

With such an astounding amount of material it seems incredible for Metzger to say that "satisfactory editions of the works of many of the Fathers have not yet been produced". What does he really want?! *Read the following carefully*!

The work of assembling files of patristic evidence, however necessary in itself, is merely a preliminary stage in ascertaining the form or forms of biblical text current in the patristic period. Instead of a bare collection of patristic quotations ... what is of far greater help to the textual critic is the *reconstruction* of the New Testament text (or texts) used by an individual Father. (p. 172, emphasis mine).

Notice he says *reconstruction,* and not "construction". What else could he mean but that the great mass of gathered material as it now stands is not favorable to his kind of text, and must therefore be *reconstructed*!

Yes, the further we go, the more illusive Fee's "good critical edition" becomes! It should be noted that Metzger does not even mention the Berlin and Vienna editions Frederic Kenyon staked so much upon.

KURT ALAND

The late Kurt Aland was this generation's acknowledged leader in Textual Criticism. His *Institute for New Testament Textual Research* has on film most of the extant Greek manuscripts, and it is his influence that has led to the acceptance of a unified text (he calls it the "Standard Text") in the two popular editions of this critical Greek New Testament - The Nestle Aland 26th ed., and the United Bible Societies 3rd ed.

In 1983 a *Corrected* Third Edition was published. The preface informs us:

> In view of the fact that the 26th Edition of the Nestle-Aland text... has had the advantage of fresh collations of manuscript evidence, the citations of evidence in the apparatus of the. . .Third Edition have been corrected by members of the Institut. . .This has been done in order to conform to the Nestle—Aland 26th Edition at those points in which the two types of apparatuses might differ. (p.x).

However, these "corrections" do not extend to patristic citations:

> Evidence for the citation of the Church Fathers has been taken almost wholly from printed editions of the Greek New Testament and has not yet been checked. (p. xxxvi).

Previously our *12th Summary, The Early Church Fathers to Chrysostom,* has shown that by noting all places in the *UBS-3* apparatus where the Byzantine Text opposed Aleph-B, the pre-400 AD Fathers voted for the Byzantine Text by a 968-733 margin. There, concern was expressed that *selective citation* had prevented a more favorable margin going to the Traditional Text. Here, though, we are about to see a demonstration on a more level playing field.

Coming now to the Preface of the *Nestle-Aland 26th ed.,* for virtually the first time in our "search" we are told:

Chapter One--Textual Criticism and the Church Fathers 323

> All the material from the writings of the Fathers in the following list has been cited from modern editions. This was not true of earlier editions [of the Greek N.T.]. (p.61*).

This is an impressive statement, and even more so when we discover that a total of 73 names and works are on Aland's list (43 from before 400 AD) But nowhere in the NA-26 does Aland give a bibliography listing these editions. He does mention a new "Paris" edition, and then gives the kind of "turn around" statement we are becoming familiar with in this inquiry.

> The Biblia patristica now being published places us in a far better position than earlier generations because it records the Biblical quotations and allusions in greater detail than any previous publication On critical analysis, however, many of these quotations (especially from the early period) are irrelevant for the textual critic. (p. 61*).

By now you probably know the reason why they are *irrelevant*! Aland then goes on to say:

> The information given in the apparatus on the Church Fathers and early Christian writers is based on a rigorous screening process. Their number could easily have been increased, but what would have been gained by adducing greater numerical support, for example, for the majority text. [!!] (p. 61*).

Again, what else can Aland be saying, but that there is substantial support in the early Fathers for the Traditional Text (and that from the modern editions!), but to this support "rigorous screening" must be applied. A survey of the NA-26 apparatus will show just how "rigorous" the "screening" has been. In comparison to the other kinds of material cited, *there is hardly any patristic citation*! Only the barest smattering! Perhaps this explains why the UBS-3 *Corrected Edition* did not alter its own citations of the Fathers to conform with NA-26.

In 1987 Aland's long awaited *The Text of the New Testament* was published in English. But, apart from a brief mention of *Vetus Latina*, nothing further is said about modern patristic editions.

> The quotations that have been most thoroughly investigated are those of the Latin Church Fathers, represented in volumes of the Vetus Latina which have appeared to date, edited by the Archabbey of Beuron. *(The Text of* the *New Testament,* p.211).

In 1989, Aland's article *The Text of the Church* appeared in English. Here he indicates that there will be a considerable trimming of the patristic citations in the next UBS edition (UBS-4). His statement is remarkable for what it *does not* say about patristic editions (old or modern). Unreliability is said to be due to other factors:

> The evidence of these quotations is frequently unreliable because allusions and paraphrases are often cited as direct quotations. but we are in the fortunate position of having reliable statistics at hand. At the Institute. . .we have been working for several years on the preparation of a fully revised Fourth Edition of *The Greek New Testament* with special concern for the patristic citations in its critical apparatus (so that in the future only demonstrably accurate data will be given there). *(Trinity Journal,* 8NS, 1987?, p.139).

Aland gives statistics for nineteen Fathers. I found the presentation very confusing, and actually seems designed to obscure support for the Traditional Text. Ever keep in mind that to the textual critic early patristic citations can only be said to be *reliable* if they support the Aleph-B kind of text.

From another standpoint, this *Text of the Church* article is a "watershed" in the entire textual debate. Here Aland admits things were so bad in Egypt and Alexandria, that Aleph, B, and even the papyri must have had their origin somewhere else! Aland, in this bewildering turn around, is actually telling us that the "Alexandrian" Text did not really come from Alexandria!! Students of the debate have long known that Alexandria was the worst place on earth to get a Bible. Now, even Kurt Aland agrees, though it virtually leaves his favorite manuscripts as "appearing out of nowhere". (see his p.138). I am not aware of others following him in this.

THE INTERNATIONAL GREEK NEW TESTAMENT PROJECT (IGNTP)

This ambitious project from liberal scholarship (with funding from the Rockefeller Foundation!) has completed volumes on Luke and John, and contains an extensive apparatus.

Regarding their sources for the Fathers, we are told:

> The Greek Patristic evidence is derived from systematic searches through the latest critical editions available. *(The New Testament in Greek, The Gospel According to St. Luke.* Oxford: Clarendon Press, 1983, Part One, p. vi).

Chapter One--Textual Criticism and the Church Fathers 325

Again, we are not told which editions were used for the Greek-speaking Fathers. We have information about all the other lines of evidence cited in the apparatus, but for this main branch of patristic evidence we are directed elsewhere! In order to interpret the abbreviations used in the apparatus for the Greek Fathers and their editions, we are directed to *A Patristic Greek Lexicon* by G.W.H. Lampe (1961-68); and for the Latin Fathers, to *Vetus Latina*. This doesn't make it very easy, and means that we must first draw from the apparatus and then go to these other sources in order to find which "latest critical editions" were used.

The following line from the executive director of the project betrays a familiar ring, and makes us wonder further about the editions they consulted:

> It may well be that as more, recent, and better editions of the Fathers are published. . . (J.K.Elliott, "The International Project to Establish A Critical Apparatus to Luke's Gospel,"New *Testament Studies,* No. 29, p.536).

In fact, a survey of the apparatus shows that J. P. Migne's *Patrologiae Cursus Completus* is probably cited more frequently than any of the modern editions! Migne was used by Burgon; now, nearly a century later, the IGNTP must also depend upon it. Perhaps there was a wish to avoid advertising this fact in the Introduction.

M. J. Suggs, who became Chairman of the Committee on Patristic Quotations for IGNTP (1963-71) expresses the usual bias against the Traditional Text, but lets slip an important admission:

> It is greatly to the advantage of present-day scholars that their studies may be based upon critical texts of many of the most important patristic works. This <u>sometimes</u> results in a direct reversal of Tischendorf's evidence. The service rendered Biblical scholarship by the Berlin Academy's monumental editions of Die griechischen christlichen.. . (GCS) is, therefore, incalculable. For sources that are available only in the less critical printings of Mai and Migne, it is doubtful whether any single reading may be cited with certainty; on the other hand, all the non—Byzantine variants found in such a source may present a fairly accurate picture of the Fathers text. (emphasis mine, "The Use of Patristic Evidence in the Search for a Primitive New Testament," *New Testament Studies,* Jan. 1958, p.141).

Tischendorf, like Burgon, made extensive use of Migne's edition, yet only "sometimes" do the modern editions indicate a reversal of evidence. Obviously it is not "most of the time" nor "many times" or Suggs would have quickly said so. Actually Suggs is forced to agree with the statement we saw earlier by Edward Hills that the newer editions "differ little" from the earlier ones. His statement shows that it is by presupposition rather than factual evidence that the Traditional Text is "ruled out of court."

GORDON FEE

This Professor from Gordon-Conwell Theological Seminary, and successor to M.J. Suggs as Chairman of the Patristic Committee for the IGNTP has been a leading voice against the renewed support for the Traditional Text. At the beginning of this chapter I cited his statement against the standard editions of the Fathers. But, as with Kenyon, Metzger, Aland, and IGNTP, Fee does not clearly point us to the kind and amount of evidence necessary to overturn the advantage the Traditional Text enjoys in the standard editions.

Typically, much is made of a little:

> It is lucidly illustrated by the discovery at Turat publication of several OT commentaries of Didymus the Blind. (Gordon D. Fee, "Modern Textual Criticism and the Revival of the Textus Receptus," *Journal of the Evangelical Theological Society*, No. 21, 1978, p.27).

Fee gave this *one* example in the article quoted by Wallace at the beginning of this section to support his contention that "a good critical edition or the discovery of early MSS always moves the Fathers text of the NT away from the TR". But a fifty year old discovery of *Old* Testament commentary portions is simply not "lucid" enough. It will take a great deal more than this.

Further, as one looks at Gordon Fee's articles, it becomes clear that he is concentrating his energies on "keeping the Traditional Text out of Egypt". The reason is clear: if a strong case cannot be made for the Aleph-B Text on its own home ground, then where can it find support? If Alexandrian Fathers give substantial notice to the TR, then at this "last ditch" Fee finds himself in real trouble. (Note that he does not feel the same about Egypt as Aland!).

Fee assures us:

> The point is that the Byzantine text simply did not exist in Egypt. (*Ibid*, p.27).
>
> I know eleven different studies on Origen alone that contradict all of Pickering's discussion. ("A Critique of W. N. Pickering's *The Identity of the N.T. Text*", *Westminister Theological Journal*, No. 41, 1978/9, p. 415, note 32).

Chapter One--Textual Criticism and the Church Fathers

By using the UBS-3 as the source, I show 27/18 support for the Traditional Text in Didymus of Alexandria, and a 115/163 disadvantage in the quotations of Origen. These figures as we saw were derived by checking all places in the apparatus where the Byzantine Text opposes Aleph-B.

Using the same criteria for other Alexandrian Fathers - Clement, Dionysius, Peter, Athanasius - the UBS-3c shows the Traditional Text to be at only a 46/66 disadvantage against Aleph-B. Thus, even in this "worst case scenario", the TR does not come off that badly. Fee will have to muster considerably more from his "good critical editions" to demonstrate that the Traditional Text was *not* substantially present in early Egypt, let alone elsewhere.

CONCLUSION

It is chiefly through the "latest critical edition" that Textual Criticism has sought to get rid of early patristic evidence for the Traditional Text. But, it has been far more rhetoric than actual demonstration. The overall picture presented in the standard editions has not been substantially altered; and, the authorities cited above give tacit acknowledgment of this. Where changes have been made in the newer editions, we need to ask to what extent an editor's proclivity to the Westcott and Hort Theory effected the change. (We should *also* ask this same question about the editions of the early versions!)

The word which best summarizes Textual Criticism's approach to the mass of patristic evidence is: *reconstruction*!

> What is of far greater help to the textual critic is the <u>reconstruction of the New Testament text used by an individual Father.</u> (emphasis mine, Metzger, *Text of N.T..* p.172).

The following pages show that the Doctrinal Text of the Authorized Version is presented very strongly in a leading edition of the early Fathers. It will take a great deal of *reconstruction* to alter this fact.

CHAPTER TWO
SOME INFLUENTIAL PATRISTIC WORKS

The available manuscripts, editions, and citations of a Father in other early works of literature, are sources that a patristic scholar goes to in preparing his edition. In comparison to the N.T., only a small number of manuscripts of a Fathers work are generally available. And, there is little indication that current editions are able to claim a significant advance in manuscript data over those of the past century.

There are three important early works, which while not being an actual collection, do frequently provide a good synopsis, and act as a kind of "fence" or corrective to later presentations.

EUSEBIUS

The idea of collecting the theological views of Christian writers began with Eusebius of Caesarea (died 339) and his *Ecclesiastical History*. In the introduction he states that he intends to report about "the number of those who in each generation were the ambassadors of the word of God" and those who were driven to an "extremity of error". He lists all writers and writings so far as he knew them, and gives quotations from most of them. Though the relative brevity of the work limits the number of Scripture quotations that can be gathered, it is a very important initial source, and contains for some authors the only known source of reference.

JEROME

The translator of the Latin Vulgate was the first to produce a history of theological literature. His *De Viris Illustribus* was written at Bethlehem in 392, and enlarges upon Eusebius' work.

> ...the work remains the basic source for the history of ancient Christian literature. For a certain number of ecclesiastical writers such as.. .Tertullian, Cyprian, Novatian, and others, it is the only source of information which we possess. Through more than a thousand years all historians of ancient Christian literature

regarded *De Viris Illustribus* as the main basis of their studies and their sole endeavor was to write continuations of this great work. (Johannes Quasten. *Patrology,* Westminister, Maryland: Christian Classics Inc., 1986, p.1).

Eusebius also dealt with the three Fathers mentioned, but Jerome gives a presentation and evaluation of their literature. Quasten lists four editions of Jerome's work, by: J.P. Migne 1844-55; C.A. Bernoulli 1895; E.C. Richardson 1896; G. Herding 1924.

GENNADIUS

One of the important early enlargements of Jerome was that of Gennadius of Marseilles in 480. To it is also given the name *DeViris Illustribus.* The four editors listed above by Quasten also compiled editions of Gennadius' work.

"A CATHOLIC ENTERPRISE"

Others over the next one thousand years were to bring out a continuation of Jerome's work; most were but a propaganda attempt to show a "lineal descent" of Romanism from the early Fathers. The work by the Benedictine, Sigebert, is an eleventh century example; another by Johannes Trithemius in 1494, gives bibliographical details of 965 writers.

While individual copies of a Father's literary works were to be had here or there, the really full collections were not undertaken until well after the Reformation, and these usually by Catholic editors. Part of the motivation for such huge publishing ventures was to influence an increasingly Protestantized Europe to read the Fathers instead of the Bible. Little did they realize that these same gatherings would be used by a later generation to defend the Received Text!

When Catholic editors, at great expense and labor, gathered and published these literary remains, it was to be discovered that not only in the Greek East but also the Latin West the Scriptures quoted pointed to the Traditional Text - certainly not the text of Alexandria. Perhaps this explains why Migne's massive set began to come into disfavor with the Roman authorities and makes us wonder about the fire which was to destroy his publishing house.

There are a number of editions which came from this period, including an influential work by French Benedictines of St. Maur. It is, however, those of Mai and Migne that need to be given special notice.

Chapter Two--Some Influential Patristic Works 331

ANGELO MAI

An Italian Jesuit (!) and teacher in their college, Angelo Mai was made prefect of the Vatican Library in 1819 and became cardinal in 1838. With credentials like these he could only be a bitterest enemy of the Reformation. Yet, within his thirty-six volumes there is a vast amount of early patristic quotation that points strongly to the Reformation Text! "Surely the wrath of man shall praise Thee", Psalms 76:10.

JACQUES PAUL MIGNE

Migne, a French Catholic, scholar, and professor, was also something of a maverick. After getting into trouble with his bishop over a book he wrote on "priestly liberty", he moved to Paris in 1833. There he established a publishing company, which, with a large staff of editors and printers, churned out enormous amounts of ecclesiastical literature. It is his *Patrologiae Cursus Completus* which to this day remains the most extensive collection of patristic material in print. It includes works from the early Fathers to writers of the Middle Ages. The Latin Series contains 221 volumes, and the Greek 167 volumes. Scripture quotations from the Latin Series as well as the Greek move strongly toward the Received Text. Therefore, with respect to the text of Scripture, if Catholicism is to defeat "the paper pope" of the Protestants, it will have to look to some other means than this!

Migne came into disfavor with the archbishop of Paris: the official reason was that "he was making too much money". In 1868 his establishment burned to the ground. And in 1874 a Vatican decree forbade any continuation of the work.

Despite many later disclaimers about not being a "critical edition", Mignes work gives a powerful demonstration that the text of the Latin West is not that much different than the hated Received Text. For centuries this fact made no difference as Rome kept the Bible from her people. If she is to undermine Europe's faith in the Reformation Bible, she must look for a different engine of war. Rome was prepared to look for such a weapon in the radical Aleph-B text, even though it meant declaring works like those massive patristic collections to be obsolete. In fact she has distanced herself so completely from *Mignes Series* that many do not realize it is a Catholic production. The most notable attempt by Catholicism to bring her patristic studies into line with the "changed state" is to be seen in two editions we have mentioned previously.

THE BERLIN AND VIENNA EDITIONS

Quasten, a Roman Catholic, writes:

> To the Academies of Vienna and Berlin falls the honor of having started two series of patristic writings that endeavour to combine philological accuracy and completeness. Both series, the Greek as well as the Latin, are still in progress of publication *(Patrology, p.14)*.

The Berlin edition of the Greek Fathers (GCS) was begun in 1897 and now comprises 41 volumes. The Vienna Latin Edition (CSE) commenced in 1866, with 70 volumes published thus far. As we saw from Hills, Kenyon, and others, neither seems to alter the overall picture.

DEAN BURGON'S INDEX

When Westcott and Hort swept Europe, and fundamentalists in America made little effort to understand the implications of the issue, John Burgon became a solitary defender of the Traditional Text in England. Much has been written about the Anglican Dean of Chichester; we have already given an account of his patristic index. The best account (must reading!) is to be found in *The Traditional Text of the Holy Gospels* by Edward Miller, Burgon's posthumous editor. This is available from *The Bible for Today*.

In 1992, I went to the then British Museum Library to see the Index. It is contained in sixteen *massive* volumes, which Burgon worked on between the years 1872-88 (the year of his death). The work is not a collection of patristic quotations, but rather an index giving the source of 86,489 quotations in other editions (mainly Migne). Each set of references, containing the chapter and verse of Scripture, followed by the volume and page where it is found in an edition, are pasted on the page in Biblical order under each Father. Burgon used color coding on the slips to indicate information about each quotation. Many colors were used, and thus any reproduction of the work would have to be in color. Quotations from 76 Fathers, covering the entire New Testament are referenced.

At the beginning of each Father there is a book by book tabulation giving the total number of quotations. I did not, however, see summaries of the times a Father quoted for or against the TR. Miller, no doubt, by interpreting and counting the colored slips, gives such a summary for the Gospels in his *Traditional Text* (pp. 99-121). These show a 3/2 margin to the TR.

Gordon Fee has disputed those findings, arguing that in quotations which had a parallel in other Gospels, Burgon could not be certain which Gospel

Chapter Two--Some Influential Patristic Works

the Father was quoting. Fee probably overstates the case, and Burgon would certainly have been careful to avoid this kind of error:

> ... having gone over the whole field a second time, and having employed all the care in either scrutiny that I could command. (p.95).

The context, previously quoted passages, and actual wording can usually determine which Gospel a Father is quoting. Nevertheless, in our own demonstration which follows, I have decided not to use many passages that have a parallel.

As for the other criticism that he used an "uncritical" edition, Burgon says:

> I have used copies of the Fathers in which the quotations were marked, chiefly those in Migne's Series, though I have also employed other editions ... But all doubtful quotations ... were discarded.
> ... Variant readings of quotations, occurring in different editions of the Fathers are found, according to my experience, much less frequently than might have been supposed. Where I saw a difference between MSS. noted in the Benedictine or other editions ... I regarded the passage as doubtful and did not enter it ... The habit of quotation of authorities from the Fathers by Tischendorf and all Textual Critics shows that they have always been taken to be in the main trustworthy. It is in order that we may be on sure ground that I have rejected many passages on both sides, and in a larger number of cases ... on the Traditional side. (pp. 96, 98).

THE ROBERTS, SCHAFF EDITIONS

By far the most respected and comprehensive work to appear in English are the combined editions known as *The Ante-Nicene Fathers* (originally, *The Ante-Nicene Christian Library*), and *A Select Library of Nicene and Post-Nicene Fathers*. The former was first published in Edinburgh (1866-72) under the editorship of Alexander Roberts and James Donaldson. An American revision, edited by A.C. Coxe, was published in 1884-86. The Nicene and Post-Nicene Series was brought out in America (1886-1900) with the intention to "complete the scheme" begun in the former. Today they are published as one set by Eerdmans and contain thirty-eight large volumes. The set has an excellent Scripture index, and all Biblical quotations and allusions can be easily found.

The fact that the set (ANPF hereafter) demonstrates a clear advantage to the Traditional Text in the writings of the early Fathers will probably disqualify it from being termed "a modern critical edition". However, after looking at it's scholarly contributors ("competent Patristic Scholars of Great Britain and the United States" - Preface to *First Series)*, its lengthy introductions, and its copious footnotes, you might be excused if you thought otherwise! While I cannot comment on the personal textual views of Roberts and Donaldson; a bias against the Received Text can be clearly seen in the introductions and footnotes of the volumes they edited. See for example - 7:423,477,517; 8:59,289. And, there can certainly be no doubt about the editor who succeeded them in the latter 28 volumes. Here we have the notorious liberal Philip Schaff: the Chairman of the American Revision Committee, the man who has done as much or more than any to establish the Aleph-B text on these shores.

ANPF seems to have many of the right credentials to be called a "modern critical edition". Yet, by using this source, I show a 2.3 to 1 advantage to the AV-Doctrinal Text against Aleph-B.

CHAPTER THREE
GUIDELINES FOR THE DEMONSTRATION

In determining whether the early Fathers voted more frequently on the side of the doctrinally full text of the AV/TR or the denuded Aleph-B Text, the following plan was followed:

1. The Test Passages were taken from among the 356 doctrinal readings cited in first section *Early Manuscripts and the Authorized Version*. These had been either removed or diminished in the NIV/NASV.

More than half of the readings were not used in the demonstration. Those omitted were:

(1) Readings from verses not indexed by ANPF. Scripture quotations from the early Fathers are very scattered and incomplete.

(2) Many of the Gospel readings that are paralleled in one or more of the other Gospels.

(3) Readings that have only the support of Aleph or B. Thus, only readings in which Aleph and B unite against the TR are presented. In the instances where B was not extant, one of the other early uncials must support Aleph if the passage is to be used. Therefore the demonstration presents a clear *contest* between the TR and Aleph-B.

(4) A few readings that were likely to tend toward ambiguity in a Fathers quotation were not used.

After these constraints, the number of doctrinal passages checked for patristic support was 149.

2. Only Fathers who died before 400 AD are cited. Therefore, several voluminous writers who died shortly after, as Augustine, Chrysostom, and Jerome, were not used.

3. Methods used to cite ANPF in the Digest:

(1) All references in the Scripture Indices of ANPF to pre-400 AD Fathers were checked for each of the 149 Test Passages. Many were found to be allusions and not distinct enough to be used.

(2) If only the reference is given in the Digest, it is to be assumed that the quotation is reasonably explicit. If it is less than explicit, it is written out. Quotations that differ from both the TR and Aleph-B are sometimes placed below the line and are not included in the totals. Additional information is also placed there.

(3) The Father, his work, and source in ANPF are given in each reference. Thus:

Irenaeus, Against Heresies (I 1:497)
Ambrose, Duties of Clergy (III 10:39)

(4) *I*, refers to the Roberts-Donaldson volumes, and, *III*, to the *Second Series* of the Schaff volumes. *II*, is not referenced, as Schaff's *First Series* contains the material of prominent Fathers who died shortly after 400. The Roman numeral is followed by the volume and page number in ANPF.

(5) An asterisk (*) indicates that the Scripture quotation ends at the place where the disputed words would appear. Thus, though credited to the Aleph-B side in the totals, it is not completely certain that the words in question were missing from the Biblical text the Father was quoting. These occurrences are always written out. In the following example, "even Christ" appears after "Master" in the TR. Did Cyprian cut the quotation short before talking about something else, or were the words missing from his text?

*Cyprian, Treatises (I 5:534) " 'For one is your Master.' Also in the Gospel..."

Even in the places where words are missing within, rather than at the end of a Scripture quotation, it is not unreasonable to question whether the Father failed to quote the passage fully or whether it was missing from the source he quoted. But, in all such cases, the Aleph-B side is given the benefit of any doubt in the totals.

(6) Quotations are listed in chronological order.

(7) The reader is referred to ANPF for information about the sources used in the presentation of a Fathers work.

4. Methods used in giving the totals for the Summary:

(1) The summaries show the number of times a Father votes for the TR or Aleph-B readings in the 149 Test Passages.

(2) Individual works are cited in the summaries. But only one quotation per work, per verse, is counted. Thus, Hilary, in his work on the Trinity, quotes John 1:18 "the only begotten Son" four times, but he is counted only once. If he quotes the words in other works, they would be counted. On occasion a Father from the same work will quote both the TR and Aleph-B reading. Ireneus in *Against Heresies* has both "only begotten Son" and "only begotten

Chapter Three--Guidelines for the Demonstration 337

God". Here a vote would be given to both sides. In one or two instances two votes are allowed from the same work if the quotation is significantly different. Thus, Irenaeus has "only begotten Son" and "only begotten Son of God". But, this occurrence in the Digest and Summary is rare.

(3) Only those works which were found to quote a Test Passage are listed in the Summary.

CHAPTER FOUR
THE SUMMARY, WITH
BIOGRAPHICAL SKETCHES

We are always thankful for wherever Biblical faith and fidelity to God's Word is to be found. Certainly these could be seen in some of the Fathers. But generally *even* the early Fathers give us a graphic fulfillment of Matthew Thirteen, and of Galatians 1:6.

> I marvel that ye are so soon removed from him that called you into the grace of Christ unto another gospel.

And, *How is the gold become dim! How is the most fine gold changed!* Lam. 4:1. Here we discover that many of the so-called "orthodox" Fathers were only orthodox in the sense that they held basically sound views on the Godhead. But, by bringing water and the wafer into the plan of salvation they were heretical (a term often reserved for believers who opposed Rome).

In looking at a Father, two questions need to be asked: To what extent *were they influenced* by Alexandria and Origen; and to what ends *did they influence* the emerging Papal system.

The following pages list alphabetically the pre-400 AD Fathers cited in the Digest, and show the number of times their works support the TR or Aleph-B Texts:

Alexander, Alexandria (273—328)

The Bishop of Alexandria from 313, he was an active opponent of Arianism and excommunicated its leader Anus who had been one of his own presbyters. With the energetic support of his deacon and successor, Athanasius, Alexander took a leading part at the Council of Nicea (325).

1 quotation is cited in the Digest

	TR	Aleph-B
Epistles on the Arian Heresy	1	0

Ambrose, Milan (339-97)

A lawyer and governor, he became bishop of Milan in 374. He was known for his preaching, and defense against Arianism, and is given partial credit for the conversion of Augustine (386), who greatly revered him. Knowledge of Greek enabled him to introduce a much of the Eastern theology into the Latin West. Ambrose, though a strong defender of morality and certain main aspects of the Faith, did much to establish Rome as the "universal" ecclesiastical power.

31 Quotations from 8 works are cited in the Digest

	TR	Aleph-B
Duties of Clergy	0	1
On the Holy Spirit	2	6 (2*)
On Belief in the Resurrection	0	3
On the Christian Faith	6	3
On the Mysteries	1	1
On Repentance	4	0
Concerning Widows	0	1
Letters	3	0
TOTALS	16	15 (2*)

Aphrahat, Syria (died 367)

Referred to as the "first" of the Syriac Church Fathers, and the "Persian Sage", he evidently held an important ecclesiastical office in the East. His writings, while basically orthodox, put great stress on asceticism and especially celibacy.

1 quotation is cited in the Digest		
Demonstrations	1	0

Athanasius, Alexandria (296-373)

After receiving theological training in Alexandria's Catechetical School (!), Athanasius became deacon and secretary to the Bishop, Alexander. He stood with Alexander against Arianism at the Council of Nicea (325), and succeeded him in 328. He is famous for a lifelong defense of the full deity and perfect manhood of Christ, as well as the deity of the Holy Spirit. In other areas he was not so sound: he aided the ascetic movement in Egypt, and was the first to introduce the knowledge of monasticism to the West.

31 quotations from 9 works are cited in the Digest		
	TR	**Aleph-B**
Defense of the Nicene Council (De Decretis)	3	1
Defense (Opinion) of Dionysius	1	0
Life of Antony	1	0
To the Bishops of Africa	1	0
Defense of His Flight (De Fuga)	1	0
Against the Arians	7	7 (1*)
On the Council of Ariminum and Selucia (De Synodius)	1	0
Letters	1	6 (1*)
Excluded Letters	0	1
TOTALS	16	15 (2*)

Athenagoras, Athens (work written 177)

Is described as "the Christian Philosopher of Athens". Athenagoras wrote to Marcus Arelius in behalf of Christians that had suffered more under his rule than any emperor since Nero. As a writer he was one of the ablest of the Apologists, and is the first we know of to have written an elaborate defense of the Trinity.

1 quotation is cited in the Digest		
	TR	**Aleph-B**
A Plea for the Christians	1	0

Basil the Great, Cappadocia in Asia Minor (330-379)

One of the "Cappadocian Fathers", he was the brother of Gregory of Nyssa and close friend to Gregory of Nazianzus. He became Bishop of Caesarea in Cappadocia (370) and fought against the Arian party led by one Eunomius. He also contended with the "Pneumatomachi", a group that denied the deity of the Holy Spirit. Over issues of polity, Basil was in conflict with the Bishops of Rome (Damasus), and Alexandria (Athanasius). He was suspected by some of Apollinarianism because of his correspondence with Apollinarius, and his stress upon the unity of the Person of Christ rather than the separateness of His two natures.

13 quotations from 4 works are cited in the Digest		
The Spirit	3	4
The Hexaemeron	0	1*
The Letters	3	1
On Colossians 1:15	1	0
TOTALS	7	6 (1*)

Chapter Four--The Summary, with Biographical Sketches 343

Clement, Alexandria, (150-215)

He was probably an Athenian by birth, who, after studying Christianity and philosophy in several places, became a pupil of Pantaenus, the head of the Catechetical School of Alexandria, whom he succeeded in 190. Clement revered Pantaenus as the "deepest Gnostic", and that system along with Greek philosophy colored his theology. For Clement, Christ came not so much to die a substitutionary death for sinners but to give a supreme revelation, that through Him men might partake of immortality. In this, the "sacraments" of baptism and the Lord's Supper play a chief part. Clement further believed in a kind of universal salvation, and eventual blessedness for even the most erring. A literal hell was not part of his theology.

15 quotations from 3 works are cited in the Digest		
	TR	**Aleph-B**
The Instructor	1	1
The Stromata, or Miscellanies	3	9
Fragments	1	0
TOTALS	5	10

Cyprian, Carthage in North Africa (200-258)

An ardent disciple of Tertullian (though not attaining to his stature), Cyprian became Bishop of Carthage so soon after his conversion that it was the cause of much dissatisfaction among the other clerics. Though a man of great personal sanctity, and having a genuine pastor's heart, it is Cyprian who did more than any other in that day to exalt the supremacy of the Roman Church as the "Cathedra Petri". He also furthered Tertullian's views on the saving efficacy of baptism.

32 quotations from 3 works are cited in the Digest		
The Epistles	7	1

	The Treatises	10	11 (2*)
Carthage	The Seventh Council of	1	1
	TOTALS	18	14 (2*)

Cyril, Jerusalem (315-386)

He became Bishop of Jerusalem from about 349. Though a strong opponent of Arianism, he was suspected of weakening somewhat. Accordingly, the Council of Antioch in 379 sent Gregory of Nyssa to report on the situation. He brought back word that while the life of the Jerusalem Church was morally corrupt and full of factions, "its faith was sound". Like many Fathers who seemed to be sound on the Godhead, Cyril promoted error in other areas. He stressed the "real presence" in the communion elements, and the saving efficacy of baptism.

14 quotations are cited in the Digest

	TR	**Aleph-B**
Catechetical Lectures	11	3

Dionysius the Great, Alexandria (200-264)

A pupil of Origen, Dionysius became head of the Catechetical School from about 233, and Bishop of Alexandria from 247. His orthodoxy was defended by Athanasius, but rejected by Basil of Cappadocia. He denied that the Apostle John wrote the Fourth Gospel and Book of Revelation.

1 quotation is cited in the Digest

The Promises	1	0

Chapter Four--The Summary, with Biographical Sketches 345

Ephraem Syrus, Syria (306-373)

A Biblical writer from Nisibis in Syria, who after it's cession to Persia, withdrew to Edessa where most of his extant works were written. He refuted the Arians, and the heretical teachers, Marcion and Manes. The doctrine of Last Things was stressed in Ephraem's works, and , as he usually wrote in verse, his writings had a great influence on early hymnology. Catholicism has claimed that he was favorable to prayers to saints and the immaculate conception of Mary, but this is more likely an example of their re-writing history than to fact.

1 quotation is cited in the Digest

Three Homilies	0	1

Eusebius, Caesarea (2606339)

Eusebius was Bishop of Caesarea, and the author of *Ecclesiastical History* which won for him the renown, "Father of Church History". He was a pupil of the scholar Pamphilus, who trained him in the tradition of Origen. During the Arian controversy he was the leader of the "moderate" party, and at the Council of Nicea where he seems to have been on trial for orthodoxy he proposed a compromise to the Nicene Creed. In his writings on the O.T. passages of prophecy, the Psalms and Isaiah, he displays Origen's allegorical methods. Eusebius quoted Papias (died 160) in an attempt to show that the Apostle John did not write Revelation, thus to him the book was not of apostolic authority. In his *Life of Constantine* he gives an account of being commissioned by the Emperor to provide fifty copies of the Scriptures for the churches of Constantinople.

3 quotations are cited in the Digest		
	TR	Aleph-B
Ecclesiastical History	1	2*

Gregory, Nazianzen in Cappadocia (329-390)

Known as "the Theologian", and one of the Cappadocian Fathers, Gregory's preaching led to the restoration of the Nicene faith at the Council of Constantinople in 381. The Council appointed him as Bishop of Constantinople, but he resigned shortly after. On the negative side, he built upon the writings of Origen in his *Theological Orations,* and with Basil the Great and Gregory of Nyssa sought to "save the reputation of Origen for orthodoxy".

9 quotations are cited in the Digest		
Select Orations	7	2

Gregory, Nyssa in Cappadocia (330-394)

Another of the Cappadocian Fathers, and younger brother of Basil the Great, who like many of his contemporaries was favorable to monasticism. He supported the Nicene Creed, yet was also strongly influenced by Origen, and we find in his writings "the mystical sense of Scripture". Worse, his eschatology was that of Origen! He held that ultimately both the souls in hell and the demons will return to God.

7 quotations from 2 works are cited in the Digest		
	TR	Aleph-B
Against Eunomius	4	1
On the Baptism of Christ	2	0
TOTALS	6	1

Gregory-Thaumaturgus, Pontus in Asia Minor (213-270)

Another instance of an early Father who fell under the spell of Origen. In 233 this Gregory was "converted" under Origen at Caesarea in Israel, and became his disciple for the next five years. Soon after his return to his native Pontus, he was made it's bishop. Virtually his entire teaching ministry was based upon Origen. Long after his death a number of miracles and legends were attributed to him, and he was surnamed "Thaumaturgus" or wonder-worker.

Chapter Four--The Summary, with Biographical Sketches 347

2 quotations from 2 works are cited in the Digest		
Canonical Epistle	0	1
Twelve Topics on the Faith	1	0
TOTALS	1	1

Hilary, Potiers in France (315—367)

Called the "Athanasius of the West" and "the leading and most respected Latin theologian of his age", he bears the familiar enigma: a foe of Arianism, a friend of Origen. His commentaries on Matthew and Psalms closely follow Origen. Hillary, like liberals today, stressed the Incarnation rather than the Cross as the means of mans reconciliation to God. He was elected Bishop of Potiers in 353.

15 quotations from 1 work are cited in the Digest		

	TR	Aleph-B
On the Trinity (De Trinitate)	8	7 (1*)

Hippolytus, Rome (170—235)

Considered the most important third century theologian of the Roman Church. His best known work is *The Refutation of All Heresies,* yet, as stated in *The Oxford Dictionary of the Christian Church,* he seems not to have taken his own medicine:

> "Whether this Logos is really a Divine Person remains vague; Hippolytus seems to regard Him rather as an instrument of creation whose personality is completed only in the Incarnation when He receives the title of Son..." And further, "his defective teaching on the Holy Ghost, to whom he refuses the title of 'Person'".

Hippolytus seems to have been influenced by Origen's visit to Rome in 212.

6 quotations are cited in the Digest

The Refutation of All Heresies	6	0

Ignatius, Antioch (35-110)

A leader of the church in Antioch, from which center came the early missionary movement, the Received Text, and the literal interpretation of Scripture - all in marked contrast to Alexandria. Nothing is known of Ignatius' life beyond his journey to martyrdom from Antioch to Rome under a guard of ten soldiers. He was allowed to stay for a while en route with Polycarp at Smyrna from where he wrote four letters, and then at Troas he wrote three further letters. At last, reaching Rome, he was put to death under Trajan (according to tradition, in the Colosseum). His letters display a sound view of the Deity and Humanity of Christ, but place an unscriptural stress upon the office of bishop, and speaks of a "real presence" in the communion elements. Though he speaks of the special importance of the church of Rome, he makes no reference to its bishop. Because of the emphasis on church hierarchy, Protestant scholars have long suspected the authenticity of the seven epistles, or at least of their present form.

3 quotations from 2 works are cited in the Digest

	TR	**Aleph-B**
Epistle to the Ephesians	2	0
Epistle to the Magnesians	1	0
TOTALS	3	0

Irenaeus, Lyons (130-202)

As a boy he heard Polycarp at Smyrna, he studied at Rome, and later became Bishop of Lyons. His statements that "Mark wrote from the mouth of Peter," and "Peter preached at Rome" helped forward the cause of the emerging Catholicism. He attacked premillennialism! Irenaeus is known for his *Five Books Against Heresies* in which he shows himself a foe of Gnosticism, yet his own speculative views on the Godhead are none too sound. He comes down to us as "the first great *Catholic* theologian".

Chapter Four--The Summary, with Biographical Sketches

20 quotations from 2 works are cited in the Digest		
Five Books Against Heresies	14	5 (1*)
Fragments	1	0
TOTALS	15	5 (1*)

Justin Martyr, Palestine, Ephesus, Rome (100-165)

He was born of pagan parents in Samaria. After a long search through the pagan philosophies he embraced Christianity (c.130). For a time he taught at Ephesus, where he wrote his well-known *Disputation with Trypho the Jew* (c.135). Later he opened a Christian school at Rome, having Tatian as one of his pupils, and wrote his *First Apology* (c.155) to the Emperor. Justin was scourged and beheaded in 165, after which he was surnamed "Martyr". The obvious courage and character of the early Fathers has caused many to gloss over the serious doctrinal error they introduced, and the lasting effects of that error. It is to Justin's credit that he taught a form of premillennialism, and that baptism was to be administered only to believers. But, his views on the Godhead were tinged with Gnosticism and Platoism. He viewed Christ's death, as not so much to satisfy Divine justice, but to enlighten men and turn them from the worship of demons.

1 quotation is cited in the Digest		
	TR	Aleph-B
The First Apology	1	0

Malchion, Antioch, (Council of Antioch, 270)

A leader in the church at Antioch, and chosen to interrogate Paul of Samosata as to his heretical views on the Godhead. This latter taught that Jesus *became* the Christ. See the discussion on "ADOPTIONISM".

| 1 quotation is cited in the Digest |

| Against Paul of Samosata | 0 | 1 |

Methodius, Pottery in Asia Minor and other places (260—312)

Epiphanus (died 403) in his writings against Origen makes great use of Methodius and speaks of him as "a learned man and a most valiant defender of the truth". In contrast to many of the Fathers I have listed, Methodius is chiefly known as the antagonist of Origen and strongly attacked his views. In his work, *On the Resurrection,* he refutes Origin's notion of a spiritual resurrection, which was of course a denial of bodily resurrection. These debates became known as the Origenistic Controversies, with Pamphilus and Eusebius siding with Origen.

5 quotations from 3 works are cited in the Digest		
The Banquet of the Ten Virgins	2	1*
Concerning Free Will	1	0
Oration Concerning Simeon and Anna	1	0
TOTALS	4	1*

Novatian, Rome (210-280)

Novatian (and the group that bore his name) was opposed to readmitting to the church those who denied the faith while under persecution. When the Novatianists failed to carry their point they withdrew fellowship from the Church of Rome, a move supported by the church at Antioch and considerable elements in Asia Minor and North Africa. They were opposed in Alexandria. They are often associated with the Montanists doctrinally (except for the Montanist teaching on extra-Biblical revelation). They were pre-millennial and orthodox on the Godhead.

	TR	Aleph-B
Treatise Concerning the Trinity	2	1

3 quotations are cited in the Digest

Origen, Alexandria and Caesarea (185-254)

The most influential of the early Fathers, the successor to Clement at Alexandria's Catechetical School, a Biblical critic, exegete, and theologian, who gave rise and force to many of the errors which corrupt Christendom today. (I have listed a number of these in *Missing in Modern Bibles,* p.58). In 231 he founded a school at Caesarea and remained there until the time of his death. Ambrosius, a wealthy Gnostic purchased for Origen a vast library at Caesarea. (A. H. Newman, *Manual of Church History,* I, p.281). As Alexandria was the source of textual corruption in North Africa and the West, so Caesarea became the corruptive fountain to the East.

31 quotations from 5 works are cited in the Digest

De Principiis	2	2
To Africanus	1	0
Against Celsus	4	5 (1*)
Commentary on the Gospel of John	6	3
Commentary on the Gospel of Matthew	5	3
TOTALS	18	13 (1*)

Polycarp, Smyrna (69—156)

Irenaeus (died 202) says that Polycarp "had associations with John and with the rest of those who had seen the Lord". He seems to have been the leading Christian figure in Asia Minor during the middle of the second century and a staunch defender of the Faith. At the age of 86 he was burned to death at Smyrna. Much of our knowledge of Polycarp comes from his *Epistle to the Philippians*

> "This is eminently scriptural, almost every doctrinal expression being in the words of the New Testament. Docetism is denounced, but in the words of John (I John 4:3)....It is remarkable that though Polycarp wrote after Ignatius, nothing of a hierarchial tendency occurs in his writing." (Newman. I, p.223).

5 quotations are cited in the Digest

	TR	Aleph-B
Epistle to the Philippians	4	1

Pontius the Deacon, Carthage (3rd Century)

An otherwise unknown deacon who wrote a biography of his bishop, Cyprian (died 258).

1 quotation is cited in the Digest

The Life and Passion of Cyprian, Bishop and Martyr	1	0

Tatian, Mesopotamia and Rome (Diatessaron written c.170)

An account of Tatian and his Gospel Harmony, the *Diatessaron,* has been given in the previous section. Here we will only note those among the early Fathers who were his opponents: Irenaeus, Tertullian, Clement of Alexandria, Hippolytus and Origen. Thus, while the views of Tatian have been brought into serious question, it is important to realize that his chiefest opposers were often mired in theological and textual corruption.

77 quotations are cited in the Digest

	TR	Aleph-B
The Diatessaron (Arabic text)	66	11

Tertullian, Carthage in North Africa (160-220)

At the very forefront of the early Fathers in influence, a voluminous writer, and called "the Father of Latin Christianity". Tertullian was sound on the Godhead, and in his *Against Praxeas* he exposes the error that the Trinity was merely three different modes (Modalism). In contrast to Origen, he generally took a literal approach to Scripture. He was associated with the Montanists, and like them was premillennial, but also shared some of their views on prophetic revelation. His most damaging influence upon succeeding generations was that he followed Irenaeus in teaching episcopal succession from the apostles, and also that sins were "washed away through baptism".

44 quotations from 13 works are cited in the Digest

The Apology (Elucidations)	1	0
On Idolatry	1	0
An Answer to the Jews	2	0
The Prescription Against Heretics	1	0
The Five Books against Marcion	8	1*
On the Flesh of Christ	2	0
On the Resurrection of the Flesh	6	0
Against Praxeas	10	1
On Baptism	1	0
On Prayer	0	1
On Patience	1	0
On Monogamy	0	1
On Modesty	3	4 (1*)

| TOTALS | 36 | 8 (2*) |

Victorinus, Pettau near Lyons (Died 304)

That there was an early bias against the premillennial position can be seen in the Oxford note on Victorinus.

". . . the earliest known exegete of the Latin Church, but nearly all his works are lost, probably on account of his millenarianist tendencies which caused them to be condemned. . . Jerome finds fault with both his style and his erudition." *(Oxford Dictionary of the Christian Church).*

He was apparently martyred under Diocletion.

| 2 quotations from 2 works are cited in the Digest |

	TR	Aleph-B
On the Creation of the World	1	0
Commentary on the Apocalypse of the Blessed John	0	1
TOTALS	1	1

ANONYMOUS WORKS

The Shepherd of Hermas (c.160)

This is supposed to be a kind of *Pilgrims Progress* for the early church. Clement of Alexandria and Irenaeus said it was inspired, while Origen thought its author was the Hermas of Rom. 16:14. Many viewed it as a manual for Christian growth. Tertullian and the Montanists rejected both its inspiration and value as a "new converts course". The narrator represents himself as a slave sold by his master to a Roman lady named Rhoda. Developing a desire for her, he is granted a vision in which the same woman appears, who, after rebuking him, declares how to live the Christian life, etc. It is no Pilgrims Progress! The errors of ADOPTIONISM and baptismal regeneration are found in its pages. It is affixed to the N.T. portion of Codex Sinaiticus.

1 quotation is cited in the Digest

	TR	Aleph-B
The Shepherd of Hermas	1	0

Two Epistles Concerning Virginity (c 250)

The title further informs us that the author was "the blessed Clement, the Disciple of Peter the Apostle"; and is followed by a salutation "to the blessed brother virgins.. .and to the holy *sister* virgins". Of course, Catholic scholarship has long argued that Clement of Rome (died 100) actually wrote this propaganda for celibacy. He did not!

2 quotations are cited in the Digest

Two Epistles Concerning Virginity	2	0

A Treatise Against the Heretic Novatian (c.255)

The author, a contemporary and supporter of Cyprian, writes against those who refused to allow the *lapsed* (professing Christians who denied the Faith while under persecution) back into the Church. See "Novatian". Stay with Novatian in this dispute!

2 quotations are cited in the Digest		
A Treatise Against the Heretic Novatian	2	0

A Treatise on Re-Baptism (c.255)

Written under the same circumstance but the opposite standpoint as the above. For Cyprian, restoration to the church of a *lapsed* Christian meant their re-baptism. This treatise attacks that practice, and seems to be especially directed at Cyprian himself.

1 quotation is cited in the Digest		
	TR	**Aleph-B**
A Treatise on Re-Baptism	0	1

The Clementine Homilies (c.270?)

By the third century, Judaism had been outlawed in the Empire, and held in contempt by Gentile Christians. It occurred to some of the Ebionites (Judaizing Christians, and far worse!) to compose several works purporting to be written by Clement of Rome (died 100). Among these are the *Recognitions* and the *Homilies*. They are blasphemous fabrications, and present a wide range of error including the adoptionist heresy that Jesus became the Christ at His baptism. (Newman, *Manual of Church History*, I, p.179).

Chapter Four--The Summary, with Biographical Sketches 357

3 quotations are cited in the Digest		
The Clementine Homilies	2	1

The Apostolic Constitutions (380)

Eight books of ecclesiastical ordinances, said to be composed in Syria. Though a latter 4th Century date is usually given for this work, the *Constitutions* are a reworking of much earlier material. Books 1-6 are based on what is known as *Didascalia*, a work written in northern Syria during the earlier part of the 3rd Century. Part of the seventh book has the well-known *Didache* which goes back to about the year 120 A.D. This latter is supposed to be a manual on Church practice and conduct. The full work covers a range of topics, and has sections dealing with the Lord's return, Antichrist, and baptism by immersion ("in living water"!). While there is some value in the *Constitution* (it bears witness to John 7:53-8:11), there is an enormous amount of chaff (Arianism, etc.) of which many in the early Church were only too ready to receive. It is similar to an Egyptian/North African work known as the *Apostolical Church Order*.

7 quotations are cited in the Digest		
	TR	**Aleph-B**
The Apostolic Constitutions	7	0

FIVE APOCRYPHAL WORKS

	TR	Aleph-B
The Gospel of Pseudo-Matthew (3rd Century)	1	1
The Gospel of the Nativity of Mary (4th Century)	1	0
The History of Joseph the Carpenter (3rd Century)	1	0
The Gospel of Nicodemus (3rd Century)	3	0

The Revelation of Esdras (4th Century)	1	0
TOTALS	7	1

Chapter Four--The Summary, with Biographical Sketches 359

CHRONOLOGICAL SUMMARY

The 401 Scripture quotations cited in the Digest from a total of 86 works of early ecclesiastical literature are tabulated below:

NAME	DATE OF DEATH	TR	Aleph B
Ignatius	110	3	0
Polycarp	156	4	1
Shepherd of Hermas	c160 written	1	0
Justin Martyr	165	1	0
Tatian	170 writing	66	11
Athenagoras	177 writing	1	0
Irenaeus	202	15	5 (1*)
Clement of Alexandria	215	6	10
Tertullian	220	36	8 (2*)
Hippolytus	235	6	0
Epistles Concerning Virginity	c250 written	2	0
Origen	254	18	13
Against Novatian	c255 written	2	0
Treatise on Re-Baptism	c255 written	0	1

360 Early Manuscripts, Church Fathers, & the Authorized Version

Cyprian	258	18	14 (2*)
Pontius	c260 writing	1	0
Dionysius	264	1	0
Gregory-Thaumaturgus	270	1	1
Malchion	270	0	1
Clementine Homilies	c270? Written	2	1
Novatian	280	2	1
Pseudo-Matthew	III written	1	1
Gospel of Nicodemus	III written	3	0
Joseph the Carpenter	III written	1	0
Victorinus of Pettau	304	1	1
Methodius	312	4	1*
Alexander of Alexandria	328	1	0
Eusebius	339	1	2*
Aphrahat	367	1	0
Hilary of Potiers	367	8	7 (1*)
Ephraim Syrus	373	0	1
Athanasius	373	16	15 (2*)
Basil the Great	379	7	6 (1*)

Chapter Four--The Summary, with Biographical Sketches 361

Apostolic Constitutions	c380 written	7	0
Cyril of Jerusalem	386	11	3
Gregory of Nazianzen	390	7	2
Gregory of Nyssa	394	6	1
Ambrose	397	16	15 (2*)
Nativity of Mary	IV, written	1	0
Revelation of Esdras	IV, written	1	0
Totals		279	122 (14*)

The above demonstrates that the 2.3 to 1 majority to the Received Text is not the result of a "late rush" of 4th Century support. Evidence is equally as strong in the 2nd and 3rd Centuries.

GEOGRAPHIC SUMMARY

It is an impressive fact of Textual History that the Received Text flourished in precisely those areas most associated with the missionary travels and Epistles of the Apostle Paul (Syria, Asia Minor, Macedonia, Achaia). Yet, most of the early ecclesiastical literature available for examination is from outside this area in Alexandria (and Caesarea), North Africa, and the West - areas that have shown a greater tendency to depart from the doctrinal heart of Scripture in both text and theology. Therefore, in any comparison, the Received Text labors under something of a disadvantage. Yet, in these regions, and in the writings of Fathers who were frequently the "servants of corruption" (II Peter 2:19), the Received Text is shown to prevail

The following demonstrates that with the exception of Alexandria, early Fathers from throughout the Roman Empire voted conclusively on the side of the Doctrinal Text.

THE EAST

	TR	Aleph-B
Ignatius, Polycarp, Athenagoras, *Concerning Virginity,* Gregory-Thaumaturgus, Malchion, *Cleinentine Homilies, Gospel of Nicodemus,* Methodius, Aphrahat, Ephraim, Basil, *Apostolic Constitutions,* Cyril, Gregory of Nazianzen, Gregory of Nyssa	44	18 (2*)

Chapter Four--The Summary, with Biographical Sketches

ALEXANDRIA AND CAESAREA

Clement, Origen, Dionysius, *Joseph the Carpenter,* Alexander, Eusebius, Athanasius	44	40 (4*)

THE WEST

Shepherd of Hernias, Irenaeus, Tertullian, Hippolytus, *Against Novatian, Re-Baptism,* Cyprian, Pontius, Novatian, *Pseudo—Matthew,* Victorinus, Hilary, Ambrose, *Nativity of Mary, Revelation of Esdras*	109	53 (8*)

EAST AND WEST

Justin Martyr (one citation), Tatian	67	11
TOTALS	279	122 (14*)

CHAPTER FIVE
THE DIGEST: 149 DOCTRINAL PASSAGES
"DISTINCTLY BYZANTINE"

The early Fathers are now called to vote on 149 passages that affect the doctrinal heart of Scripture. Bear in mind that in each instance[1] the AV reading is opposed by Aleph and B. Therefore, Textual Criticism would have to admit that in nearly every instance these 149 AV readings are what they term *distinctly Byzantine*. Ponder also, that for the past one hundred years Textual criticism has told us that few, if any, of these readings are found in the writings of the early Fathers.

> The ante-Nicene fathers unambiguously cited every text type except the Byzantine. (D.A. Carson. *The King James Version Debate*. Grand Rapids: Baker Book House, 1979, p.47).

Who, indeed, is right!

AN INVITATION

When Seminary teachers as Carson undermine faith in the Standard Bible by making this kind of statement, we must ask whether they have taken the time to verify these facts! The material in this digest has been presented plainly. It can be checked. It can be compared with other editions. If any can show (using the same Fathers on the same passages) that this 2.3 to 1 advantage to the Traditional Text can be can be overturned, we will be glad to see the evidence.

The Word endures in the place where the grass withers and the flower fades - **i.e. on earth.   (Isaiah 40:8)**

---

[1] Except in the places where B is not extant, in which case Aleph must have the support of other early uncials or papyri.

149 DOCTRINAL PASSAGES

The full manuscript support for these passages can be seen in the previous Digest and *KJVMT*.

AV	NIV
MATTHEW 1:25	
And knew her not til she had brought forth her <u>firstborn</u> son	But he had no union with her until she gave birth to a son
TATIAN *Diatessaron* (I 10:45) BASIL THE GREAT *On Col. 1:15* (III 8:xii) CYRIL OF JER. *Cat. Lectures* (III 7:46)	
MATTHEW 5:22	
That whosoever is angry with his brother <u>without a cause</u> shall be in danger of the Judgment	that anyone who is angry with his brother will be subject to judgment
TATIAN *Diatessaron* (I 10:57) IRENAEUS *Against Heresies* (I 1:482) *Apostolic Constitutions* (I 7:419,460)	ORIGEN *De Principiis* (I 4:305,368) ATHANASIUS *Letter Xl* (III 4:535)

AV	NIV
MATTHEW 5:27	
Ye have heard that it was said <u>by them of old time</u>, thou shalt not commit adultery	you have heard that it was said, Do not commit adultery
IRENAEUS *Against Heresies* (I 1:477)	TATIAN, Diatessaron (I 10:57)

368 Early Manuscripts, Church Fathers, & the Authorized Version

AV	NIV
MATTHEW 5:44	
Love your enemies, <u>bless them that curse you; do good to them that hate you</u> and pray for them which despitefully use you, and persecute you	Love your enemies and pray for those who persecute you
POLYCARP *Epistle* (I 1:36) "Pray also...for those that...hate you" JUSTIN MARTYR *First Apology* (I 1:167) TATIAN *Diatessaron* (I 10:58) ATHENAGORAS *Pleas for Cstns.* (I 2:134), "bless them that curse you; pray for them that persecute you" IRENAEUS *Against Heresies* (I 1:447), "Love your enemies, and pray for those that hate you" TERTULLIAN *On Idolatry* (I 3:74), "according to the precept, not to return a curse.. but clearly to bless in the name of God" TERTULLIAN *On Patience* (I 3:711), "bless your cursers, and pray for your persecutors" GREGORY OF NYSSA *Baptism of Christ* (III 5:524)	ORIGEN *Against Celsus* (I 4:652) CYPRIAN *Treatises* (I 5:546) AMBROSE *Duties of Clergy* (III 10:39)

Lk. 6:27,28 "Love your enemies, do good to them which hate you, bless them that curse you, and pray for them which despitefully use you" ANPF indexes the above quotes to Matthew rather than Luke.

Chapter Five--The Digest: 149 "Byzantine" Doctrinal Passages

AV	NIV

MATTHEW 6:1

Take heed that ye do not your <u>alms</u> before men	Be careful not to do your <u>acts of righteousness</u> before men
TATIAN *Diatessaron* (I 10:58) ORIGEN *Matthew* (I 10:444)	

MATTHEW 6:13

but deliver us from evil: <u>for thine is the kingdom, and the power and the glory, forever. Amen</u>	but deliver us from the evil one
TATIAN *Diatessaron* (I 10:58) *Apostolic Constitutions* (I 7:379), "for Thine is the power and the glory for ever"	*Clementine Homilies* (I 8:331), " Deliver us from the evil one. And in another place..."

Lk. 11:4 "but deliver us from evil". The content indicates that it is Matthew rather than Luke that is quoted, the ANPF indices concur.

MATTHEW 6:33

But seek ye first the kingdom <u>of God</u> and his righteousness	But seek first his kingdom and his righteousness
TATIAN *Diatessaron* (I 10:59) CYPRIAN *Treatises* (I 5:478,535)	TERTULLIAN *On Prayer* (I 3:683) "Seek ye first the kingdom, and then even these shall be added"
CLEMENT OF ALEX. *The Instructor* (I 2:268), "Seek first the kingdom of heaven"	

AV	NIV

MATTHEW 12:6	
That in this place is <u>one</u> greater than the temple	(NASV) that <u>something</u> greater than the temple is here
TATIAN *Diatessaron* (I 10:55). "here is what is greater than the Temple." Note #2, "In all probability agrees with the masculine reading found in the TR." IRENAEUS *Against Heresies* (I 1:472)	

MATTHEW 13:51	
Jesus saith unto them. Have ye understood all these things? They say unto him, Yea, <u>Lord</u>	Have you understood all these things? Jesus asked. Yes, they replied
TATIAN *Diatessaron* (I 10:70)	VICTORINUS *Apocalypse* (I 7:345)

AV	NIV

MATTHEW 16:3

And in the morning, it will be foul weather today: for the sky is red and lowering. O ye hypocrites ye can discern the face of the sky; but can ye not discern the signs of the times?	Footnote: "Some early manuscripts do not have..."
TATIAN *Diatessaron* (I 10:66)	

I saw no indication in ANPF of a pre-400 AD Father joining verses 2 and 4, while omitting verse 3. The indices make no reference to verse 2; Origen makes a lone reference to verse 4 (I 10:451,452).

MATTHEW 17:20

Because of your <u>unbelief</u>: for... if ye had faith as a grain of mustard seed	Because you have <u>so little faith</u>...if you have faith as a mustard seed
TATIAN *Diatessaron* (I 10:81)	ORIGEN *Matthew* (I 10:426)

372 Early Manuscripts, Church Fathers, & the Authorized Version

AV	NIV

MATTHEW 17:21	
Howbeit this kind goeth not out but by prayer and fasting	----------
PSEUDO-CLEMENT OF ROME *Concerning Virginity* (I 8:59) ORIGEN *Matthew* (I 10:479) AMBROSE *Letters* (III 10:459)	

MK. 9:29 "This kind can come forth by nothing. but by prayer and fasting". The ANPF indexes the quotations to Matthew.

MATTHEW 18:11	
For the Son of man is come to save that which was lost	----------
TATIAN *Diatessaron* (I 10:85) TERTULLIAN *On Modesty* (I 4:83), "The Lord had come of course, to save that which 'had perished'"	

Lk 19:10 "For the son of Man is come to seek and to save that which was lost". Luke is referring to the encounter with Zacchaeus. ANPF indexes the above quotations to Matthew. While the indices give a number of references to 18:10, 18:11, 18:12, and 18:11,12: there are none to 18:10,12.

Chapter Five--The Digest: 149 "Byzantine" Doctrinal Passages

AV	NIV

MATTHEW 18:15

If thy brother shall trespass <u>against thee</u>, go and tell him his fault	Footnote: "Some manuscripts do not have..."
TATIAN *Diatessaron* (I 10:85) ORIGEN *Matthew* (I 10:492) BASIL THE GREAT *Letters* (III 8:312) AMBROSE *Letters* (III 10:441)	

LK 17:3 "if thy brother trespass against thee, rebuke him". ANPF indexes to Matthew.

MATTHEW 20:16

So the last shall be first and the first last: <u>for many be called but few chosen</u>	so the last will be first, and the first will be last
TATIAN *Diatessaron* (I 10:89) IRENAEUS *Against Heresies* (I 1:480,500) CLEMENT OF ALEX. *Stromata* (I 2:448) *Clementine Homilies* (I 8:271)	

Mt. 22:14 "For many are called, but few are chosen". The context indicates that the above were quoting 20:16, and is so indexed by ANPF.

374 Early Manuscripts, Church Fathers, & the Authorized Version

AV	NIV
MATTHEW 23:8	
But be not ye called Rabbi: for one is your Master, <u>even Christ</u>	But you are not to be called Rabbi, for you have only one Master
NOVATIAN *Trinity* (I 5:643), "And Christ is called the 'one Master'." GREGORY OF NYSSA *Against Euromius* (III 5:226)	TATIAN *Diatessaron* (I 10:105) CYPRIAN *Treatises* (I 5:534), " 'For one is your Master.' Also In the Gospel..."
MATTHEW 24:36	
But of that day and hour knoweth no man, no not the angels of heaven, but my father only.	No one knows about that day or hour. not even the angels in heaven, <u>nor the Son</u>, only the Father
TERTULLIAN *Against Praxeas* (I 3:623)	
Mk. 13:32 "neither the son, but the Father". ANPF indexes Tertullian's quotation to Matthew	

Chapter Five--The Digest: 149 "Byzantine" Doctrinal Passages

AV	NIV

MATTHEW 24:48

that evil servant shall say in his- heart, My lord delayeth <u>his coming</u>	NIV, NASV remove "his coming"
TATIAN *Diatessaron* (I 10:109) IRENAEUS *Against Heresies* (I 1:497) *Clementine Homilies* (I 8:249)	IRENAEUS *Against Heresies* (I 1:519)

LK 12:45 "that servant say in his heart, My Lord delayeth his coming". ANPF indexes to Matthew, the passage in Luke is in a different context.

MATTHEW 25:13

ye know neither the day nor the hour <u>wherein the son of man cometh</u>	you do not know the day or the hour
	TATIAN *Diatessaron* (I 10:110) *HILARY OF POTIERS *Trinity* (III 9:178) "'...day nor the hour.' When He bids them watch..." *ATHANASIUS *Against Arians* (III 4:418), "'...neither the day nor the hour.' He who said..."

Mt. 24:32 "Watch therefore: for ye know not what hour your Lord doth come". ANPF indexes to Mt. 25:13.

376 Early Manuscripts, Church Fathers, & the Authorized Version

AV	NIV

MATTHEW 25:31	
and all the holy angels with him	and all the angels with him
TATIAN *Diatessaron* (I 10:110) "all the pure angels" HIPPOLYTUS *Appendix* (I 5:252)	CYPRIAN *Treatises* (I 5:482,528,532) CYRIL OF JER. *Cat. Lectures* (III 7:111) AMBROSE *Cstn. Faith* (III 10:257)

MATTHEW 26:42	
if this cup may not pass away from me	NASV omits
TATIAN *Diatessaron* (I 10:117) HILARY OF POTIERS *Trinity* (III 9:192)	

Chapter Five--The Digest: 149 "Byzantine" Doctrinal Passages

AV	NIV

MATTHEW 27:34

they gave him <u>vinegar</u> to drink mingled with gall	There they offered him <u>wine</u> to drink, mixed with gall
TATIAN *Diatessaron* (I 10:122) "Wine and myrrh, and vinegar which had been mixed with the myrrh" *Gospel of Nicodemus* (I 8:436) *Revelation of Esdras* (I 8:572)	

MK 15:23 "And they gave him to drink wine mingled with myrrh". Thus the Aleph-B rather than the Traditional Text may have been paralleled to Mark.

MATTHEW 27:35

And, they crucified him, and parted his garments, casting lots: <u>that it might be fulfilled which was spoken by the prophet, they parted my garments among them, and upon my vesture did they cast lots</u>	When they had crucified him, they divided up his clothes by casting lots
TERTULLIAN *Ans. to the Jews* (I 3:165)	

John 19:24 "that the Scriptures might be fulfilled which saith, they parted...lots". The context of the two passages are not parallel.

AV	NIV

MATTHEW 28:6

Come, see the place where the <u>Lord</u> lay	Come and see the place where he lay
TATIAN *Diatessaron* (I 10:125)	

MK 16:6 "behold the place where they laid him". The Aleph-B text may have been paralleled to Mark, but not the Traditional.

MARK 1:2

As it is written <u>in the prophets</u>, Behold, I send my messenger before thy face	It is written <u>in Isaiah the prophet</u> I will send my messenger ahead of you
IRENAEUS *Against Heresies* (I 1:431) TERTULLIAN *Ans. to the Jews* (I 3:163)	ORIGEN *Against Celsus* (I 4:431)

The parallel accounts In Matthew and Luke quote one prophet, Isaiah. But Mark makes reference to the "prophets", because Malachi <u>and</u> Isaiah are quoted.

MARK 3:15

And to have power <u>to heal sicknesses</u> and to cast out devils	and to have authority to drive out demons
TATIAN *Diatessaron* (1 10:56)	

Chapter Five--The Digest: 149 "Byzantine" Doctrinal Passages

AV	NIV

MARK 3:29

hath never forgiveness, but is in danger of eternal <u>damnation</u>	will never be forgiven; he is guilty of an eternal <u>sin</u>
TATIAN *Diatessaron* (I 10:65), "eternal punishment"	CYPRIAN *Epistles* (I 5:290,542)

Mt. 12:32 "shall not be forgiven him, neither in this world, neither in the world to come"
LK. 12:10 "It shall not be forgiven"

MARK 9:24

<u>Lord</u>, I believe	I do believe
TATIAN *Diatessaron* (I 10:81) CYRIL OF JER. *Cat. Lectures* (III 7:31)	

MARK 9:44

<u>Where their worm dieth not and the fire is not quenched</u>	----------
TATIAN *Diatessaron* (I 10:82) GREGORY OF NAZIANZEN *Orations* (III 7:373)	

There are no indications in the ANPF indices of a pre-400 Father skipping from verse 43 to 45 in his quotation.

Early Manuscripts, Church Fathers, & the Authorized Version

AV	NIV

MARK 10:24

children how hard it is <u>for them that trust in riches</u> to enter into the kingdom of God	children, how hard it is to enter the kingdom of God
TATIAN *Diatessaron* (I 10:87)	

Mt. 19:23 "a rich man shall hardly enter into the kingdom of heaven" Lk. 18:24 "How hardly shall they that have riches enter into the Kingdom of God". The Aleph-B rather than the Traditional reading could have been paralleled here.

MARK 11:26

<u>But If you do not forgive neither will your father which is in heaven forgive your trespasses</u>	----------
TATIAN *Diatessaron* (I 10:94)	

The context is completely different from the similar statements in Mt. 6:15; 18:35. I saw no indication in ANPF of a pre-400 AD Father skipping from verses 25 to 27 with the disputed portion missing. The indices referred to verse 25 in I 5:425,454 6:161 8:481 10:512; and to verse 27 in III 10:281.

Chapter Five--The Digest: 149 "Byzantine" Doctrinal Passages

AV	NIV

MARK 15:28

And the Scripture was fulfilled which saith, And he was numbered with the transgressors	----------
TATIAN *Diatessaron* (I 10:122)	

The similar reference in Luke 22:37 is in the context of events before the Crucifixion. There are no indications in the ANPF indices of a pre-400 Father skipping from verse 27 to 29 in his quotation.

382 Early Manuscripts, Church Fathers, & the Authorized Version

AV	NIV
MARK 16:9-20	
Now when Jesus was risen........ confirming the word with signs following. Amen	Footnote: "The two most reliable early manuscripts do not have Mark 16:9-20."
TATIAN *Diatessaron* (I 10:125,126,128,129), quote in entirety IRENAEUS *Against Heresies* (I 1:426) quotes 16:19 TERTULLIAN *Resurrection of Flesh* (I 3:584) quotes 16:19 TERTULLIAN *Against Praxeas* (I 3:627), quotes 16:19 CYPRIAN *7th Council* (I 5:569), refers to 16:17,18 *Gospel of Nicodemus* (I 8:422,432,436,445), quotes 16:15-19 APHRAHAT *Demonstrations* (III 13:351), quotes 16:15-19 *Apostolic Constitutions* (1 7:457,479) quotes 1 6:16-19 AMBROSE *The Holy Spirit* (III 10:133,134) quotes 16:15-18 AMBROSE *Cstn. Faith* (III 10:216) quotes 16:15 AMBROSE *Repentance* (III 10:335) quotes 16:17,18	
There is no indication in the indexes of ANPF of a pre-400 A.D. Father quoting up to verse 8, and then stopping!	

Chapter Five--The Digest: 149 "Byzantine" Doctrinal Passages

AV	NIV

LUKE 1:28

the Lord is with thee: "<u>blessed art thou among women</u>	The Lord is with you
TATIAN *Diatessaron* (I 10:44) *Gospel of Nativity of Mary* (I 8:386), "blessed art thou above all women"	

LUKE 2:14

Glory to God in the highest and on earth peace, <u>goodwill toward men</u>	Glory to God in the highest, and on earth peace <u>to men on whom his favour rests</u>
TATIAN *Diatessaron* (I 10:46) GREGORY-THAUMATURGUS, *Twelve Topics* (I 6:52), "good will among men" METHODIUS *Simeon and Anna* (I 6:386) *Apostolic Constitutions* (I 7:478), "good will among men" GREGORY OF NAZIANZEN *Ovations* (III 7:423)	CYRIL OF JER. *Cat. Lectures* (III 7:81), "peace among men of His good pleasure" *Pseudo-Matthew* (I 8:374), "peace to men of good will"

AV	NIV

LUKE 2:22

And when the days of <u>her</u> purification according to according to the law of Moses were accomplished, they brought him to Jerusalem	When the time of <u>their</u> purification according to the Law had been completed, Joseph and Mary took him to Jerusalem
Pseudo-Matthew (I 6:375) "Now after the days of the purification of Mary were fulfilled'	TATIAN *Diatessaron* (I 10:46)

IRENAEUS *Against Heresies* (I 1:425), "And still further does Luke say in reference to the Lord: 'When the days of purification were accomplished'" HIPPOLYTUS *Fragments* (I 5:194), "When they brought Him to the temple...they offered the oblations of purification. For if the gifts of purification according to the law were offered for Him, in this indeed He was made under the law"

LUKE 2:33

And <u>Joseph</u> and his mother marvelled of those things which were spoken of him	The child's <u>father</u> and mother marveled at what was said about him
TATIAN *Diatessaron* (I 10:46)	CYRIL OF JER. *Cat. Lectures* (III 7:46)

AV	NIV

LUKE 2:40	
And the child grew, and waxed strong <u>in spirit</u>	And the child grew and became strong
TATIAN *Diatessaron* (I 10:48)	

LUKE 2:43	
The child Jesus tarried behind in Jerusalem; and <u>Joseph and his mother</u> knew not of it	While <u>his parents</u> were returning home...
TATIAN *Diatessaron* (I 10:48)	

LUKE 4:41	
And devils...saying. Thou art <u>Christ</u> the Son of God	Moreover demons... shout - you are the Son of God
TATIAN *Diatessaron* (I 10:53)	

Mk. 3:11 "Thou art the Son of God". A different context from the above.

AV	NIV

LUKE 9:55

But he turned and rebuked them, <u>and said, ye know</u> not what manner of spirit ye are of	But Jesus turned and rebuked them
TATIAN *Diatessaron* (I 10:102) CLEMENT OF ALEX. *Fragment* - not in the Oxford ed., (I 2:584) AMBROSE *Repentence* (III 10:343)	

LUKE 9:56

<u>For the Son of man is not come to destroy men's lives, but to save them.</u> And they went into another village	and they went to another village
TATIAN *Diatessaron* (I 10:102) CYRPRIAN *Epistles* (I 5:354) AMBROSE *Repentance* (III 10:343)	

LUKE 12:39

that if the goodman of the house had known what hour the thief would come, <u>he would have watched</u>	If the owner of the house had known at what hour the thief was coming
	TERTULLIAN *Against Marcion* (I 3:398)

Chapter Five--The Digest: 149 "Byzantine" Doctrinal Passages

AV	NIV

LUKE 13:25

Lord, <u>Lord</u> open to us	Sir, open the door for us
	TATIAN *Diatessaron* (I 10:91)

LUKE 14:5

Which of you shall have an <u>ass</u> or an ox fallen into a pit	if one of you has a <u>son</u> or an ox that falls into a well
	TATIAN *Diatessaron* (I 10:89)

LUKE 17:3

If thy brother trespass <u>against thee</u>, rebuke him	If your brother sins, rebuke him
CLEMENT OF ALEX. *The Instructor* (I 2:293)	TATIAN *Diatessaron* (I 10:85)

LUKE 21:36

and pray always, that ye <u>may be accounted worthy</u> to escape all these things that shall come to pass	(NASV) at all times, praying in order that you may <u>have strength</u> to escape all these things that are about to take place
TATIAN *Diatessaron* (I 10:109) TERTULLIAN *Resurrection of the Flesh* (I 3:561)	

AV	NIV

LUKE 22:68	
And if I also ask you, ye will not answer me, nor let me go	and If I asked you, you would not answer
TATIAN *Diatessaron* (I 10:119)	

LUKE 23:42	
And he said unto Jesus, Lord, remember me	Then he said, JESUS, remember me
TATIAN *Diatessaron* (I 10:123)	

LUKE 23:45	
And the sun was darkened	(NASV) the sun being obscured (lit. eclipsed)
TATIAN *Diatessaron* (I 10:123)	

LUKE 24:46	
Thus it is written, and thus it behoved Christ to suffer	This is what is written: The Christ will suffer
TATIAN *Diatessaron* (I 10:127) CYPRIAN *Treatises* (I 5:509)	

Chapter Five--The Digest: 149 "Byzantine" Doctrinal Passages

AV	NIV

LUKE 24:47	
And that repentance <u>and</u> remission of sins should be preached	(Literal) And that repentance <u>unto</u> remission of sins should be preached
Joseph the Carpenter (I 8:388)	TATIAN *Diatessaron* (I 10:127)

JOHN 1:18	
the only begotten <u>Son</u>....hath declared him	the only begotten <u>God</u>...has explained Him

IRENAEUS *Against Heresies* (I 1:427), "the only-begotten Son of God"
IRENAEUS *Against Heresies* (I 1:489), "the only-begotten Son"
TERTULLIAN *Against Praxeas* (I 3:611)
HIPPOLYTUS *Against Noetus* (I 5:225)
ORIGEN *Against Celsus* (I 4:460)
ARCHELAUS *Disputations with Manes* (1 6:205)
METHODIUS *Free Will* (I 6:356), "glorifying in the Spirit, Jesus, who is in His bosom"
ALEX. OF ALEXANDRIA *Arian Heresy* (I 6:292,297)
HILARY OF POTIERS *Trinity* (III 9:73,84,95,113)
ATHANASIUS *De Decretis* (III 4:158,164)
ATHANASIUS *Against Arians* (III 4:382,439,443)
ATHANASIUS *De Synodius* (III 4:461), "Son of God, Only-begotten"
BASIL THE GREAT *Letters* (III 8:274)
CYRIL OF JER. *Cat. Lectures* (III 7:46), "the Only-begotten alone hath declared"
GREGORY OF NAZIANZEN *Orations* (III 7:307)
AMBROSE *Cstn. Faith* (III 10:246)
AMBROSE *Letters* (III 10:437)

IRENAEUS *Against Heresies* (I 1:491), "The Only-Begotten God"
CLEMENT OF ALEX. *Stromata* (I 2:463)
ORIGEN *John* (I 10:343)
ATHANASIUS *Against the Heathen* (III 4:26)
BASIL THE GREAT *The Spirit* (III 5:9,11,18)
GREGORY OF NYSSA *Against Eunomius* (III 5:102,104,125,140)

TATIAN *Diatessaron* (I 10:49), "the only Son, God which..."
ARCHELAUS *Disputations with Manes* (I 6:182). "Only-begotten Christ"
ATHANASIUS *De Synodis* (III 4:457) "God, Only-begotten"

AV	NIV

JOHN 1:27

He it is, who coming after me <u>is preferred before me</u>	He is the one who comes after me
TATIAN *Diatessaron* (I 10:49) HIPPOLYTUS *Theophany* (I 5:235) CYPRIAN *Treatises* (I 5:524), "...is made before me"	*ORIGEN *Against Celsus* (I 4:548). " 'He it is who cometh after me.' And it is absurd, when..."

JOHN 1:51

<u>Hereafter</u> ye shall see heaven open	you shall see heaven open
TATIAN *Diatessaron* (I 10:51)	ORIGEN *Against Celsus* (I 4:417)

AV	NIV

JOHN 3:13

And no man hath ascended up to heaven, but he that came down from heaven, even the Son of man which is in heaven	No one has ever gone into heaven except the one who came from heaven — the Son of man
TATIAN *Diatessaron* (I 10:93) HIPPOLYTUS *Against Noetus* (I 5:225) NOVATIAN *The Trinity* (I 5:622) HILARY OF POTIERS *The Trinity* (III 9:186) GREGORY OF NAZIANZEN *Orations* (III 7:438)	
APHRAHAT *Demonstrations* (III 1 3:382). "...who was in heaven"	

AV	NIV

JOHN 3:15

That whosoever believeth in him <u>should not perish</u> but have eternal life	that everyone who believes in him may have eternal life
TATIAN *Diatessaron* (I 10:93)	CYPRIAN *Treatises* (I 5:524)

JOHN 4:42

and know that this is indeed <u>the Christ</u>, the Saviour of the world	and we know that this man really is the Saviour of the world
TATIAN *Diatessaron* (I 10:77)	

JOHN 5:3,4

In these lay a great multitude of impotent folk, of blind, halt, withered, <u>waiting for the moving of the</u> water, <u>for an angel.. made whole of whatsoever disease he had</u>.	Here a great number of disabled people used to lie - the blind, the lame, the paralyzed
TATIAN *Diatessaron* (I 10:77) TERTULLIAN *Baptism* (I 3:671,672) GREGORY OF NAZIANZEN *Orations* (III 7:372) AMBROSE *Mysteries* (III 10:320)	

The indexes of ANPF do not show any pre-400 AD Father quoting John 5:2,5 with the disputed portion omitted. There are no references to 5:2. There are four references in the Ante-Nicene volumes to 5:5. These are 1:393 6:395 8:419,428.

394 Early Manuscripts, Church Fathers, & the Authorized Version

AV	NIV
JOHN 5:16	
And therefore did the Jews persecute Jesus, <u>and sought to slay him</u>	so, because Jesus.. the Jews persecuted him
TATIAN *Diatessaron* (I 10:78) HILARY OF POTIERS *The Trinity* (III 9:170)	ATHANASIUS *Against the Arians* (III 4:355)
JOHN 5:17	
And <u>Jesus</u> answered them, My Father worketh hitherto, and I work	(NASV) "Jesus' is removed from this declaration of union with the Father.
TATIAN *Diatessaron* (I 10:78)	
JOHN 5:30	
the will of the <u>Father</u> which hath sent me	him who sent me
	TATIAN *Diatessaron* (I 10:78)

Chapter Five--The Digest: 149 "Byzantine" Doctrinal Passages

AV	NIV

JOHN 6:14

When they had seen the miracle that <u>Jesus</u> did	(NASV) "Jesus" is removed from immediate association with "that prophet"
TATIAN *Diatessaron* (I 10:72)	

JOHN 6:39

And this is the <u>Father's</u> will which hath sent me	And this is the will of him who sent me
	TATIAN *Diatessaron* (I 10:73) ATHANASIUS *Against Arians* (III 4:377) AMBROSE *Resurrection* (III 10:1 88)

JOHN 6:47

He that believeth <u>on me</u> hath everlasting life	I tell you the truth, he who believes has everlasting life
TATIAN *Diatessaron* (I 10:74)	

AV	NIV

JOHN 6:65	
except it were given unto him of my Father	unless the Father has enabled him
CYPRIAN *Epistles* (I 5:584)	TATIAN *Diatessaron* (I 10:74)

JOHN 6:69	
the Christ, the Son of the living God	... the Holy One of God
TATIAN *Diatessaron* (I 10:74) IRENAEUS *Against Heresies* (I 1:428), "By whom also Peter, having been taught recognized Christ as the Son of the living God" CYPRIAN *Epistles* (I 5:374) "...are sure, that thou art the Son of the living God"	

Mt. 16:16 "Thou art the Christ, The Son of the living God". The ANPF Indexes point the above quotations to John rather than Matthew

Chapter Five--The Digest: 149 "Byzantine" Doctrinal Passages

AV	NIV
JOHN 7:53-8:11	
And every man went unto his own house.....go and sin no more	Footnote: "the earliest and most reliable manuscripts do not have 7:53 - 8:11"
Apostolic Constitutions (I 7:408), refers to the account and quotes 8:11.	

Though the early fathers seem to be silent concerning this account, it is also a fact that there is no indication in ANPF of a pre-400 AD Father omitting the disputed portion by joining 7:52 directly to 8:12. There were thirteen references in the indices to the "Light of the World" passage in 8:12 (I 2:313 5:363,494,519 6:120 7:15 10:536; III 4:377,395,476 7:352 10:224 12:348), and one reference to 7:52 (III 10:234).

JOHN 8:26	
I do nothing of myself; but as <u>my</u> Father hath taught me, I speak these things	I do nothing on my own but speak just what the Father has taught me
TATIAN *Diatessaron* (I 10:98) TERTULLIAN *Against Praxeas* (I 3:617)	HILARY OF POTIERS *The Trinity* (III 9:171)

AV	NIV

JOHN 8:29	
the Father hath not left me alone	he has not left me alone
TATIAN *Diatessaron* (I 10:98)	HILARY OF POTIERS *The Trinity* (III 9:171)

JOHN 8:59	
but Jesus hid himself, and went out of the temple going through the midst of them, and so passed by	but Jesus hid himself, slipping away from the temple grounds
TATIAN *Diatessaron* (I 10:98) IRENAEUS *Fragments* (I 1:576) ATHANASIUS *De Fuga* (III 4:259) GREGORY OF NAZIANZEN *Orations* (III 7:351)	

AV	NIV

JOHN 9:4

I must work the works of him that sent me	we must do the works of him who sent me
TATIAN *Diatessaron* (I 10:99) TERTULLIAN *Against Praxeas* (I 3:618) AMBROSE *Cstn. Faith* (III 10:249)	ORIGEN *John* (I 10:311), "He says to those who partake of His light, 'work while it is day'"

JOHN 9:35

Dost thou believe on the Son of God?	do you believe In the Son of man?
TATIAN *Diatessaron* (I 1 0:99) TERTULLIAN *Against Praxeas* (I 3:618) HILARY OF POTIERS *The Trinity* (III 9:106,116)	

AV	NIV

JOHN 10:29

My Father, which gave them me, is greater than all	Footnote: "What my Father has given me is greater than all."
TATIAN *Diatessaron* (I 10:100)	HILARY OF POTIERS *The Trinity* (III 9:127) AMBROSE *The Holy Spirit* (III 10:97,151)

JOHN 10:32

Many good works have I shewed you from my Father	I have shown you many great miracles from the Father
TATIAN *Diatessaron* (I 10:100) ATHANASIUS *Against Arians* (III 4:439)	HILARY OF POTIERS *The Trinity* (III 9:128)

JOHN 13:3

Jesus knowing that the Father had given all things into his hands	Italicized NASV
TATIAN *Diatessaron* (I 10:111) TERTULLIAN *Against Praxeas* (I 3:619)	

Chapter Five--The Digest: 149 "Byzantine" Doctrinal Passages 401

AV	NIV

JOHN 13:32

AV	NIV
<u>If God be glorified in him,</u> God shall also glorify him in himself	Footnote: "Many early manuscripts do not have..."
TATIAN *Diatessaron* (1 10:112) TERTULLIAN *Against Praxes* (I 3:619), "And God, says He, 'shall also glorify Him in Himself'...because He has Him within Himself" HILARY OF POTIERS *The Trinity* (III 9:168)	

JOHN 16:10

AV	NIV
because I go to <u>my</u> Father	because I am going to the Father
TATIAN *Diatessaron* (I 10:115)	

AV	NIV

JOHN 16:16

and again, a little while and ye shall see me, <u>because I go to the Father</u>	and then after a little while you will see me
TATIAN *Diatessaron* (I 10:115)	

JOHN 17:12

While I was with them <u>in the world</u>. I kept them	While I was with them, I protected them
TATIAN *Diatessaron* (I 10:116)	HILARY OF POTIERS *The Trinity* (III 9:193)

JOHN 17:17

Sanctify them through <u>thy</u> truth	Sanctify them by the truth
TATIAN *Diatessaron* (I 10:116) ATHANASIUS *Against Arians* (III 4:404) *Apostolic Constitutions* (I 7:486)	AMBROSE *The Holy Spirit* (III 10:139)

Chapter Five--The Digest: 149 "Byzantine" Doctrinal Passages

AV	NIV

JOHN 19:26

he saith unto <u>his</u> mother, Woman, behold thy son	(Literal) he saith unto the mother, Woman, behold thy son
TATIAN *Diatessaron* (I 10:123) ORIGEN *John* (I 10:300)	

JOHN 20:17

for I am not yet ascended to <u>my</u> Father	for I have not yet returned to the Father
TATIAN *Diatessaron* (I 10:125) TERTULLIAN *Against Praxeas* (I 3:621) PSEUDO-CLEMENT OF ROME *Epistles Concerning Virginity* (I 8:65) GREGORY OF NYSSA *Against Eunomius* (III 4:240) AMBROSE *Cstn. Faith* (III 10:265)	IRENAEUS *Against Heresies* (I 1:560)

AV	NIV
ACTS 2:30	
that of the fruit of his loins, according to the flesh he would raise up Christ to sit on his throne	that he would place one of his descendants on his throne
TERTULLIAN *Flesh of Christ* (I 3:540)	
ACTS 3:20	
And he shalt send Jesus Christ which before was preached unto you	(NASV) and that He may send JESUS the Christ appointed for you
TERTULLIAN *Resurrection of Flesh* (I 3:562)	
ACTS 6:8	
And Stephen. full of faith and power	(NASV) And Stephen full of grace and power
CYRIL OF JER. *Cat. Lectures* (III 7:130)	

Chapter Five--The Digest: 149 "Byzantine" Doctrinal Passages

AV	NIV
ACTS 8:37	
And Philip said, if thou believest with all thine heart, thou mayest. And he answered and said, I believe that Jesus Christ is the Son of God	----------
IRENAEUS *Against Heresies* (I 1:433), "the believing eunuch himself.. said 'I believe Jesus Christ to be the Son of God'" CYPRIAN *Treatises* (I 5:545), "Then said Philip, If thou believest with all thine heart, thou mayest" PONTIUS *Life of Cyprian* (I 5:268), "the eunuch is described as at once baptized by Philip because he believed with his whole heart"	

I found no indication in ANPF of a pre-400 AD Father quoting the above general passage with the disputed words omitted. There were no references to verses 36 and 38 in the indices.

406 Early Manuscripts, Church Fathers, & the Authorized Version

AV	NIV
ACTS 15:11	
through the grace of the Lord Jesus Christ we shall be saved	through the grace of our Lord Jesus that we are saved
	TERTULLIAN *On Modesty* (I 4:99)
ACTS 17:30	
God...now commandeth all men everywhere to repent	(NASV) God is now declaring to men that all...should repent
ATHANASIUS *Opinion of Dionysius* (III 4:178)	
ROMANS 1:16	
For I am not ashamed of the gospel of Christ	For I am not ashamed of the gospel
TERTULLIAN *Against Marcion* (I 3:457), "I am not ashamed of the gospel (of Christ)"	HILARY OF POTIERS *The Trinity* (III 9:244) BASIL THE GREAT *Hexaemeron* (III 8:101) "'...not ashamed of the gospel,' Those who have written.."

AV	NIV

| ROMANS 10:15 ||

How beautiful are the feet of them that <u>preach the gospel of peace</u>, and bring glad tidings of good things	How beautiful are the feet of those who bring good news
IRENAEUS *Against Heresies* (I 1:436) TERTULLIAN *Against Marcion* (I 3:340)	CLEMENT OF ALEX. *Stromata* (I 2:353)

| ROMANS 14:10 ||

For we must all stand before the judgment seat <u>of Christ</u>	For we will all stand before <u>God's</u> judgment seat
POLYCARP *Epistle* (I 1:34)	

| ROMANS 15:29 ||

I shall come in the fulness of the blessing <u>of the gospel</u> of Christ	I will come in the full measure of the blessing of Christ
	CLEMENT OF ALEX. *Stromata* (I 2:459)

AV	NIV

I CORINTHIANS 5:4

AV	NIV
with the power of our Lord Jesus Christ	and the power of our Lord Jesus
	BASIL THE GREAT *The Spirit* (Ill 8:43) *AMBROSE *The Holy Spirit* (III 10:124), "'...power of the Lord Jesus,' Do we then..."

I CORINTHIANS 5:7

AV	NIV
Christ...is sacrificed <u>for us</u>	Christ...has been sacrificed
CLEMENT OF ALEX. *Stromata* (I 2:460) TERTULLIAN *Against Marcion* (I 3:443) OR1GEN *John* (I 10:388) AMBROSE *Repentance* (III 10:343)	CYPRIAN *Treatises* (I 5:434,536) ATHANASIUS *Letters* (III 4:507,512,513,520,524,531,538, 541,542,552). In most of the foregoing the quotation ends with "sacrificed".

AV	NIV

I CORINTHIANS 6:20

glorify God in your body <u>and in your spirit, which are God's</u>	honour God with your body
	*IRENAEUS *Against Heresies* (I 1:540), "'Glorify God in your body'. Now God..." *TERTULLIAN *Modesty* (I 4:91), "'glorify and extol the Lord in your body', see whether..." *CYPRIAN *Treatises* (I 5:450,500,536,551), "Glorify the Lord in your body." (end of quote) *ATHANASIUS *Letters* (III 4:520. "'Glorify God with your body'; and the prophet commands..."

TERTULLIAN *Resurrection of Flesh* (I 3:556), "'Therefore glorify and exalt God in your body' - being certain that such efforts are actuated by the soul"

AV	NIV

I CORINTHIANS 7:39

| The wife is bound <u>by the law</u> as long as her husband liveth | A woman is bound to her husband as long as he lives |
| | TERTULLIAN *Monogamy* (I 4:68)
ORIGEN *Matthew* (I 10:510)
CYPRIAN *Treatises* (I 5:550)
AMBROSE *Widows* (III 10:391) |

I CORINTHIANS 9:1

| have I not seen Jesus <u>Christ</u> our Lord | Have I not seen Jesus our Lord? |
| TERTULLIAN *Against Praxeas* (I 3:611)
TERTULLIAN *On Modesty* (I 4:88), "have not seen Christ Jesus our Lord" | |

I CORINTHIANS 9:18

| I make the gospel <u>of Christ</u> without charge | the gospel I may offer it free of charge |
| | GREGORY OF NAZIANZEN *Orations* (III 7:216), "the living by my own hands, the gospel without charge" (*sic*) |

Chapter Five--The Digest: 149 "Byzantine" Doctrinal Passages

AV	NIV

I CORINTHIANS 9:22	
To the weak became I <u>as</u> weak	to the weak I became weak
CYPRIAN *Epistles* (I 5:331) AMBROSE *Cstn. Faith* (III 10:284)	ORIGEN *John* (I 10:384) ATHANASIUS *Excluded Letters* (III 4:580)

I CORINTHIANS 11:24	
he brake it and said, <u>Take eat</u>...	he broke it and said
	CYPRIAN *Epistles* (I 5:361)

I CORINTHIANS 15:47	
The first man is of the earth earthy: the second man is <u>the Lord</u> from heaven	The first man was of the dust of the earth, the second man from heaven
TERTULLIAN *Against Marcion* (I 3:451) TERTULLIAN *Flesh of Christ* (I 3:529) HIPPOLYTUS *Fragments* (I 5:167) VICTORINUS OF PETTAU *Creation* (I 7:342) BASIL THE GREAT *The Spirit* (III 8:30)	CYPRIAN *Treatises* (I 5:436,495,520,536) HILARY OF POTIERS *The Trinity* (III 9:186) ATHANAS1US *Against the Arians* (III 4:382)

AV	NIV

II CORINTHIANS 4:10	
Always bearing about in the body the dying of <u>the Lord</u> Jesus	we always carry around in our body the death of Jesus
TERTULLIAN *Resurrection of the Flesh* (I 3:577) ORIGEN *John* (I 10:312)	IRENAEUS *Against Heresies* (I 1:540) ORIGEN *Against Celsus* (I 4:626) ORIGEN *John* (I 10:316,484) ATHANASIUS *Letters* (III 4:523,527) BASIL THE GREAT *The Spirit* (III 8:20) BASIL THE GREAT *Letters* (III 8:263)

Chapter Five--The Digest: 149 "Byzantine" Doctrinal Passages

AV	NIV

II CORINTHIANS 5:17	
old things are passed away; behold, all things are become new	the old has gone. the new has come
IGNATIUS *To the Magnesians - longer* (I 1:62) TERTULLIAN *Against Marcion* (I 3:361,456) ATHANASIUS *De Decretis* (III 4:162) ATHANASIUS *To the Bishops of Africa* (III 4:491) *Apostolic Constitutions* (I 7:458)	
METHODIUS *Simeon and Anna* (I 6:383), "'old things are passed away' - things new burst forth into flowers"	

II CORINTHIANS 11:31	
The God and Father of our Lord Jesus Christ	The God and Father of the Lord Jesus
CLEMENT OF ALEX. *Stromata* (I 2:453)	

AV	NIV
GALATIANS 4:7	
an heir of God <u>through Christ</u>	God has made you also an heir
	CLEMENT OF ALEX. *Instructor* (I 2:218) BASIL THE GREAT *The Spirit* (III 8:7) "... 'heir of God.' And like as..." AMBROSE *The Holy Spirit* (III 10:127), "an heir also through God"

AV	NIV
GALATIANS 5:19	
Now the works of the flesh are manifest, which are these; <u>Adultery</u>	The acts of the sinful nature obvious;
IRENAEUS *Against Heresies* (I 1:537) CYPRIAN *Treatises* (I 5:452,551) BASIL THE GREAT *Letters* (III 8:273)	CLEMENT OF ALEX. *Stromata* (I 2:420) TERTULLIAN *Modesty* (I 4:92), "Among the first he has set, 'fornication, impurity, lasciviousness'" ORIGEN *De Principiis* (I 4:338) CYPRIAN *7th Council* (I 5:566)
EPHESIANS 1:1	
to the saints which are at <u>Ephesus</u>	Footnote: "Some early manuscripts do not have..."
IGNATIUS *To the Ephesians- longer* (I 1:53)	

416 Early Manuscripts, Church Fathers, & the Authorized Version

AV	NIV

EPHESIANS 1:18

the eyes of your <u>understanding</u> being enlightened	the eyes of your <u>heart</u> may be enlightened
TERTULLIAN *Against Marcion* (I 3:465) CYRIL OF JER. *Cat. Lectures* (III 7:143)	EPHRAIM SYRUS *Three Homilies* (III 13:319)

EPHESIANS 3:9

God, who created all things <u>by Jesus Christ</u>	God, who created all things
	*TERTULLIAN *Against Marcion* (I 3:467), "'God, who created all things,' The falsification, however..." *AMBROSE *The Holy Spirit* (III 10:124), "'...created all things;' and again"

Chapter Five--The Digest: 149 "Byzantine" Doctrinal Passages

AV	NIV

EPHESIANS 3:14

AV	NIV
bow my knees unto the Father <u>of our Lord Jesus Christ</u>	for this reason I kneel before the Father
HIPPOLYTUS *Refutation of all Heresies* (I 5:89) METHODIUS *Ten Virgins* (1 6:337)	

EPHESIANS 5:9

AV	NIV
For the fruit of the <u>Spirit</u> is in all goodness	for the fruit of the light consists in all goodness
	GREGORY-THAUMATURGUS *Canonical Epistle* (I 6:18)

EPHESIANS 5:30

AV	NIV
For we are members of his body, <u>of his flesh, and of his bones</u>	For we are members of his body
IRENAEUS *Against Heresies* (I 1:528) METHODIUS *Ten Virgins* (I 6:317)	

418 Early Manuscripts, Church Fathers, & the Authorized Version

AV	NIV
EPHESIANS 6:12	
against the rulers of the darkness <u>of this world</u>	"Omitted in some early manuscripts"
IGNATIUS *To the Ephesians - longer* (I 1:55) CLEMENT OF ALEX *Stromata* (I 2:469) TERTULLIAN *Elucidations* (I 4:114) ORIGEN *Against Celsus* (I 4:652) ORIGEN *De Principiis* (I 4:329,332) ORIGEN *Matthew* (I 10:458) CYPRIAN *Epistles* (I 5:350) CYPRIAN *Treatises* (I 5:556) ATHANASIUS *Antony* (III 4:201) ATHANASIUS *Letters* (III 4:507) GREGORY OF NYSSA *Against Eunomius* (III 5:134)	
Variation in the above, but all include the word "world".	

Chapter Five--The Digest: 149 "Byzantine" Doctrinal Passages

AV	NIV

PHILIPPIANS 4:13

AV	NIV
I can do all things through <u>Christ</u> which strengtheneth me	I can do everything through <u>him</u> who gives me strength
ORIGEN *De Principiis* (I 4:333) ORIGEN *Against Celsus* (I 4:666), "through Christ Jesus our Lord" ORIGEN *John* (I 10:317) "through Jesus Christ...(and again) Christ Jesus" ORIGEN *Matthew* (I 10:457), "through Christ Jesus" CYRIL OF JER. *Cat. Lectures* (III 7:150)	CLEMENT OF ALEX. *Stromata* (I 2:427)

COLOSSIANS 1:14

AV	NIV
In whom we have redemption <u>through his blood</u>	in whom we have redemption
	ATHANASIUS *De Decretis* (III 4:161)

COLOSSIANS 2:10

AV	NIV
intruding into those things which he <u>hath not</u> seen	goes into great detail about what he <u>has</u> seen
ORIGEN *Against Celsus* (I 4:546)	

AV	NIV

I THESSALONIANS 2:15		
Who both killed the Lord Jesus, and <u>their own</u> prophets	Who killed the Lord Jesus and the prophets
TERTULLIAN *Against Marcion* (I 3:461), "The Jews had slain their prophets" ORIGEN, To Africanus (I 4:389).	

I THESSALONIANS 2:19		
in the presence of our Lord Jesus <u>Christ</u> at his coming	In the presence of our Lord Jesus when he comes
TERTULLIAN *Resurrection of the Flesh* (I 3:562)	

I THESSALONIANS 3:11		
our Lord Jesus <u>Christ</u>, direct our way unto you	Our Lord Jesus clear the way for us to come to you
ATHANASIUS *Against the Arians* (III 4:400) AMBROSE *Cstn. Faith* (III 10:235)	

Chapter Five--The Digest: 149 "Byzantine" Doctrinal Passages

AV	NIV

I THESSALONIANS 3:13

AV	NIV
at the coming of our Lord Jesus Christ	When our Lord Jesus comes
TERTULLIAN *Resurrection of the Flesh* (I 3:562) BASIL THE GREAT *The Spirit* (III 8:33)	AMBROSE *The Holy Spirit* (III 10:149)

I TIMOTHY 1:17

AV	NIV
immortal, invisible, the only <u>wise</u> God	immortal, invisible, the only God
GREGORY OF NYSSA *Against Eunomius* (III 5:119) GREGORY OF NAZIANZEN *Ovations* (III 7:314)	TERTULLIAN *Against Praxeas* (I 3:611) NOVATIAN *The Trinity* (I 5:614)

I TIMOTHY 3:16

AV	NIV
<u>God</u> was manifest in the flesh	<u>He</u> appeared in a body
GREGORY OF NYSSA *Against Eunomius* (III 5:101,155,176,232)	HILARY OF POTIERS *The Trinity* (III 9:199,205)

AV	NIV

I TIMOTHY 4:12	
be thou an example.. in charity, in spirit	Set an example...in love
	CLEMENT OF ALEX. *Stromata* (I 2:427) ATHANASIUS *Letters* (III 4:511)

I TIMOTHY 5:16	
If any man or woman that believeth have widows, let them relieve them	If any woman who is a believer has widows in her family, she should help them
	ATHANASIUS *Against Arians* (III 4:351)
AMBROSE *Duties of the Clergy* (III 10:54), "If any that believeth hath widows"	

I TIMOTHY 5:21	
I charge thee before God, and the Lord Jesus Christ	I charge you, in the sight of God and Christ Jesus
BASIL THE GREAT *The Spirit* (III 8:13) CYRIL OF JER. *Cat. Lectures* (III 7:32)	CLEMENT OF ALEX. *Stromata* (I 2:300)

Chapter Five--The Digest: 149 "Byzantine" Doctrinal Passages

AV	NIV
I TIMOTHY 6:5	
Supposing that gain is godliness: from such withdraw thyself	who think that godliness is a means of financial gain
CYPRIAN *Epistles* (I 5:318,387)	MALCHION *Against Paul of Samosata* (I 6:169) *EUSEBIUS *Eccl. Hist.* (III 1:314) "'...gain is godliness' - or in that he is haughty"
I TIMOTHY 6:7	
For we brought nothing into this world, and it is certain we can carry nothing out	For we brought nothing into the world, and we can take nothing out of it
	POLYCARP *Epistle* (I 1:34), "Knowing therefore, that 'as we brought nothing into the world, so we can carry nothing out' CYPRIAN *Treatises* (I 5:550)
CYPRIAN *Epistles* (I 5:453,479) "nor indeed can we carry anything out"	

424 Early Manuscripts, Church Fathers, & the Authorized Version

AV	NIV
II TIMOTHY 2:19	
Let everyone that nameth the name of <u>Christ</u>	Everyone who confesses to the name of <u>the Lord</u>
	ATHANASIUS *Letters* (III 4:536)

HEBREWS 1:3	
When he had <u>by himself</u> purged our sins	After he had provided purification for sins
Shepherd of Hermas (I 2:35), "He Himself then, having purged away the sins of the people" ATHANASIUS *Against Arians* (III 4:338)	CYRIL OF JER. *Cat. Lectures* (III 7:102) *AMBROSE *Cstn. Faith* (III 10:254), "In the first place, 'having made purification'"

AV	NIV

| **HEBREWS 3:1** ||

| Consider the Apostle and High Priest of our profession, <u>Christ</u> Jesus | fix your thoughts on Jesus, the apostle and high priest whom we confess |
| HILARY OF POTIERS *Trinity* (III 9:74), "Jesus Christ" ATHANASIUS *Against Arians* (III 4:337) | ATHANASIUS *Against Arians* (III 4:348,353) AMBROSE *Cstn. Faith* (III 10:255) |

| **HEBREWS 10:30** ||

| Vengeance belongeth unto me, I will recompense, <u>saith the Lord</u> | it is mine to avenge; I will repay |
| *Against Novatian* (I 5:659) *Gospel of Nicodemus* (I 8:421) CYRIL OF JER. *Cat. Lectures* (III 7:61) | |

| **HEBREWS 10:34** ||

| knowing in yourselves that ye have <u>in heaven</u> a better and an enduring substance | because you knew that you yourselves had better and lasting possessions |
| | CLEMENT OF ALEX. *Stromata* (1 2:428) |

AV	NIV
I PETER 4:14	
Christ.. <u>on their part he is evil spoken of, but on your part he is glorified</u>	...Christ...
CLEMENT OF ALEX. *Stromata* (I 2:418) CYPRIAN *Epistles* (I 5:348) CYPRIAN *Treatises* (I 5:501)	
I PETER 5:5	
Yea, all of you <u>be subject</u> one to another	... toward one another
POLYCARP *Epistle* (I 1:35)	
I JOHN 1:7	
and the blood of Jesus <u>Christ</u> his Son	and the blood of Jesus, his Son
	TERTULLIAN *Modesty* (I 4:96)

Chapter Five--The Digest: 149 "Byzantine" Doctrinal Passages 427

AV	NIV

I JOHN 2:7	
The old commandment is the word which ye have heard <u>from the beginning</u>	The old command is the message you have heard
ATHANASIUS *De Decretis* (III 4:153)	

I JOHN 2:20	
but ye have an unction from the Holy One, and <u>ye know all things</u>	(NASV) But your have an anointing from the Holy One, and <u>you all know</u>
CYRIL OF JER. *Cat. Lectures* (III 7:150)	

I JOHN 2:28	
<u>When</u> he shall appear	(NASV) <u>If</u> he should appear
CYRIL OF JER. *Cat. Lectures* (III 7:149)	

AV	NIV
I JOHN 4:3	
And every spirit that confesseth not that Jesus <u>Christ is come in the flesh</u> is not of God	But every spirit that does not acknowledge Jesus is not from God
POLYCARP *Epistle* (I 1:34) TERTULLIAN *Against Heretics* (I 3:259) CYPRIAN *Treatises* (I 5:519)	

AV	NIV

I JOHN 5:7,8	
For there are three that bear record <u>in heaven, the Father, the Word, and the Holy Ghost: and these three are one. And there are three that bear witness in earth</u>, the Spirit, and the water and the blood: and these agree in one.	For there are three that testify: the Spirit, the water and the blood
CYPRIAN Treatises (I 5:423), "and again' it is written of the Father, and of the Son, and of the Holy Spirit, 'And these three are one'"	ORIGEN *John* (I 10:372), "John speaks in his Epistles of the Spirit, and the water, and the blood as being one." *Treatise on Re-Baptism* (I 5:677), "the Apostle John, who says that 'three' bear witness, the Spirit, and the water, and the blood; and these three are one' GREGORY OF NAZIANZEN *Orations* (III 7:323), "What about John then, when.,. he says that there are three that bear witness, the Spirit and the water and the blood" AMBROSE *On the Holy Spirit* (III 10:103,144), "for there are three witnesses, the Spirit, the water and the blood; and these three are one" AMBROSE *Mysteries* (III 10:319)

430 Early Manuscripts, Church Fathers, & the Authorized Version

AV	NIV

JUDE 1

| to them that are <u>sanctified</u> by God the Father | (NASV) to those who are the... <u>beloved</u> in God the Father |
| | ORIGEN *Matthew* (I 10:491) |

REVELATION 1:9a

| and in the kingdom and patience of Jesus <u>Christ</u> | in the....kingdom and patient endurance that are ours in Jesus |
| DIONYSIUS *Promises* (I 7:83) EUSEBIUS *Eccl. Hist.* (III 1:310) | |

REVELATION 1:9b

| and for the testimony of Jesus <u>Christ</u> | and the testimony of Jesus |
| | EUSEBIUS *Eccl. Hist.* (III 1:310) "'...testimony of Jesus.' And towards the close...." |

Chapter Five--The Digest: 149 "Byzantine" Doctrinal Passages 431

AV	NIV

REVELATION 11:15

AV	NIV
The kingdoms of this world are become the <u>kingdoms</u> of our Lord	The kingdom of the world has become the <u>kingdom</u> of our Lord
	AMBROSE *Resurrection* (III 10:191)

REVELATION 11:17

AV	NIV
which art, and wast, <u>and art to come</u>	Who is and who was
	CYPRIAN *Treatises* (I 5:540)

REVELATION 14:5

AV	NIV
for they are without fault <u>before the throne of God</u>	they are blameless
	*METHODIUS *Ten Virgins* (I 6:313), "'for they are without fault', he says, 'and they follow the Lamb...'"

AV	NIV

REVELATION 20:12

And I saw the dead, small and great stand before <u>God</u>	And I saw the dead, great and small, standing before <u>the throne</u>
Against Novatian (I 5:663), "standing before the sight of the Lord's throne"	AMBROSE *Resurrection* (III 10:194)

REVELATION 22:14

Blessed are they <u>that do his commandments</u>, that they may have right to the tree of life	Blessed are those <u>who wash their robes</u>, that they may have the right to the tree of life
TERTULLIAN *On Modesty* (I 4:96) CYPRIAN Treatises (I 5:525)	ATHANASIUS *Against Arians* (III 4:444), "Blessed are they who make broad their robes"

May God add His blessing to the completion of this work, and to all who seek to spread His full, preserved Word around the world.

Jack Moorman

Select Bibliography

Authors Cited

Aland, Kurt, and Barbara Aland. *The Text of the New Testament*, Grand Rapids: Eerdmans, 1987.

Aland, Kurt. "The Text of the Church," *Trinity Journal,* 8NS, 1987.

Brock, Sebastian, "The Resolution of the Philoxenian/Harclean. Problem, *"New Testament Textual Criticism ... Essays in Honor of Bruce Metzger"*, Eds. Eldon J. Epp and Gordon D. Fee, Oxford: Clarendon Press, 1981.

Brown, Kenneth I. *The Church Fathers and the Text of the New Testament,* published by author, 1978.

Bruggen, Jakob, van. *The Ancient Text of the New Testament*, Winnipeg: Primier, 1976.

Burgon, John W. and Edward Miller. *The Traditional Text of the Holy Gospels,* Collingswood NJ: The Bible for Today Press, 1998.

Carson. D. A. *The King James Version Debate*, Grand Rapids: Baker Book House, 1979.

Elliott, J. K. "A Second Look at the United Bible Societies' Greek N.T.", *The Bible Translator*, 26, 1975.
— "The United Bible Societies Greek New Testament: A Short Examination of the Third Edition", *The Bible Translator*, 30, 1979.
— "An Examination of the Twenty - Sixth Edition of Nestle Aland Novurn Testamentum Graece," *Journal of Theological Studies*, 32, 1981.
— "The International Project to Establish A Critical Apparatus to Luke's Gospel," *New Testament Studies,* No. 29, 1983.

Fee, Gordon D. "Modern Textual Criticism and the Revival of the Textus Receptus," *Journal of the Evangelical Theological Society,* No. 21, 1978.
— "A Critique of W. N. Pickering's *The Identity of the N.T. Text"*, *Westminister Theological Journal,* No. 41, 1978/9.

Grant, Robert M. "The Heresy of Tatian", *Journal of Theological Studies*, 5, 1954.

Hills, Edward. *The King James Version Defended*, Des Moines: The Christian Research Press, 1984.

Kelly, J.N.D. *Early Christian Doctrines*, London: Adam & Charles Black, 1958.

Kent, Homer. *The King James Only*. Winona Lake, IN: Grace Theological Seminary.

Kenyon, Frederick. *Recent Developments in Textual Criticism of the Greek Bible*, London: Oxford University Press, 1933.

Kenyon, Frederic. *Handbook to the Textual Criticism of the New Testament* 2nd ed. Grand Rapids: Eerdmans, 1951.

Letis, Theodore. *Edward Freer Hill's Contribution to the Revival of the Ecclesiastical Text*, M.. T. S. Thesis, Emory University, 1987.

Metzger, Bruce H. , *The Text of the new Testament*, 2nd edition, Oxford: Clarendon Press, 1968.
— *The Early Versions of the New Testament: Their Origin, Transmission, and Limitations*, Oxford: Clarendon, 1977.
— "Patristic Evidence and the Textual Criticism of the New Testament," *New Testament Tools and Studies*, Leiden: E. J. Brill, 1980.

Miller, H. S. *General Biblical Introduction*, Houghton: The Word-Bearer Press, 1960.

Milne, H.J.M. and T.C. Skeat. *Scribes and Correctors of Codex Sinaiticus*, London: British Museum, 1938.

Moorman, Jack A. *Modern Bibles, The Dark Secret,* (Revised edition of *Missing in Modern Bibles*, 1988), Collingswood, NJ: The Bible For Today Press, 2004.
— *When the KJV Departs from the "Majority" Text*, Collingswood, NJ: BFT, 1988.
— *Early Manuscripts and the Authorized Version, A Closer Look!*, Collingswood, NJ: BFT, 1990.
— *Early Church Fathers and the Authorized Version, A Demonstration!*, Collingswood, NJ: BFT, 1992.
— *8000+ Differences Between the Textus Receptus and Nestle-Aland Texts*, Collingswood, NJ: BFT, 2003.

Select Bibliography

Newman, Albert H. *A Manual of Church History,* Philadelphia: American Baptist Publication Society, 1899.

Pickering, Wilbur. *The Identity of the New Testament Text*, Nashville: Thomas Nelson, 1980.

Quasten, Johannes. *Patrology,* Westminister, Maryland: Christian Classics Inc., 1986.

Robinson, Maurice A. *How Many Manuscripts are Necessary to Establish the Majority Text*, unpublished paper, 1978.

Scrivener, F. H. A. *A Plain Introduction to the Criticism of the New Testament*, Cambridge: Deighton, Bell, 1883.

Suggs, M. J. "The Use of Patristic Evidence in the Search for a Primitive New Testament," *New Testament Studies,* Jan. 1958.

Voobus, Arthur. *Early Versions of the New Testament,* Stockholm: Estonian Theological Society in Exile, 1954.

Wallace, Daniel B. "The Majority Text and the Original Text", *Bibliotheca Sacra,* April-June 1991.

Westcott, B. F. and F. J. A. Hort. *The New Testament in the Original Greek Introduction and Appendix*, New York: Harper Bros., 1882.

Other Works Cited

"ADOPTIONISM", *Hastings Encyclopedia of Religion and Ethics.*

"Hippolytus, Victorinus" *Oxford Dictionary of the Christian Church*

"An Index of Syriac Manuscripts containing the Epistles and the Apocalypse", *Studies and Documents*, xxxiii, Salt Lake City, 1968.

"Interconfessional Bibles", *Trinitarian Bible Society Quarterly Record*, April-June 1989.

Apparatuses Consulted, including for *KJVMT*

Aland, Kurt. *Synopsis Quattuor Evangeliorum*, Stuttgart: Wurttembergeshe Bibelanstal,1964.

Aland, Kurt; Black, Matthew; Martini, Carlo; Metzger, Bruce; Witgren, Allen; (eds.), *The Greek New Testament*, 3rd Edition Corrected, New York: American Bible Society, 1983.
Hodges, Zane C. and Arthrur L. Farstad (eds.). *The Greek New Testament According to the Majority Text*, Nashville: Thomas Nelson, 1982.

Hoskier, Herman C. *Concerning the Text of the Apocalypse*, London: Bernard Quartich, 1914.

Legg, S. C. E. (ed.), *Novum Testamentum Graece Secundum Textum Westcotto-Hortianum. Evangelium Secundum Marcum.* Oxonii: E. Typographero Clarendoniano, 1935.
— *Novum Testamentum Graece Secundum Textum Westcotto-Hortianum, Evangelium Secundum Mattaeum*, Oxonii: E. Typographero Clarendoniano, 1935.

Nestle, Irwin and Kurt Aland. *Novum Testamentum Graece*, 26th Edition, Stuttgart: Wurttembergeshe Bibelanstal, 1979.

Soden, Hermann F. von. *Die Schriften des Neuen Testaments,* Gottingen: Vandenhoeck und Ruprecht, 1911.

The American and British Committees of the International Greek New Testament Project. *The New Testament in Greek,* The Gospel According to Luke, (Part One, Chs. 1-12), Oxford: Clarendon Press, 1984.

Tischendorf, Constantine von. *Novum Testamentum Graece*. Editio octava critica maior. Lipsae: Giesecke and Devrient, 1869.

Index of Words and Phrases

A Select Library of Nicene and Post-Nicene Fathers 333
A.C. Coxe 333
A.D. Uscan 99
ABBREVIATIONS 4, 119, 320, 325
ACHMIMIC 91-94, 121
ADOPTIONISM 2, 13, 108, 355
aeons 20, 107
Against Heresies 336, 348, 349, 366-368, 370, 373, 375, 378, 382, 384, 389, 390, 396, 403, 405, 407, 409, 412, 415, 417
Aksenaga 81
Aland, K.   5, 25, 26, 30, 31, 33, 38, 42, 45, 49, 52, 63, 64, 74, 79, 80, 119, 120, 322-324, 326, 433, 434, 437
Aleph B text 25
Aleph-correctors 33
Alexander 6, 81, 114, 228, 333, 339, 341, 360, 363
Alexander Roberts 333
Alexandria 21, 66, 78, 80, 81, 88, 90, 99, 104, 107, 111, 113-117, 314, 315, 324, 327, 330, 339, 341-344, 348, 350-352, 355, 359, 360, 362, 363, 389
Alexandrian 21, 23, 30, 33, 34, 37, 40, 88-90, 106, 109, 314, 315, 317, 326, 327
Alexandrian Text 23, 30, 37, 40, 88, 109, 314
Alexandria's Catechetical School 341, 351
Allen Wikgren 25
Alphabet 52, 96, 98
Ambrose ... 6, 116, 336, 340, 361, 363, 368, 372, 373, 376, 382, 386, 390, 393, 395, 399, 400, 402, 403, 408, 410, 411, 414, 416, 420-422, 424, 425, 429, 431, 432
American Bible Society 25, 437
American Committee of the International Greek N.T. Project 321
American Revision Committee 334
ANONYMOUS WORKS 6, 355
ANPF 334-336, 368, 369, 371-375, 379-382, 393, 396, 397, 405
ante-Nicene 104, 105, 333, 365, 393
Ante-Nicene Fathers 104, 105, 333, 365
Antioch 67, 78, 97, 111, 113, 114, 344, 348-350

440 Early Manuscripts, Church Fathers, & the Authorized Version

Antiochan Text 67
Aphrahat 6, 340, 360, 362, 382, 392
Apocrypha 33, 74
Apollinarianism 342
Apollinarius 342
Apostolic Constitutions ... 357, 361, 362, 366, 369, 382, 383, 397, 402, 413
Arabic Diatessaron 109
Aramaic 67, 83
Arianism 97, 339-341, 344, 347, 357
Armenian 4, 38, 96, 98, 99, 101-103, 109, 110, 112, 121
Athanasius .. 6, 115, 327, 339, 341, 342, 344, 360, 363, 366, 375, 389, 390,
394, 395, 398, 400, 402, 406, 408, 409, 411-413, 418-420,
422, 424, 425, 427, 432
Athenagoras 6, 111, 342, 359, 362, 368
Attic form 30
Augustine 72, 96, 212, 335, 340
authorized ... 1, 3, 2, 5, 9-11, 13, 23, 33, 38, 40, 45, 63, 64, 67, 76, 83, 92,
100, 103, 104, 119, 120, 313-315, 317, 327, 335, 434
Authorized Version .. 1, 3, 2, 5, 9-11, 13, 23, 33, 38, 40, 45, 63, 64, 67, 76,
83, 92, 100, 103, 104, 119, 120, 313-315, 317, 327, 335,
434
baptism ... 20, 140, 228, 298, 343, 344, 346, 349, 353, 356, 357, 359, 363,
368, 393, 429
Barbara Aland 25, 38, 433
Basil the Great . 115, 342, 346, 360, 366, 373, 390, 408, 411, 412, 414, 415,
421, 422
Bauer 40
Berlin 5, 319, 320, 322, 325, 332
Bible Societies 25, 26, 30, 38, 120, 315, 322, 433
Biblia patristica 323
Bishop of Edessa 78
Black, M. 21, 25, 96, 434, 437
Bohairic 4, 88-94, 121
breakthrough 10
British and Foreign Bible Society 26, 79, 100
Brock 81, 82, 433
Brown, K. 317, 433
Bruce Metzger 5, 25, 82, 88, 320
Burgon, J. 4, 10, 64, 104-106, 111, 113, 114, 117, 119, 212, 319, 320, 325,
332, 333, 433
Burgon and Miller 4, 104-106, 111, 319
Burgon's Index 5, 318, 332

Index of Words and Phrases

Byzantine . 23, 24, 38-40, 45, 65, 67, 84, 104-106, 111, 317, 322, 326, 327, 365
Byzantine Text 40, 84, 105, 317, 322, 326, 327
C. H. Gwilliam 79
C. R. Gregory's 78
Caesarean 23, 65, 317
Caesarean texts 23
Cappadocian Fathers 345, 346
Carlo Martini 26, 315
Carson, D. 104, 105, 365, 433
Casearean 37
Catholic Church 25, 26, 68, 74, 164
CHRONOLOGICAL SUMMARY 6, 359
Chrysostom 4, 38, 104, 117, 317, 322, 335
Clement . 6, 74, 88, 107, 113, 114, 327, 343, 351, 352, 355, 356, 359, 363, 369, 372, 373, 386, 387, 390, 403, 407, 408, 413-415, 418, 419, 422, 425, 426
Clementine Homilies 356, 357, 360, 369, 373, 375
Codex A 49, 50, 273
Codex Argenteus 97
Codex C 50, 51
Codex Fuldensis 110, 112
Codex Sinaiticus 2, 30, 33, 355, 434
Codex Vaticanus 30, 33, 91
colophon 81
Constantinople 98, 115, 117, 345, 346
Coptic 4, 38, 88-92, 94, 95, 120, 121
Corrected Edition 323
correctors 33-35, 45, 49, 434
Council of Nicea 339, 341, 345
Coxe 333
Critical Text 2, 21, 29
CSE 332
Cureton, W. 80
Curetonian 3, 78, 80, 83, 85, 86, 120
Cyprian 6, 113, 228, 329, 336, 343, 352, 356, 360, 363, 368, 369, 374, 376, 379, 382, 388, 391, 393, 396, 405, 408-411, 415, 418, 423, 426, 428, 429, 431, 432
D. A. Carson 104, 365
Dallas Theological Seminary 317
Damasus 74, 342
Daniel B. Wallace 317
de Dieu manuscript 82, 87

442 Early Manuscripts, Church Fathers, & the Authorized Version

Deity 11, 13, 14, 17, 20, 191, 197, 252, 262, 274, 310, 341, 342, 348
Deity of Christ 11, 252, 262, 274
derived text 23
Detroit Baptist Divinity School 317
Diatessaron 4, 106-110, 112, 206, 352, 353, 366-403
Dionysius the Great 113, 344
disassociate 20, 21
disassociation 2, 20, 298
Disputation with Trypho the Jew 349
Docetism 352
Docetists 88
Doctrinal Text . 38, 44, 52, 55, 61-64, 66, 92, 104, 314, 315, 317, 327, 334, 362
Donaldson, J. 333, 334, 336
Early Christian Doctrines 21, 434
Ecclesiastical History 100, 329, 345
eclectic 29, 30
edition . 25, 26, 30, 31, 65, 73-75, 79, 81-84, 89, 90, 99, 100, 106, 109, 110, 120, 190, 314, 317, 320, 322-327, 329, 332, 333, 433, 434, 437
Edward Hills 40, 105, 326
Edward Pococke 83
Eerdmans 25, 49, 319, 333, 433, 434
Egypt 21, 40, 44, 62, 80, 88-90, 96, 114, 115, 252, 315, 324, 326, 327, 341
Egyptian 40, 88, 89, 91-94, 121, 202, 357
Elliott, J. 30, 31, 325, 433
Encratites 88, 107
Encyclopedia of Religion and Ethics 20, 437
Ephraem 6, 109, 110, 112, 115, 345
Ephraem Syrus 345
Ethiopic 4, 38, 96, 99-103, 121
Eugene Nida 25
Eusebius 5, 6, 100, 107, 114, 329, 330, 345, 350, 360, 363, 423, 430
Eutychites 88
FAYYUMIC 91-94, 121
Fee, G. 5, 82, 317, 318, 326, 327, 332, 333, 433
Ferrar, W. 65
Franz Praetorius 100
Frederic Kenyon 5, 104, 318, 322
Frumentius 99, 100
G.W.H. Lampe 325
GCS 325, 332

Index of Words and Phrases

Gennadius of Marseilles 330
GEOGRAPHIC SUMMARY 6, 362
George Homers 90
Gnostic 20, 21, 91, 107, 202, 252, 263, 351
Gnosticism 21, 348, 349
Gordon Fee 5, 317, 318, 326, 332
Gordon-Conwell Theological Seminary 326
Gothic 4, 38, 96-98, 101-103, 121
Greek text 26, 29
Gregory, C.   6, 113, 115, 116, 342, 344-346, 360-362, 368, 374, 379, 383,
              390, 392, 393, 398, 403, 410, 417, 418, 421, 429
Gregory of Nazianzus 342
Gregory of Nyssa ... 342, 344, 346, 361, 362, 368, 374, 390, 403, 418, 421
Gregory-Thaumaturgus 6, 346, 383, 417
Gwilliam, C. 79
Gwynn, J. 79
H.S. Miller 98, 99
Harclean 3, 81-83, 85-87, 120, 433
Harris, R. 105, 319
Harry Sturz 40
Hastings 20, 437
Hellenized 89
heresy 20, 21, 67, 108, 298, 340, 356, 389, 434
heretical 40, 41, 339, 345, 349
Herman Hoskier's 37
Hieronymian 321
Hilary .. 6, 115, 336, 347, 360, 363, 375, 376, 389, 392, 394, 397-402, 406,
         411, 421, 425
Hills, E. 40, 105, 196, 212, 216, 319, 320, 326, 332, 434
Hippolytus .. 6, 113, 274, 347, 352, 359, 363, 376, 384, 389, 391, 392, 411
Holy Spirit ... 9, 20, 218, 293, 340-342, 382, 400, 402, 408, 414, 416, 421,
                                                                          429
Homer Kent 13
Homers, G. 90
Hort, F. 23, 25, 29-31, 65, 71, 73, 104, 106, 190, 317, 327, 332, 435
Hortian theory 318
Hoskier, H. 38, 273, 437
Ignatius 6, 274, 348, 352, 359, 362, 413, 415, 418
IGNTP 5, 38, 324-326
inspiration 9, 355
Institute for New Testament 25, 64, 322
interconfessional text 26

444 Early Manuscripts, Church Fathers, & the Authorized Version

Irenaeus . 6, 108, 113, 228, 336, 337, 348, 351-353, 355, 359, 363, 366-368,
370, 373, 375, 378, 382, 384, 389, 390, 396, 398, 403, 405,
407, 409, 412, 415, 417
Italia 72
J. P. Migne's 325
JACQUES PAUL MIGNE 5, 331
James Donaldson 333
Jerome 5, 74, 329, 330, 335, 354
Johann Widmanstadt 79
Johannes Quasten 330
Johannes Trithemius 330
John Gwynn 79
John Zohrab 99
Justin 6, 107, 111, 349, 359, 363, 368
Justin Martyr 6, 107, 111, 349, 359, 363, 368
Kelly, J. 20, 434
Kelly's 21
Kenneth I. Brown 317
Kenyon, F. 5, 104, 318-320, 322, 326, 332, 434
Khirbet Mird 84
King Haitho 98, 99
Kirsopp Lake 33, 65
Kurt Aland 5, 25, 26, 322, 324, 437
Lake, K. 33, 34, 65, 79, 434, 437
Lampe, G. 325
lectionaries 83
Letis, T. 83, 320, 434
Leudsen and Schaff 79
Liege 110, 112
Logos 107, 347
M. J. Suggs 325
Mabbug 81, 82
Mai 5, 325, 330, 331
majuscule 63
Malchion 6, 349, 360, 362, 423
Manuscript A 71
Manuscript Digest .. 4, 20, 33, 35, 38, 40, 42, 50, 52, 55, 63, 65, 73, 78, 79,
88, 91, 96, 106, 119, 121
Marcionites 88
Mardinesis 79
Martini, C. 26, 315, 437
Matthew Black 25
Mechitarist Monastery 99

Index of Words and Phrases

Memphitic 90, 98
Merk 25
Methodius 6, 113, 350, 360, 362, 389, 417, 431
Metzger, B.   5, 25, 65, 72, 74, 79, 80, 82, 83, 88-91, 97, 99, 100, 107-109,
320-322, 326, 327, 434, 437
Migne, J. 5, 325, 330-332
Miller, E or H... 4, 98, 99, 104-106, 111, 113, 114, 117, 319, 332, 433, 434
Milne, ... 33, 34, 434
Modalism 353
Monophysites 78
Montanist 350
Moses 79, 81, 82, 119, 173, 226, 384
Moses Mardinesis 79
Munster Institute 64
NA apparatus 45
National of Scotland 26
NA-25 30
NA-26 .... 30, 31, 323
Nestle, E. 25, 26, 30, 31, 33, 38, 42, 45, 63, 74, 79, 119, 120, 322, 433, 434,
437
Nestle Aland 25, 26, 30, 31, 33, 38, 42, 45, 63, 74, 79, 120, 322, 433
Nestle text 25
Nestorians 78
Netherlands Bible Society 26
New American Standard Versions 11
Nicene and Post-Nicene Series 333
Nida, E. 25
Novatian 6, 329, 350, 356, 359, 360, 363, 374, 392, 421, 425, 432
Novum Testamentum Graece 437, 438
omission 13, 203
omissions 13
Origen 113, 326, 327, 339, 344-347, 350-353, 355, 359, 363, 366, 368,
369, 371-373, 378, 389-391, 399, 403, 410-412, 415, 418-
420, 429, 430
Ostrogothic 97
palimpsest 50, 80, 273
Pamphilus 114, 345, 350
paper pope 315
Papias 345
papyri 3, 21, 37, 40, 42, 44, 120, 324, 365
Patrologiae Cursus Completus 325, 331
Persian Harmony 110, 112
Person of Christ 20, 298, 342

Peshitta 3, 78-83, 85-87, 89, 94, 98, 108, 120, 229
Philip Schaff 334
Philoxenian 3, 81-83, 85, 86, 120, 433
Philoxenus 81, 82
Pickering, W. 63, 104, 105, 107, 319, 435
Platoism 349
Platt 100-103, 121
pleroma 20
Pococke, E. 83
Polycarp 6, 81, 82, 348, 351, 352, 359, 362, 368, 407, 423, 426, 428
Polyglot Bibles 83
polyglots 84
Pontifical Biblical Institute of Rome 26
Pontius the Deacon 352
Pope Sixtus V 74
Pope Sylvester 68
Praetorius, F. 100, 121
premillennialism 348, 349
Proto-Bohairic 92-94, 121
Ptolemy 20, 21
Quasten, J. 330, 332, 435
Rabbula 78
receptus 9, 119, 314, 315, 318, 320, 326, 433, 434
reconstruction 321, 322, 327
Reformation 25, 79, 315, 330, 331
Reformation Bibles 315
Rendel Harris 105, 319
Richard Simon 315
Roberts, A. 5, 333, 334, 336
Roman Catholic Church 26, 74
Romanism 314, 330
Rufinus 100
Sahidic 4, 88-94, 121
Schaff, P. 5, 79, 333, 334, 336
scriptorium 33, 34
Scrivener, F. 33, 78, 81, 98, 273, 274, 435
Second Coming 11, 172
selective citation 4, 61, 105, 117, 322
Shepherd of Hermas 20, 21, 355, 359, 424
Sigebert 330
Simon, R. 190, 294, 315
Sinaitic 3, 78, 80, 83, 85, 86, 120
Sixtine Edition 74

Index of Words and Phrases

Skeat 33, 34, 434
Soter 108
St. Catharines Monastery 80
Stuggart 110
Sturz, H. 40
Suggs, M. 325, 326, 435
Swedish Evangelical Society 100
SYMBOLS 4, 119
Syriac 3, 38, 67, 78-81, 83, 84, 87, 94, 95, 98, 108-110, 112, 120, 340, 437
Tatian 6, 107-109, 117, 206, 349, 352, 359, 363, 366-403
Tertullian .. 6, 113, 206, 228, 329, 343, 352, 353, 355, 359, 363, 368, 369, 372, 374, 377, 378, 382, 386, 387, 389, 393, 397, 399-401, 404, 406-413, 415, 416, 418, 420, 421, 426, 428, 432
Tetraevangelium 79
Textual Criticism .. 2, 5, 23, 29, 31, 33, 34, 37, 40, 45, 63, 65, 80, 81, 104, 273, 314, 317-320, 322, 326, 327, 365, 433, 434
The Ante-Nicene Fathers 104, 105, 333, 365
THE INTERNATIONAL GREEK 317, 321, 324, 437
The Text of the Church 324
The Text of the New Testament 25, 38, 49, 65, 317, 320, 323, 433, 434
Thebaic 89
Theodore P. Letis 83, 320
theory 23, 31, 64, 73, 81, 104, 318, 319, 327
Thomas of Harkel 81
Thomas Pell Platt 100
Thomas' version 82
Tischendorf 30, 33, 34, 38, 79, 82, 89, 90, 325, 333, 438
TR .. 106, 315, 318, 326, 327, 332, 335, 336, 339-349, 351-357, 359, 362, 370
Traditional ... 4, 9, 10, 23, 24, 30, 33, 35, 37, 38, 44, 45, 49, 52, 65, 67-69, 71-74, 78, 90, 91, 96-99, 105-109, 111, 117, 120, 318, 319, 322-327, 330, 332-334, 365, 377, 378, 380, 433
Traditional Majority 23, 120
Traditional Text . 4, 9, 10, 23, 24, 33, 35, 37, 38, 44, 45, 49, 52, 65, 67, 68, 72, 74, 78, 90, 91, 96-99, 105-108, 111, 117, 318, 319, 322-327, 330, 332, 334, 365, 377, 433
Trinitarian Bible Society 26, 437
Trinity . 11, 324, 336, 342, 347, 351, 353, 374-376, 389, 392, 394, 397-402, 406, 411, 421, 425, 433
Trithemius, J. 330
Tuscan 110, 112
Tyndale 67

UBS-3 .... 30, 104, 322, 323, 327
UBS . 26, 29, 30, 38, 65, 67, 82, 83, 100, 104, 106, 109-111, 113, 114, 117,
        120, 123, 127, 129, 141, 143, 152, 157-160, 166, 167, 170,
        184, 187, 189, 194, 197-201, 211, 232, 242, 250, 259, 261,
        267, 283, 315, 322-324, 327
UBS-1 315
Ulfilas 96-98
Uncials 3, 35, 37, 38, 45, 49-53, 55, 56, 61, 62, 224, 335, 365
United Bible Societies 25, 26, 30, 38, 120, 315, 322, 433
Uscan, A. 99, 101, 102, 121
van Unnik 40
Vaticanus 30, 31, 33, 45, 46, 63, 65, 91, 314
Vaudois 68
Venetian 110, 112
Vetus Latina 321, 323, 325
Victorinus 6, 114, 354, 360, 363, 370, 411
Vienna 5, 319, 320, 322, 332
Vogels 25, 74, 110
Voobus 83, 84, 90, 97, 100, 108, 110, 435
Vulgate 3, 37, 38, 73-77, 96, 98, 99, 103, 110, 120, 173, 314, 329
Waldensian 68
Waldensians 68, 288
Wallace, D. 317, 326, 435
Westcott, B. 23, 25, 26, 30, 31, 73, 106, 190, 216, 317, 327, 332, 435
Westcott and Hort's 26, 30
Westcott and Hort 23, 25, 30, 31, 73, 106, 190, 317, 327, 332
Western 23, 67, 190, 314, 317
Widmanstad, J.t 79
Wikgren, A. 25
Wilbur Pickering 63, 319
William Cureton 80
William Hugh Ferrar 65
Wurtemberg 26
Wycliffe 67
Zohrab, J. 99, 101-103, 121

Order Blank (p. 1)

Name:_____

Address:_____

City & State:_____ Zip:_____

Credit Card #:_____ Expires:_____

Books By Dr. Jack Moorman

[ ] *Early Manuscripts, Church Fathers, & the Authorized Version* by Dr. Jack Moorman, $25+$5 S&H. Hardback
[ ] Send *Forever Settled--Bible Do*cuments *& History Survey* by Dr. Jack Moorman, $20+$4 S&H. Hardback book.
[ ] Send *When the KJB Departs from the So-Called "Majority Text"* by Dr. Jack Moorman, $16 + $4 S&H
[ ] Send *Missing in Modern Bibles--Nestle-Aland & NIV Errors* by Dr. Jack Moorman, $8 + $4 S&H
[ ] Send *The Doctrinal Heart of the Bible--Removed from Modern Versions* by Dr. Jack Moorman, VCR, $15 +$4 S&H
[ ] Send *Modern Bibles--The Dark Secret* by Dr. Jack Moorman, $5 + $2 S&H
[ ] Send *Samuel P. Tregelles--The Man Who Made the Critical Text Acceptable to Bible Believers* by Dr. Moorman ($2+$1)
[ ] Send *8,000 Differences Between TR & CT* by Dr. Jack Moorman [$54 + $5 S&H] Over 500 large pages of data

Books By or About Dean Burgon

[ ] Send *The Revision Revised* by Dean Burgon ($25 + $4 S&H) A hardback book, 640 pages in length.
[ ] Send *The Last 12 Verses of Mark* by Dean Burgon ($15+$4 S&H) A hardback book 400 pages.
[ ] Send *The Traditional Text* hardback by Burgon ($16 + $4 S&H) A hardback book, 384 pages in length.
[ ] Send *Causes of Corruption* by Burgon ($15 + $4 S&H) A hardback book, 360 pages in length.

Send or Call Orders to:
THE BIBLE FOR TODAY
900 Park Ave., Collingswood, NJ 08108
Phone: 856-854-4452; FAX:--2464; Orders: 1-800 JOHN 10:9
E-Mail Orders: BFT@BibleForToday.org; Credit Cards OK

Order Blank (p. 2)

Name:_____

Address:_____

City & State:_____Zip:_____

Credit Card #:_____Expires:_____

Other Books By or About Dean Burgon

[ ] Send *Inspiration and Interpretation*, Dean Burgon ($25+$4 S&H) A hardback book, 610 pages in length.
[ ] Send *Burgon's Warnings on Revision* by DAW ($7+$3 S&H) A perfect bound book, 120 pages in length.
] Send *Westcott & Hort's Greek Text & Theory Refuted by Burgon's Revision Revised--Summarized* by Dr. D. A. Waite ($7.00 + $3 S&H), 120 pages, perfect bound.
[ ] Send *Dean Burgon's Confidence in KJB* by DAW ($3+$3)
[ ] Send *Vindicating Mark 16:9-20* by Dr. Waite ($3+$3 S&H)
[ ] Send *Summary of Traditional Text* by Dr. Waite ($3 +$2)
[ ] Send *Summary of Causes of Corruption*, DAW ($3+$2)
[ ] Send *Summary of Inspiration* by Dr. Waite ($3 + $2 S&H)

Books by Dr. D. A. Waite

[ ] Send *Defending the King James Bible* by Dr. Waite $12+$4 S&H) A hardback book, indexed with study questions.
[ ] Send *Four Reasons for Defending KJB* by DAW ($3+$3)
[ ] Send *The Case for the King James Bible* by DAW ($7 +$3 S&H) A perfect bound book, 112 pages in length.
[ ] Send *Foes of the King James Bible Refuted* by DAW ($10 +$4 S&H) A perfect bound book, 164 pages in length.
[ ] Send *Central Seminary Refuted on Bible Versions* by Dr. Waite ($10+$3 S&H) A perfect bound book, 184 pages
[ ] Send Fuzzy *Facts From Fundamentalists* by Dr. D. A. Waite ($8.00 + $3.00) printed booklet

Send or Call Orders to:
THE BIBLE FOR TODAY
900 Park Ave., Collingswood, NJ 08108
Phone: 856-854-4452; FAX:--2464; Orders: 1-800 JOHN 10:9
E-Mail Orders: BFT@BibleForToday.org; Credit Cards OK

Order Blank (p. 3)

Name:_____

Address:_____

City & State:_____ Zip:_____

Credit Card#:_____ Expires:_____

More Books by Dr. D. A. Waite

[ ] Send *Fundamentalist Distortions on Bible Versions* by Dr. Waite ($6+$3 S&H) A perfect bound book, 80 pages
[ ] Send *Fundamentalist MIS-INFORMATION on Bible Versions* by Dr. Waite ($7+$3 S&H) perfect bound, 136 pages
[ ] Send *Westcott's Denial of Resurrection*, Dr. Waite ($4+$3)
[ ] Send *26 Hours of KJB Seminar* (4 videos) by DAW ($50.00)
[ ] Send *Theological Heresies of Westcott and Hort* by Dr. D. A. Waite, ($7+$3 S&H) A printed booklet.
[ ] Send *Holes in the Holman Christian Standard Bible* by Dr. Waite ($3+$2 S&H) A printed booklet, 40 pages
[ ] Send *Contemporary Eng. Version Exposed*, DAW ($3+$2)
[ ] Send *NIV Inclusive Language Exposed* by DAW ($5+$3)
[ ] Send *Colossians & Philemon--Preaching Verse by Verse* by Pastor D. A. Waite ($12+$5 S&H) hardback, 240 pages.
[ ] Send *Philippians--Preaching Verse by Verse* by Pastor D. A. Waite ($10+$5 S&H) hardback, 176 pages.
[ ] Send *Making Marriage Melodious* by Pastor D. A. Waite ($7+$3 S&H), perfect bound, 112 pages.
[ ] Send *Ephesians--Preaching Verse by Verse* by Pastor D. A. Waite ($12+$5 S&H) hardback, 224 pages.
[ ] Send *Galatians--Preaching Verse By Verse* by Pastor D. A. Waite ($12+$5 S&H) hardback, 216 pages.
[ ] Send *First Peter--Preaching Verse By Verse* by Pastor D. A. Waite ($10+$5 S&H) hardback, 176 pages.

Send or Call Orders to:
THE BIBLE FOR TODAY
900 Park Ave., Collingswood, NJ 08108
Phone: 856-854-4452; FAX:--2464; Orders: 1-800 JOHN 10:9
E-Mail Orders: BFT@BibleForToday.org; Credit Cards OK

Order Blank (p. 4)

Name:_____

Address:_____

City & State:_____Zip:_____

Credit Card #:_____Expires:____

Books by D. A. Waite, Jr.
[ ] Send *Readability of A.V. (KJB)* by D. A. Waite, Jr. ($6+$3)
[ ] Send *4,114 Definitions from the Defined King James Bible* by D. A. Waite, Jr. ($7.00+$3.00 S&H)
[ ] Send *The Doctored New Testament* by D. A. Waite, Jr. ($25+$4 S&H) Greek MSS differences shown, hardback
[ ] Send *Defined King James Bible* lg. prt. leather ($40+$6)
[ ] Send *Defined King James Bible* med. prt. leather ($35+$5)

Newly Published Book
[ ] Send *The LIE That Changed the Modern World* by Dr. H. D. Williams ($16+$4 S&H) Hardback book

Miscellaneous Authors
[ ] Send *Guide to Textual Criticism* by Edward Miller ($7+$4) Hardback book
[ ] Send *Scrivener's Greek New Testament Underlying the King James Bible*, hardback, ($14+$4 S&H)
[ ] Send *Scrivener's Annotated Greek New Testament*, by Dr. Frederick Scrivener: Hardback--($35+$5 S&H); Genuine Leather--($45+$5 S&H)
[ ] Send *Why Not the King James Bible?--An Answer to James White's KJVO Book* by Dr. K. D. DiVietro, $10+$4 S&H
[ ] Send the "*DBS Articles of Faith & Organization*" (N.C.)
[ ] Send *Dean Burgon Society DVD's* (2004) ($35+$5 S&H)
[ ] Send Brochure #1: "*1000 Titles Defending KJB/TR*"(N.C.)

Send or Call Orders to:
THE BIBLE FOR TODAY
900 Park Ave., Collingswood, NJ 08108
Phone: 856-854-4452; FAX:--2464; Orders: 1-800 JOHN 10:9
E-Mail Orders: BFT@BibleForToday.org; Credit Cards OK

The Defined King James Bible

UNCOMMON WORDS DEFINED ACCURATELY

I. Deluxe Genuine Leather

✦Large Print--Black or Burgundy✦
1 for $40.00+$6 S&H
✦Case of 12 for✦
$30.00 each+$30 S&H

✦Medium Print--Black or Burgundy✦
1 for $35.00+$5 S&H
✦Case of 12 for✦
$25.00 each+$24 S&H

II. Deluxe Hardback Editions

1 for $20.00+$6 S&H (Large Print)
✦Case of 12 for✦
$15.00 each+$30 S&H (Large Print)

1 for $15.00+$5 S&H (Medium Print)
✦Case of 12 for✦
$10.00 each+$24 S&H (Medium Print)

Order Phone: 1-800-JOHN 10:9

About the Author

Dr. Jack Moorman studied for a while at the Indianapolis campus of Purdue University, attended briefly Indiana Bible College, and graduated from Tennessee Temple Bible School. Since his graduation, he has been involved in church planting, Bible Institute teaching, and extensive distribution of Scriptures and gospel tracts in Johannesburg, South Africa from 1968--1988, and in England and London since 1988. More recently he has been seeking to get Scripture portions into Latin Europe. He married his wife, Dorothy, on November 22, 1963.

Dr. Moorman has written the following scholarly books defending the King James Bible and the Hebrew, Aramaic and Greek Words that underlie it:

1. *Early Manuscripts, Church Fathers, and the Authorized Version* (the present volume).
2. *Forever Settled.*
3. *When the King James Bible Departs from the So-Called "Majority Text."*
4. *Missing in Modern Bibles--the Nestle-Aland Greek Text & New International Version Errors.*
5. *The Doctrinal Heart of the Bible--Removed form Modern Versions.*
6. *Modern Bibles--The Dark Secret.*
7. *Samuel P. Tregelles--The Man Who Made the Critical Text Acceptable to Bible Believers.*
8. *8,000 Differences Between the Textus Receptus and the Critical Text.*

All of these scholarly and well-documented works by Dr. Moorman are replete with manuscript and other evidence which he has gleaned from his own vast resources as well as all the references found in the British Museum and other libraries in the London area.

Pray for this humble friend of this vital cause as he continues in his research, writing, and preaching ministries.